DISTANT ECHOES

DISTANT ECHOES

OMESH SAIGAL

GYAN PUBLISHING HOUSE
NEW DELHI-110002

DISTANT ECHOES

(Journalism, Literature, Politics, Current Affairs, Sociology)

ISBN : 81-212-0653-7

Published in 2000 in India by
Gyan Publishing House,
5, Ansari Road, Darya Ganj
New Delhi-110002

Laser Typesetting at A.S. Printers, Delhi

Printed at Mehra Offset Printers, Delhi

CONTENTS

PART 8
TRYST WITH MIND

PART 9
TRYST WITH BODY

PART 10
PRE-METAPHYSICS

PART 11
OF KHANS AND BOLLYWOOD

PART 12
THE BIG-SMALL SCREEN

PART 13
OUR CITY

PART 14
TROTTING AROUND

PART 15
SHORT OF THE GOAL

PART 16
ABRACADABRA

FOREWORD

Another Sunday painter? No. A prolific writer and regular columnist.

Being a bureaucrat myself, I know how they write—but most of them are 'Sunday Painters'. They write for fun. Now, here is another bureaucrat-turned author—turned columnist, who claims to be a regular writer! Do his claims merit attention?

Omesh Saigal is one of the best known columnists who contributes to 'Mid Day' every week, quite punctually and religiously. And this is no small fact that he has been doing so for the last 8 or 9 years. This is indeed an achievement.

These are selected writings of Omesh Saigal, who writes in a light vein albeit demands a serious reading. These pieces include Essays, Articles, Travelogues and simple Commentaries, which cover a full spectrum of topics, issues and problems. He writes in style—his own. In fact, many would consider his writings as prose written in verse.

They cover a wide range—from the mundane to the profound, from tongue in cheek on the cinema to serious science writing. The range is indeed staggering.

This is neither pure satire, nor pure humour nor serious writing, but it has a punch and a moral, which is a unique phenomenon. This sort of writing attracts readers and gradually becomes their weekly habit—at a time when most of people do not bother to read anything beyond news in a daily newspaper.

Indo-Anglian literature has come of age. Contemporary

Indian writers are a remarkable breed, if not the most remarkable cultivation in the history of literature in the Third World. After having rode the waves for over a century, the open, outward-looking assimilative outlook of Indian authors has matured. Generally, Indo-Anglian writers are not inclined to use their pen for mere financial benefit. They simply write to satisfy their urge, to express themselves and to share their ideas with their readers and Omesh Saigal is no exception. He has an inbuilt acumen for writing in beautiful and impressive language, using the right diction and idiom and choosing proper words to bring his readers under his spell. His writings make one think at the end. Each of his pieces seems to have been derived from life around in a straight forward manner and the reader's heart goes out to it.

To prove my point, it wouldn't be out of place to quote none other than the author of this book. While reviewing a book by one of his colleagues, he writes:

"(His) book is a mix of a travelogue, an *aide de memoire,* a diary and a treatise on the area, in which he spent a very good part of his (early) life. It is replete with funny incidents............ If (his) book had only an account of his personal experiences, it would have had only a limited interest, but as told, it is an interesting blend of his own experience with that of earlier administrators, which makes the book an important addition to the lure of the country."

I attribute the above lines to Omesh Saigal himself and his writings.

While offering no revolutionary insight into our day to day life (which is least expected from such writings), yet it brings people close to the system, prevailing in the country and help them realise what the real state of affairs is. With a bureaucratic background, most of the chapters do hold great interest. Further, the power of pen and mind do offer new insight.

The book provides a fresh reading. In fact, in today's intellectually polluted atmosphere, such creations must be sure winners. This may not be something very serious but it certainly is thought provoking and help you get awakened. This is like an oasis in the desert of monotonous writings.

The author has come a long way and he would go ahead. At a time when writers write for the chosen readers, he writes for people—the common readers.

I am really impressed by the author's knack for creative writing. He not only laughs at others, he has the novel capability to laugh at himself too, which is rare. And so in a natural way, he must have the last laugh.

I wish he keeps winning the hearts, column by column and week by week.

JAGMOHAN

PREFACE

The other day as I was going through some of my old papers, I came across a diary of my high school days when I was all of sixteen years of age. As I flipped through the pages, I was astonished to find that page after page of the diary was full of two things: accounts of my dreams and poems. Dream after dream, poem after poem made an absolutely fascinating reading, not because I could understand what they meant (let me admit that many of the writings made no sense at all) but the fact that I had penned them at all! And the fact that they contained, as one of the poems said, 'my loves, my woes, my secret joys.'

As I went through the diary I wondered why I had stopped the habit, why I wrote this for only one year. How wonderful it would have been if I could have had a similar account of the rest of the years of my life as well. How wonderful and illuminating! I realize the reason now: you cannot write unless you make a habit of it. It was the reason why Agatha Christie wrote 10 pages every day, come what may.

It is not that what you write this way is a gem but at least you write. It is probably due to this reason, I reckon, that I responded affirmatively to John Dayal's invitation to write a weekly column for 'Midday'. I have written religiously, week after week, rain or hail, whether I am in Delhi or not, for all of the 500 weeks that have gone by. I don't know how much of this is 'creative' but there is no doubt that some of it has made an emotional impact on some of my readers, including John himself. No wonder he sent me a bouquet of flowers when I wrote an account of his going to iail for his agitation for the Christian Dalits.

Some people who are not bitten by the writing bug consider writers as some sort of freaks, even as foolish people.But most are more generous and look at writers with a bit of respect and a whole lot of awe, wondering why they don't have the same sort of talent and ability. Scarcely do they realize that it is these very doubts that inhibit their ability to write. They will surely give up their doubts if they care to remember that there is nothing unique in the education of a writer.

The initiation into the school of writing begins as soon as the child enters the kindergarten and has to mug his way through the a...b...c, the alphabet. Then you are told that some of them are called consonants and some vowels, the latter being key to the understanding as to how words are formed. Words, we soon realize, are not just an arrangement of these alphabets but have a relation to mental and empirical pictures. Remember, A for Apple, B for Bat and C for Cat, and so on?

Having gone through the words that form pictures, we now go to so called 'action' words, the words that 'do'.The words like Run, Cry, Sigh, Walk, etc., are not just 'picture' words but describe action or activity. But this is not all. Now when you come back to 'picture' words again, you find that one word is not enough for all of them. Take man: he can be white or black, snub-nosed or aquiline, pretty or ugly and so on. So you now come to 'adjectival' words that 'qualify' the 'picture' words.

Enough having been said about the intricacies of grammar and, since I do not intend this to be made into a schoolroom discourse, let us now go ahead and see how the rearrangement of the alphabet and the rules of grammar convert into the art of creative writing.

Language no doubt is a means of communication and when the art of writing was not yet born, we had to make do with verbal communication. Now that the means of writing are available to us, the question of 'how' of writing has cropped up. Superficially viewed, it is easy, once the alphabet and the rules of grammar have been mastered. All that one has to do is to transliterate the spoken word into writing and that is that but all those who have tried their hand at writing have long back realized that matters are not that simple.

Writing is not just about putting the alphabet into the shape of words and then stringing the words together into sentences and paragraphs by applying the rules of grammar. For one we have to know, even if we have decided on what to write about, how to begin, how to develop the theme, and finally, how to end it.

To illustrate what I mean, let us take an example, say of a biography. We know a lot of details of 'X's life: where he was born, where he spent his youth, his later life and where he died; we know a lot about what he did, with whom he came in contact, how he spent his time, his hobbies, interests, achievements. We also know a lot of what people with whom he came in contact felt about him, about what others who just knew him felt about him; and so on.Going this way, we realize that we have so much raw data that it could fill several volumes and still there would be much left.

It's not just selecting from what we know about the person, although that itself is no easy task which would depend on several factors, not least of all on the aspects of his life that we wish to highlight in our tome. Even when the selection has been made, we will still be left with the task of deciding which of the data that we have selected will need to be highlighted and what needs to be just mentioned in passing or in brief. Even this is not enough to make us sit on the computer keyboard and start tapping the keys; what we have to know is where we'll begin.

To just highlight just some of the problems that you'll confront, take the problem of the beginning. It could be a simple, undramatic one like 'He was born in (place) on (date)' or something more dramatic like 'Even before his genius could flower, (name) was mowed down by a hail of machine bullets' or innumerable other openings. All of these have been tried before with an equal amount of success or failure depending upon how the individual writer has been able to handle it.

Its not just the drama that is important, it is also what one wants to say, or, in other words, what is the theme. If we wish to highlight the successful struggle of a person, we may begin the story just at the moment the struggle began; or then some other writer may want to highlight the efforts through a flashback, by beginning at the point where the struggle ends. Here again, there are as many possibilities as there are writers; no mathematical formula can be given.

The theme itself has to be decided and that itself is no mean task. In writing a biography, one would like to highlight an achievement that has impressed him the most. But is there any certainty that this is really the achievement for which the personage was known or indeed wanted to be known? We could carry out a sample survey of what others think of him but then that may lead us to a theme that we do not accept at all. Wouldn't then one be dishonest in writing something that one doesn't believe in?

Let us say we have sifted the material, decided the theme, decided where we are going to begin from and what is the end. But it does not solve the problem of the 'how' of writing? I'm afraid the problem has only begun. We want at least three things to happen out of our writing: we want the reader to relate with the theme, we want him to find emotional and intellectual content in this, and, most of all, we want him to find it interesting so that he reads through it. How does one do this?

I could go on and on like this, dissecting the principles of the 'how' of writing and finding that each time we seem to solve one problem, we are led to another. One sure thing of ensuring that you don't write anything is to go on bothering about the 'how' of writing: I can safely say that this is the safest 'how not' of writing!

The safest 'how' of writing is that once you know the alphabet and the rules of grammar in the rudimentary form, just sit down on your desk, pick up the pen and start 'putting black on white'. Let me give you two preposterous tautologies: 'The only way to write is to write and to put black on white'.

You don't believe me, do you? But let me tell you that's the truth. It may not make you a great writer but at least you'll write. That's much more than what most of us can do. It is in this spirit that most of the pieces in the following pages have been penned.

Many people will say that okay, that explains how you write but still why write? Why not spend the time doing something more useful? Like helping the poor, doing social work, spending more time on files and so on. This question becomes especially important when you realize that full time writers can hardly make two ends meet.

Why write? Why indeed?

As I mull over this question, I am reminded of the answer to a similar question given to me by a friend who particularly likes me. Why do you like me? I asked. His puzzled looks might have given me the answer long before his lips did. "Ask my heart", he said; "or, if you can, read the expression in my eyes".

You'll have to do the same if you want to know why I write. Hear carefully to find if my heartbeats out an answer or if my eyes betray me. My lips just refuse to tremor in a way that will give my vocal cords the right lead.

Even as I don't have the answer to this question, I would like to counter it with another: Why shouldn't I? There's almost a unanimous chorus in reply: because you are a long serving-hard core bureaucrat.

That's the irony. A bureaucrat, who really has no other expertise other than wielding the pen on paper, should be questioned for this very activity!

Bureaucrats are really 'paper tigers' moving within the bounds of their well documented rules and regulations and through the medium of the 'red-taped' files. All our oral or telephonic orders are supposed to be followed by 'confirmation in writing' and all our meetings must be followed by written 'minutes'. All our decisions must be recorded on files and all our rules and regulations must be in writing even if they are precedents or practices. Isn't it odd, then, that a bureaucrat should be asked why he writes?

The question probably is not why I write but why I write other than 'nonsense' (the esoteric one of the variety that one often sees in files, otherwise called 'bureaucratese'); or why I indulge in what is sometimes somewhat optimistically called creative writing. Well, I'll try to answer this one.

Often it is for a very selfish, personal reason. I am basically a harmless, non-violent person but that makes me different from other human beings but I too get angry and violent at times; also vengeful and murderous. Especially when somebody, in my estimation, wrongs me. It happened to me once that a particular act of a person made me so angry that I wanted to murder him. Believe me, I was so angry that I actually wanted to kill him in a way that would attract Section 302 of the Indian Penal Code.

I am basically a meek person who, while enjoying murder mysteries and revenge movies, is not really physically equipped with the qualities of a killer. So what did I do? Picked up a pen and started writing on a piece of paper. I put him in a park early in the morning, just before day break. Here was I, with a shining sharp knife in my hand and murder in my eyes, following him waiting for the right moment to strike. My moment came when he stepped into the shade of a large tree, away from the glare of lamp posts and park lights.

I now stepped out of my hiding place and went towards him, with the stealth of a panther, determination of a tiger and grace of a fawn. Slowly and steadily I advanced, my every single nerve tense and my every single faculty focused at the task in hand. Suddenly I stopped as I noticed something strange: what was the chap doing?

He was not just standing under the tree: he was actually hugging it. In due course I noticed that he was kissing it too. And then when the truth dawned on me, my knife slipped out of my hands and my head swayed back and my lips gave out a most hearty and loud chuckle: he was having sex with the tree!

As I took my pen off the paper, I was laughing heartily too, having happily forgiven my real life tormentor too: how could such a demented fellow be blamed for his actions? It was so much fun in writing this story that I converted it into a short film for television.

This can't possibly be the only reason for writing; I can assure you there are several but none of them are apparent when one actually takes the pen, or starts tapping on the word processor keyboard. And sure as hell, it isn't. I remember when I returned from the cremation ground after collecting the mortal remains of my mother, I had a deadline and I had to write the article. So it was when I returned home after the 'bidaii' of my daughter or when I found amongst some old articles my photograph at the age of seventeen. On these occasions the writing bug starts biting you.

The bug bites you when there is tension or frustration; or when failure stares you in the face or the fear of rejection or anything like this. I don't know if what you produce at such times is a Nobel winning gem or just plain trash but there is no doubt that it does provide an 'escape'.

Writing is escapist, it may be protested. I'm not sure, as I said earlier, that what one writes in such moments is escapist fare or not but there is no doubt that writing does provide a means of escape. But that cannot be the sole purpose for which one writes. Why else?

One of the most native and innate urges in man is self-expression. Even the baby in the cradle is trying to do that. That's the reason why one wears clothes of a certain variety, the reason why one meets people or carries out other social interactions. Actors act because of this urge and leaders give speeches for this. And I suppose you can't blame writers if they wish to fulfill this innate urge through putting 'black on white'

Freud called dreams as 'wish fulfillment'. So I suppose is writing in many ways. A man suffers from many frustrations and failures in real life: in fact, a whole life is nothing but a string of failures strung together with knots or tied together through individual incidents. As one stumbles from one failure to another, one's need for rationalization of the meaning of existence becomes more and more important. Writing provides this rationalization, the *raison d'etre* of life.

But there is even a greater reason why one writes. Man is not an island; not only is he surrounded by a sea of humanity but also by many obstacles and hindrances. I write so that I can share these hindrances with others and also get the realization that I am not alone in my trials and tribulations. For me this alone is my *raison d'etre* not just of writing but of life itself.

That may give some hint of what to write but does not answer it entirely. The 'Why' of writing is not as unconnected with the 'What' of writing as may appear at first thought but still the connection is not that obvious. After a life time of writing I am pretty clear about why I write though I cannot say the same for what I write. Or, for that matter, what I ought to be writing.

It may be interesting to find out what are the subjects on which others write. At least that would give us a clue to where to start from.

Even with my limited range of reading I can without hesitation say that the range of what people write is indeed staggering. From the absolute trash and muck to the profound and esoteric the range is very wide, almost as much as it is amongst human characters itself.

Is there anything that has not been written upon? Biography, fiction, fact; detective, mystery, murder, sex; intrigue, roguery, deception; science fact, human nature, biology; reading the palm, mythology, religion; and what not. You name it and there it is, almost every subject under the sun. A mere survey of the writing scene does not give any idea of what one ought to be writing about; in fact if that is what you are trying to determine in the survey, you will get so confused and disgusted that you may have to give up writing altogether!

But writing is one of the innate urges of man and, while like life, it does not need a justification, a *raison d'etre* from without, like Kant's *categorical imperative* or Krishna's *nishkama karma* it is its own justification. The what of writing has to flow out of this essential fact.

Man is not an island and even if he were he would soon have found that he has hardly any control on the essential feature of his environment. He is not only surrounded by a sea of humanity but also by many obstacles and hindrances over which he hardly has any control. His life therefore, is bound to be dotted with a whole lot of frustrating obstacles. Many of us see in our writing a way of sharing these hindrances with others and also to get the realization that one is not alone.

One of the most dreaded moments of life is the death of one's mother. More than a flesh and blood person, mother is a feeling, a warmth, a comforting thought—rarely seen as such but felt nevertheless. For full nine months before birth and then for the rest of your life you bask in the comfort of her radiance, hardly ever thinking that this comfort could ever be lost. We take her for granted, just as we do heat and light, water and air. But, alas! she too is only human and just like the rest of us death is an inalienable reality for her too.

Any death is an unnerving experience but most of all it is the death of mother. It's like water and air vanishing from the world; for a moment it seems that the world would come to a stop. This happened to me too; right through the last rites, journey to Nigambodh, the collection of the wood, laying her limp body on the heap, the chanting of mantras and, finally, the lighting of the pyre—all this seemed a mechanical, administrative process. But on the fourth day when we went back to collect the bones from the dead fire that it suddenly came to me: the comfort was no more.

The 'what' of writing was clear to me: The death of my mother. I cried as I wrote and as I'm told, did a large number of my readers who read that piece. I suddenly realized I was not alone in this world; even if people were not partaking in my life in any other way, at least we were one in expressing our grief.

It's not just death that causes apprehensions in our life; there are many smaller happenings and events which cast the shadow of dread much before they arrive. An interview or exam, the first day in class, facing a new boss, a speech or public talk, and what not. In each of these 'dreads' one thinks that one is unique and alone. The mere realization that one is not alone in this regard lessens the impact of the dread. And one way of getting this realization is to pen it down, making it one of the 'What' of writing.

I remember the first time my daughter came and told me about the man she loved. Here was the moment I had 'dreaded' all my life and finally when it came true I realized how irrational my dread was and how easily I coped up with the issue! Isn't it true of most other dreads as well? I quickly made it the what of my writing. When 'Father of the Bride' appeared in the paper, dozens of people rang up to say how they had felt the same way too.

The same was true of 'Bidaii of my Daughter' as well. This was another event that I had dreaded all my life. I cry very easily, even while watching a movie. However will I cope up with parting with my dear darling daughter? As it is, I didn't cry, I wasn't even heavy within: I was overwhelmed with the fact that far from losing a daughter I was actually gaining a son. People still remember this article of mine and mention it to me in parties and on other occasions.

Just about anything can constitute the 'what' of writing. It is better if the event or occurrence has made an emotional impact on you but what if it hasn't? It can still give you a means of self-expression. Book reviews and writing about films would be covered in this category.

I remember the time when the fast aging Amitabh Bachchan was desperately trying to stage a comeback. I saw one of the movies he made at that stage. All the time as I saw the pictures on the large screen I saw none but the Amitabh of my class in Boys High School, Allahabad as he sat quietly on the back bench. What a contrast! As against the simple, unpretentious youngster of my class, there was this tragic figure on the screen trying to outdo the Shahrukhs and Salmans of the present day.

I penned down this comi-tragedy and posted a copy to the aging superstar. I don't know how he reacted to the article but he did send a warm acknowledgement.

I'm not trying to motivate you to shower praise on my writings. All I'm saying is that any subject is good enough for writing; all you have to do is to take out your pen and start writing. The results of some of these efforts are here with you as you will flip through the pages of 'Distant Echoes'. Each one of the pieces is written more with the heart than with the head and because of this they will reverberate in your mind long after the words and lines are forgotten. At least that is what I hope.

Writing has been a labour of love for me. There is not a single line I have ever written with the hope that I will be read. I have enjoyed every moment that the pen is in my hand, loved every word that has flowed out of it. If I manage to communicate even a part of the pleasure that I have derived out of my writing to the reader I will consider the effort and labour to have been well spent. Both mine and that of the publisher.

OMESH SAIGAL

PART 1

MAN OF THE MILLENNIUM

1

MAN OF THE MILLENNIUM-I

When somebody asked me recently as to who our man of the millennium is, I had no hesitation whatsoever in blaring out the answer: Mahatma Gandhi, of course. Who else could it be?

But then when I started thinking, I found that the answer is not as simple as all this; after all the millennium is a thousand years old and it is a long time in the history of a nation that now has more than a billion people. In these thousand years we have seen the likes of Kabir and Ghalib or Tulsidas not to speak of Tagore and Bankim. And who can forget thinkers and leaders like Guru Nanak and Guru Govind Singh or great rulers of the caliber of Akbar? Raman, Chandrashekhar, Teresa......the list really is endless.

Is Mohandas Karamchand Gandhi really the obvious choice for the Man of the Millennium? I wonder. And as I do that all the arguments against him come rushing to the fore. For one, he was a bad husband and even a worse father. His wife Kasturba loved and adored him. Not that he did not love: by his own admission he was equally fond of her. But then how do you account for his behaviour in South Africa when she had refused to clean the latrine of a Dalit Christian guest?

Love, if nothing else, implies understanding and faith. Surely he understood that his wife, too like him, stood for certain principles. And as much as she admired him for this, he too should have at least understood the underlying purity of faith for the ones she stood for. He should have understood that this was the least that ahimsa, in which he had so abiding and complete a faith, demanded of him.

Why did he then recourse to ahimsa to the extent of driving her out of his house, knowing fully well that she had no options being thousands of miles from her home in India? It was not just his behaviour with his wife for which he owes an explanation but his attitude towards his eldest son, Harilal, was even more devoid of merit. Harilal was not born to a Mahatma or was he anybody but the son of a briefless barrister who was forced to seek his fortune in far away Africa.

Being in a joint family and with his father away he was naturally guided in important matters by his uncles. He was barely seventeen when he fell in love with Saraswati, a girl of the same age. Coming to know of this his uncle got the two married and subsequently informed Gandhi is far away South Africa. For young Harilal it was a dream come true; it was like walking on the clouds.

How was he to know that his happiness was soon to end that his angry father would soon force him to come to Africa leaving his young wife behind? Gandhi too had married his (Harilal's) mother at a tender age (both he and Ba were thirteen at that time) and was, for that reason, terribly opposed to marriage before the age of maturity. He considered such marriages to be almost sinful. But how was Harilal to know all this?

But this did not disturb Mohandas on we bit: for him it was enough that a marriage had taken place in the family and that itself was an 'immoral', act. He summoned Harilal to Africa, forcing him to leave his young bride behind in India. When Saraswati died subsequently of an illness and Harilal wanted to marry again, Mohandas would have none of it. For him sex and immorality were almost synonyms. He wrote to Ba that Hari was born out of 'their sin' alluding to the incident narrated in his autobiography of how the sexual desire aroused him at the time he was rubbling the feet of his aling father and how, as he had sex with he, he died. All his life he was under the allusion that Harilal was the child born out of this act, forgetting that the daughter born to him approximately 9 months after this incident was stillborn!

If he had just been a bad husband and father, one may have ignored it: after all it was for his public life that we know him.

But see how he treated Netaji when, he became the Congress President despite his open opposition. The conditions that he created for him were so impossible that the poor Subhas Chandra Bose had no choice but to resign; in fact, he had to quit the party. Was this the act of a saint? Or the simple response of a plain and simple politician who has lost out on the ballot?

If this were all, one would not have thought twice over the issue but take his attitude to various human urges. He talked all the time of abstinence and self-denial. It is true that much of his life does reflect this basic philosophy of his. But how does one explain his absolute failure to check his sexual urges to take the better of him?

He admits to having sexual urges even at the age of 78! He used to sleep with women even at a ripe old age to prove to himself, and the world, that he had controlled his basic emotions but he was a failure. But are not we leaving the basic issue: he was a Mahatma not because of these virtues (or lack of them) but because of his undoubted power to influence millions and millions of people, many of whom were opposed to him. He was a true leader of men, with the power to bring round to his viewpoint not only the masses but also the elite.

He could not merely bring round people behind him but also affect them profoundly, both mentally and spiritually. His power of persuasion extended not just to the poor people of Orissa and Bihar or intellectuals like Nehru but also people like Albert Einstein was spoke the immortal lines, generations to come, it may be, will scarce believe that such a one in flesh and blood walked upon this earth. But, lest we forget, his powers of persuasion came to a scratch when it came to the crunch.

India stood at the threshold of independence. Many sectarian forces had raised their ugly head, at the head of which stood the Muslim League, with their 'two-nation theory'. Gandhi along with all the other national leaders had rejected this obnoxious theory and were willing to sacrifice their all for the unity of the motherland. To keep the unity of the country, Gandhi told the British: 'hand over power to the Muslim League and quit: we'll settle it amongst ourselves'.

It is here that almost all his supporters deserted him. Even the 'yes-yes' man Patel and the 'no-yes' man Nehru. Everyone, but his personal companions and servants, here is to his leadership!

Is this the man of the millennium? I wonder, I like you to wonder too.

2

MAN OF THE MILLENNIUM-II

In the last chapter, we have discussed Gandhi's credentials for the top slot of the millennium. A bad husband, a poor, heartless father, a leader, who cannot make his followers follow, and an anti-democracy man—could such a man be the Man of the Millennium? These were some of the questions raised; now is the time to carry the discussion on.

The first point to be delved a bit deeper is the attitude of the Mahatma to his kith and kin, mainly his own wife and eldest son. Let us contrast it with the attitude of today's generation of leaders in this regard.

Pratap Singh Kairon was questionably one of the free India's most competent chief ministers. His two sons were always in the forefront whether it involved setting up of cinemas or participating in development (naturally their own) or in setting up business empires. Kairon is not alone in this regard: what he did was followed invariably by almost all of the new breed of politicians.

Unlike Kairon, the later breed of politicians believed not just in cornering the loaves and fishes of office but also the office itself. The political mantle passed not only to the next of the line in the party or in the cadres but to wives, children and other relations. And this syndrome is confined not just to the ruling parties but extends to parties in opposition as well. Count the number of wives and children of former and present leaders, heading the political parties and governments to realize what

I'm saying. Politicians seem to have two standards: one for their family and one for others.

Gandhi too had two standards: but do you realize the difference? His standards for his own kith and kin were much more exacting and demanding and not the other way round. In this regard he stands heads and shoulders above the rest of the ilk not just in India but probably in the whole of the developing world.

Gandhi's attitude towards Netaji was no doubt anti-democratic but let us not forget that their differences were not personal or personality based (as in most political parties today) but based on certain basic principles, such as the use of non-violence as a political weapon for India's struggle for freedom. Both of them stuck to their principles and the result was the formation of a new political party, the Forward Block, to accommodate Netaji. This is how political parties were born and not the way it happens today, merely to accommodate the ambitions of some power hungry politician or the other.

As for the point made about Gandhi's failure as a leader, epitomized in the fact of his followers deserting him on the partition issue, history has given us an answer: the failure was not of the leader but of the dozens of his substandard followers who deserted him. And to get this answer, we have had to undergo not just the destruction of more than a million people in the aftermath of the partition and in the four wars we have fought with Pakistan, but also in the legacy of hatred and violence with which the subcontinent has been besotted all this while.

It was not his followers who deserted him but he who decided to undertake 'ekla chalo ekla chalo'. And history has clearly told us that he was right.

Let's pause here: does all this make him the Man of the Millennium? Surely no. What we have done so far is to see that the criticism made of him is not justified. That's all. But what he did that no Indian has done in the last 1000 years? Just being taller than the other leaders in his time does not necessarily make him the all time great! What is it that does?

His voluntary adoption of poverty may have been the act of a politician trying to identify himself with the masses to win their support. The adoration that he received from the masses was indeed unique but not any more than Hitler got from the German masses. He was a sharp politician with the acumen to build institutions but arguably not above the ability of Nehru in this regard. He held firmly to his principles and precepts but no more than what a person like Vinoba Bhave would do. He sacrificed his all, yes, but probably no more than Bhagat Singh. He was a firm nationalist who loved his country but no more than Netaji Subhas Chandra Bose or any of the other innumerable freedom fighters. He served the poor and suffering people but no more than Mother Teresa.

What is it that makes Gandhi different?

Let us take the first three or four decades of his life. These years were marked by both a mediocrity of achievement and of effort. He had a terrible handwriting, and about the art of public speaking, the less said the better. He could not even read out a brief note he had penned earlier. He was a lawyer who, in the first and probably the only brief he got in India, stood tongue tied in the court when it came to replying to the arguments of the prosecutor and lost the case miserably.

Gandhi was not just a mediocre but downright incompetent in this period. That is the reason why he was forced by his uncles to go to South Africa where at least he would be able to earn his living. Contrast with this, the later period of his life was a sharp contrast. Instead of being a stuttering high school student, he was a brilliant orator who held even hostile crowds spell-bound and cheering. A lawyer, who could barely speak in court debated and defeated some of the greatest speakers, it can be almost said that India won her freedom as much in the debating halls of Eton as from the manifold agitations he launched in India.

A mediocrity rising to brilliance is a theme of hit movies; this is Gandhi's life story too. The Einsteins and Chandrasekhars of the world are destined for greatness; they are uncommon minds. Theirs can hardly be an examples that could inspire the vast masses of the people: but for a man who is like them to rise above the limits of his mediocrity and attain greatness that is denied even to the likes of Einsteins and Gogh is what inspires and enthuses.

Much more than the achievement is the struggle and strife. All his life Gandhi was struggling with his limitations, his sexual struggles towards the later part of his life, his despairing attempts to bring back into his life his estranged son Harilal, his futile attempts to keep Nehru and Company behind him when he asked the Cripps Mission to hand over power to Jinnah and quit India, his desperate attempts to keep the first Ministers steadfast to their ideals, and so on are all part of this man's ability to keep on struggling and striving even though he was obviously losing.

In more ways than one Gandhi's life was a failure but this did not keep him away from the struggle. Even when he lay bleeding before the assassin's bullet, he said 'Hey Ram' as if he was praying to God to let him complete his task even after his death.

It was his ability to strive and struggle, much more than of any other Indian of the millennium that I know of, that makes me call him the Man of the Millennium.

3
THE RELEVANCE OF GANDHI

It is now more than five decades since India won its independence and almost the same time since the father of the nation departed. Much of what Gandhi did has already been forgotten; much of what he said is also mostly confined to his Collective Works. There is a growing feeling that he and his economic philosophy are becoming more and more irrelevant to the needs of a modern and progressive India. Much in the same way that he had become during the last few years of his life.

It is true that many people who think like this know little about the Mahatma and his views except that he was against the machine and wanted India to adapt the *charkha* or the spinning wheel as its symbol. This they feel makes him quite irrelevant considering the impact that science and technology have had on the rest of the world, including the so called Third World.

If this was indeed the case and the spinning wheel is the only legacy of Gandhi, then maybe they are right too. But is this his only or even his main legacy? Is Gandhi minus the spinning wheel nothing?

In a way, yes, but that is only if the spinning wheel is taken as a mere machine. For Gandhi it was more than that; it was a symbol. For Gandhi symbols were important; so much so that many of them became part of his very being. Like shedding his upper garments (for identification with the poor) or his vows of celibacy or the selling of a handful of salt at Dandi. For many people Gandhi has become irrelevant because they have forgotten, or not cared to know, the truth behind these symbols. In fact, it is people who care more for the symbols than for the truth behind these that have made Gandhi irrelevant.

It is my firm view that only if we care to find out the true meaning behind the symbols that we can understand the true Gandhi; it is only then that we can find solutions to many of our present day problems.

Take the evil of corruption. It now pervades every aspect of life. The same is true of casteism, communalism, nepotism and all other ills that afflict us. Can the life and views of Gandhi help us in finding solutions to these problems? Can Gandhi help? Yes, he can and that, in my view, is his true relevance today.

It is a well-known fact that Gandhi called the Sabarmati Central Jail his 'other ashram'. What is not so well known is the fact that he believed that jail's conditions be accepted as suffering for truth In that case 'we shall never weary of jail going', he wrote; 'when the whole of India has learnt this lesson, India shall be free'. In the converse, India shall be in bondage if we do not learn this lesson.

Now when, for the second time in the recent political history of the country, politicians are again being picked up for selective prosecutions and jail going, the message becomes important. But such has become the calibre of our present day leadership that this very important lesson has been forgotten. Just see how they shudder at the thought of going to jail, trying desperately for bail or even feigning sickness! How different from Gandhi who even had a major operation in jail and whose caring wife and hardworking secretaries actually died there!

Does it mean that India is now in for another period of bondage? Or is it that the jail going is for reasons other than truth? Probably the latter is truer than the former though it is a sad commentary on our political system.

Be it as it may, there is no doubt that this is the key message of the Mahatma that has relevance today. These one and all his utterances on corruption, are an issue which has come to the fore as never before. But it isn't as if corruption has come up as an issue only at the present moment or that Gandhi had never confronted it.

Gandhi first came in contact with corruption at the time of the Bengal famine. India was then under British rule and there was nothing much he could do but to exhort his party (Congress) to themselves remain above board. But the corruption that he encountered at the time of the refugee relief programme in the wake of the partition was at a time when there was a national government in power. This saddened him no end. Also how easily the Congress leadership which had spent years in jail took to the fishes and loaves of office, both in terms of posh bungalows as also in terms of other luxuries.

On the eve of the independence of the country, he was in Calcutta calming down the communal frenzy that was gripping the city. It was then that the new Bengal cabinet came to seek his blessings. Warning them of the corrupting influence of power, he advised them to be 'humble, forbearing and ceaselessly strive for truth and non-violence'. He went on: 'This is a testing time for you and now is the real test: do not be trapped by power and the pomp and show that go with it. Do not forget that power is for the service of the poor folk in the villages.' One wonders how many ministers remember this message now though, if anything, it is even more relevant now than it was at that time!

Some time back I met a minister who had quit his position in the wake of the hawala racket. He was surrounded by a large number of admirers (sycophants?) trying to give him solace. His wife, otherwise an innocent housewife, remarked: 'What are a few lacs for him! This much money is stitched to the garlands that he is given when he tours his area! He just takes the garland and gives it to one of his workers!'

Gandhi often said that all his sayings and words should be burnt at his pyre and his 'life' should be allowed to be his message. What did he do with the donations that he got? Once he was travelling for attending the Congress Session at Calcutta. The train stopped on the way, the multitudes greeted him. He spread out his palm before them for donations and all of them, according to their mite, contributed, some even as low as an anna or two.

On the way, in between stations, he would meticulously make an account of all the donations received-sometime these would number more than 5000 during the course of a single journey—writing them down on the backs of envelopes or any other paper that he had. During this Calcutta trip too he collected a lot of such donations. As soon as the train reached Howrah station, he summoned, from out of the rush assembled there, Dr. B C Roy (later to be Chief Minister of West Bengal) and asked him to take charge of the cash as also the various sundry slips of paper on which he had written the accounts.

When Dr. Roy suggested that he would do so after the public reception that had been arranged outside the station, Gandhi would have none of it. 'First the public funds should go to the public account and then anything else'. It was only after every paisa was accounted for in the books of the West Bengal Congress Committee that B.C. Roy was allowed to attend the public functions. What a lesson for the present day politicians who take the moneys given to them as donations as their personal property!

The credibility of the political leadership of the country is so low that every paisa that they take is called a bribe. Otherwise, how can the mere fact of a certain amount of money given to a politician (as reflected in the hawala diary) condemn a politician as corrupt? Is there an objective criteria for determining whether money taken by a politician amounts to a bribe?

It was early days for Gandhi in India after his last return from South Africa. He had set up an ashram near Ahmedabad on the lines of the ashrams that he had started in South Africa. Unlike South Africa, where he had the support of the rich Indian expatriates, his source of funds soon dried up. A situation came when his financial position was so precarious that he had no option but to wind up the ashram.

Most of the luggage and other items had been packed up and despatched; now he awaited the car that would take him to his new home. Suddenly a black car drove and out stepped a diminutive *dhoti* clad person. He walked to the Mahatma and bent low before him. When he straightened up, Gandhi found a wad of notes at his feet. Even before he picked up the money, the diminutive character got into his car and drove away after telling the Mahatma that running the ashram was more important than many other things that he could do with the money.

Gandhi immediately accepted the gift, got it entered in the ashram accounts and the ashram was again in business. How would you classify this gift? A bribe? A donation? Today's politicians would know better but, in my view, it became a donation the moment Gandhi got it entered in the accounts of the Ashram. Till then it could be anything, even a bribe! I'm saying this because the identity of the anonymous donor is now known: he is none other than Jamnalal Bajaj.

Most of what Gandhi said or did has relevance today, especially his views on what true freedom means. For Gandhi political freedom alone was not the *swaraj* of his dreams. In his *poorna swaraj* resolution moved on January 26, 1930 at the Lahore session, freedom meant freedom from want for the poorest of the poor. This should be quite relevant when viewed in the context of the present liberalisation of the economy. Gandhi's test for any decision was: how it would benefit the poorest of the poor. When viewed in this light, one gets a pretty dim view of the present economic policies which, at least visibly, has only meant more and more cars and more expensive consumer goods for the upper middle classes. I wonder how much of these will ever reach the common man, what to talk of the poorest of the poor!

The one most remarkable fact that confronts us in contemporary India is the fact that in no field is there any person who can merit international attention. While in a time of bondage we could have a Tagore get the Nobel Prize for literary merit and a Raman get it for science, now for a Khurana to get it he has to go and work in the states. The same applies to the political field, the social field, the government services: wherever you see there is mediocrity and lack of leadership.

Look at the sort of people that Gandhi was able to discover; from nowhere he would conjure a leader. From the Hindus and the Muslims, from the upper and the lower castes, from the poor and the affluent, from the north and the south. And see what he made of them! Rightly it is said of him:

Gandhi was a scavenger,
Mental, moral, physical,
Who swept in the dust bin of the world.
A highway for the gods to use.

(Extract from the author's 'Never Gandhi, Not Again': published by Full Circle Publications)

What many Indians today still remember Gandhi fondly, what they have forgotten is his use of symbols. Injustice exists as much today as it did in the time of Gandhi; what we have forgotten is the way Gandhi countered it. That is the true significance of his smilingly going to jail. Or his spinning of the wheel in the face of the gravest crises. Or his 'hours of silence' or his fasts or even his humility. Understand now why he got out of the train to get a cup of tea for his sleeping mate? Or why he gave his commode to Nehru when he joined him for a few days at Noakhali even though he himself found it difficult to squat? Or why he took off his leather *chappals* when he got out of the train in Noakhali and decided to complete the tour barefoot?

It is true that much of Gandhi's symbolism came out of genuine conviction and belief but it is also true that he clung to the symbol as much as he did to the belief that gave rise to it. It is also true that we in India cling to many of his symbols without believing in anything deeper. Still, the fact that we have given up many if not most of the symbols of his era is symptomatic of our drift. If nothing else, let us at least revive some of the symbols of his age.

Like wearing *khadi*. Or wearing *chappals* made at home. Even if every Indian does not find it possible to do so, at least let a beginning be made with the leaders or those who have pretensions of becoming so. At least there's one thing I beg of you; let us not just wait for him to be born again so that he can take the burden of our sins on his shoulders.

But never Gandhi, not again,
Be born upon this blighted earth;
Please do not give another chance
To us to shoot you down again.
Please Gandhi don't be born again!
We cannot bear the burden of
The weight of your beliefs and faith;
We couldn't then, how will we now?
Belief in non-violence and truth
Is more than we can bear and hold.
Please Gandhi don't be born anew:
We only want you here with us
So we can shoot you down once more.

(From 'Never Gandhi, Not Again' by the author)

4

LETTING THE WINDS BLOW IN

I want all the windows of my house open for the winds from all sides to blow in; but I refuse to be swept off my feet.

Remember who said this? The long forgotten, suffering great soul whose name was Mohandas Karamchand Gandhi. Whom four per cent less people think has influenced their life than his namesake but more recent Indira Gandhi!

Like much of what he said, we have probably forgotten this edict too. But, maybe, the crisis that we face in the wake of the huge economic invasion from the West, will make us take another look at it.

Gandhi talked of the cultural invasion that was taking place at that time and the terrible dilemma that the country faced: do you remain trapped in your ivory tower and in the process be by-passed in the international rat race; or do you get submerged in the cultural wave that the world had unleashed on you?

We are in the midst of a similar situation today except that the crisis is not cultural but economic. Will this edict help us evolve some sort of a response to the latest invasion?

After the fall of the Soviet Union, there is no way that any nation, leave alone a large one such as India, can remain with its doors and windows closed. No longer can barriers of tariffs and controls protect us from the possible ravages of an unhindered movement of goods and technology from a powerful and monopolistic industrialized world.

The winds which blow outside our house are strong, gusty

and powerful. And the tiny blocks (be they factories or business houses) that we have assembled inside during the period of protectionism may not be exactly made of cards but are puny and weak all the same.

If we open our windows and doors (allow unhindered access to foreign goods, technology and competition) there is a distinct danger that all these carefully assembled blocks may be swept away and destroyed.

On the other hand, if we do not open our doors, our house itself may remain isolated and backward in a fast advancing and progressing world.

I feel the Mahatma's edict is even more relevant today than it was at the time it was issued. Maybe it does not give an answer to the problem but it certainly gives one of the essential parameters which every possible solution must satisfy.

At first it may appear that there is no way that the two contrary situations can be reconciled; it seems an either-or situation. Either we can open the window or keep the blocks inside intact; there is no way that we can do both.

Those who think like this must be taking a pretty dim view of much of our historical developments which largely consists of attempts to reconciling the opposites and the contraries. Our entire heritage has been translated into the unity in diversity that we find in every facet of our contemporary life.

In any case, Gandhi's edict of 'refusing to be swept off my feet' must have seemed equally ridiculous at that time as trying to balance foreign technology powered growth with safeguarding of the swadeshi achievements may seem today. But see how all this could be done with remarkable success by the Mahatma!

It is true that mere injunctions and edicts are not enough; suitable tools and methodologies have to be developed. To launch his political battle, Gandhi did not go for the revival of traditional Indian institutions, political or social; on the contrary he took hold of a foreign institution (the Congress Party) founded by the foreigner Hume, as his launch vehicle.

In a matter of a few years, with a few deft strokes of his pen, he had rewritten the constitution of this party and soon made it into a powerful weapon for fighting against foreign rule. What is interesting is that Gandhiji used a foreign institution both as a shield and as a weapon against that very same foreign rule. But still that alone was not enough if he had not devised the right methods.

Take *Satyagraha*. What a powerful weapon it proved to be! At the end of British rule, it was still difficult to say who had won and who had lost. It seems—and still seems today—that both the sides had won.

Can we follow this approach today? What we need is technology, competition and what have you but not to destroy but to strengthen.

Let the competition and capital from outside, instead of threatening our own millions of small and medium businesses, strengthen them. And such should be the nature of the interaction that they themselves are gainers in the process.

I think one single example should suffice. Small businesses are known for their resilience and hard work; and large ones for their expertise and capital. Instead of pitting one against the other, is it not possible to pool the advantages and use them to the mutual benefit of both?

Gandhi showed how it can be done in the political and cultural fields; it is now our job to see that the same thing is done in the economic field as well. We have to evolve appropriate institutions, methodologies and techniques. That's all.

All this is easier said than done. *Satyagrana* was a powerful technique but it needed a Gandhi to develop it. The Congress was a strong and resilient institution but it needed a Gandhi to write its new constitution. We cannot forget that some of the greatest leaders the country has known came up at this time. But this, alas, became possible because there was a Gandhi to recognize them.

Do we have a leader who has the capacity to take upon his shoulders the mantle of Gandhi? Do we have one single leader of that calibre?

5

THE MAKING OF THE MAHATMA

Let me admit it: as I walked into the Sirifort auditorium for the Shyam Benegal film on the Mahatma, my expectations were not too high: for one I knew that the film would suffer in comparison with the Attenborough masterpiece; for another I realised it wouldn't be easy for an Indian to make a film on him. But still I was not prepared for the shock that I actually received.

Bad is not the word I would like to use for the film; in its own way it has points that would impress serious film makers. After all a film that picked up as many as three national awards cannot be devoid of any merit. But as a film on a personality and that too a well known one, the film has to be judged more for how it depicts him than for its cinematic content. It is here that the film falters and miserably fails.

It is not just that the Gandhi seen on the screen is a stranger; his so called progression to Mahatma, with which the film ostensibly deals, also remains veiled. The events are all there but still there is something missing. It is almost as if the film is a body, but a body without a soul.

A film maker is not just an observer, noting down and narrating events as they unfold before him. Let's take an example. Everybody knows the circumstances under which Gandhi was thrown out of the first-class compartment. In a film we are not satisfied with merely being informed about what we already know but like to feel and, in a way, relive the experience. This is what Attenborough did so brilliantly and, I'm afraid, Benegal miserably failed to do.

After being thrown out, we see Rajat Kapur (I still can't make myself see this actor as Gandhi, despite the national award to him) sitting on his luggage seeing the train steam off without him. As the camera, perched high above his head, trolleys with him, Kapur gets up and sits on the bench. Here he picks up a copy of the Holy Koran that has been gifted to him at Durban station. Thereafter, there are a few bars of music and the scene dissolves to show him sitting on the train again.

A number of questions crop up: if he had to take the train next day, why did he leave it the last night? Did he want to travel first class just because he had a ticket or were there other reasons? This latter question is important since we know that almost his entire life the Mahatma insisted on travelling third class. What did he do the rest of the night and what effect this experience had on his personality? What did the Koran have to do with all this?

Benegal is silent on most of the questions, except for a few movements of the camera and some bars of music. Is it because there is nothing to say? Let's see what Gandhi himself has to say in his Autobiography. I sat and shivered. There was no light in the room....I began to think of my duty. Should I fight for my rights or go back to India...? It would be cowardice to run back to India without fulfilling my obligation. The hardship to which I was subjected was superficial—only a symptom of the deep sense of colour prejudice. I should try, if possible, to root out the disease....

It is clear that the incident while characterising him also showed how he now had a focus, an objective to aim at while in South Africa. Benegal could not be ignorant of this; in fact, I wrote a long biographical poem on Gandhi quite some time ago which brought out this very aspect.

'The train steamed off, left him behind/Shaking with rage, with humbled pride/A fire burning in his heart/Young Mohan felt so like the crow/Who finds himself alone amidst/The empty widths, infinite depths/And endless heights of angry storms/He was a picture of despair/Of woe and gloom, of anger, hate/ Contempt and sorrow, hopelessness!' On his mood I write: 'I see no moon, I see no stars/I see no left, I see no right/I see none but this raging storm/I hear naught but the thunder boom/ I think not but of death beyond/I feel naught but impending doom/Forsake me not, forsake me not!'

It is after this that the enlightenment comes. "And then at once there was no rain/There was no storm, no lightning, sound/ No more the dark clouds hid the sky/No more the threat from Death appeared/The sea became a placid lake/Then like the fixed, determined star/And like the big Himalayan peaks/young Mohan stood determined, fixed/No matter what they do to me/ No matter what they say to me/I will not leave South Africa/ Till I have filled my station here/And played my part to help these folk/To see the Truth, His Colour too."

In many places Benegal almost paints Gandhi as a reactionary. Take his views on the war against the Zulus and the Boers. Overruling the arguments of his colleagues, he assists the British army in their war against these oppressed tribes, a seemingly reactionary step. Mr Benegal, I wish you had picked up Gandhi's autobiography. 'When the war was declared, my personal sympathies were all with the Boers, but I believed then that I had yet no right, in such cases, to enforce my individual convictions.'

This is the key to the understanding of the Mahatma, a characteristic that would be with him right through his life: to suppress his individual convictions for the public good.

Benegal meanders through one incident after another, without bothering to either bring out the changes that these brought out in him or even to try to understand the inner strivings that had brought them about. Benegal has merely patched up a story of Gandhi in South Africa, that's all. It is difficult to understand how the westernised individual who landed in Natal in 1883 was transformed into a Mahatma in 21 years.

Even, factually, he has made mistakes; though these may not be important to the total import of the movie, these are being mentioned to illustrate the lackadaisical manner in which the film seems to have been made. When he came to Durban in 1897, he had three children with him, Hari and Mani and the 10-year old son of his sister, not two as the film shows.

If any young chap wants to know about Gandhi, my advice is to stay away from the Benegal film till he has read Gandhi's *My Experiments with Truth*; and once he has read this, he can give the film a miss since the emotional and intellectual experience of reading the book far exceeds the one that lies in store in the cinema house where the film will be released.

6

THE MAKING OF CHARISMA

I received two jolts the other day; one when V. N. Singh, the Commissioner of Police, entered my room and the other when he left. On both the occasions he referred to my piece on the relevance of Gandhi. It is nice for a writer to hear about his writing from someone but it is doubly so if what is being referred to is also something about which one too feels strongly.

I had noted in my article how a poor student, a poor speaker who made of hash of his first case in court; one who was short in height, was a very ordinary person to look at, yet who could convert his very lack of abilities into a great asset to become the most extraordinary Indian of the millennium. It was this that V.N. found inspiring enough to remember on the two occasions and this is what sets me thinking on what makes charisma.

Well, coming down to it, let's try to determine what really does make charisma? There have been many charismatic individuals down the centuries. Starting with Buddha, Rama and Christ, we come down to our own age with people like Napoleon, Bismarck, Stalin, Hitler, Mao, Ho Chi Minh, Churchill, etc. All of them, some for good, others for bad, with their mesmerising personalities changed the course of events and influenced people long after they are dead and gone.

What is it that makes for charisma? What is it that these people had which others lacked that makes them so charismatic? Is it physical beauty? Character? Upbringing? Pedigree?

Take Napoleon. He was not even a Frenchman, having been born in the island of Corsica, miles away from the French coast. Not a brilliant student, fat and stodgy, quite ugly to look at, it was but natural that he did not have a fantastic start in life, having to be content to join the artillery as a lieutenant. In the normal course he would probably have retired as a Colonel or maybe as a general: there is no way he could have shaped the course of history, at least not in the way he actually did. In fact, one wonders if he had even been a footnote in history had it not been for the fortune that his was the only army unit available when unruly mobs gheraoed the National Assembly.

Anybody who has ever handled law and order knows that the rule is to use minimum necessary force to control an unruly mob. Also that army is called as a last resort, after persuasion, warnings, tear gas and police lathis have failed to control the unruly mobs. Post revolution Paris was an extraordinary city. Unruly mobs ruled the streets and the heads of the nobility that had ruled France for the best part of 2000 years or more were hanging from lamp posts and trees.

The gherao of the Assembly was the extraordinary culmination of the events and the Terror following the Revolution and calling in the army was the desperate last resort. When Napoleon reached the Assembly and saw the extraordinary situation there, he did the only thing that he was trained to do: open up with his artillery. History does not record how many people died, but the shock of the 'whiff of grapeshot' was so decisive that the crowd melted away and with it the aftermath of the revolution.

The child of the revolution was not just the hero of the hour O; he was destined to become the man of the century too. Promoted to the rank of general, he was soon the envy of the other senior generals who manoeuvred to send him to Italy where the revolutionary armies were engaged in a deadly combat. But Napoleon was able to turn the tables there and the rest is history. Not only did he become the leader of the post-revolutionary France but also its Emperor not much more than a decade after his 'whiff of grapeshot' brought him into prominence.

Prince Siddhartha's shaping was equally dramatic, though the path taken by him was that of renunciation and giving up the crown rather than of taking the path of war and glory. So was the path of glory taken by Emperor Ashoka who renounced the path of peace when at the height of glory as the victor of the battle of Kalinga.

Gandhi's was a more painstaking route; there's hardly one single incident that can describe his change from mediocrity to charisma. In fact, his whole life was a struggle to get out of his mediocrity. His rise to greatness was slow and 11 through his life his inhibitions threatened his growth in that direction.

Take the incident in South Africa when Kasturba was thrown out of the house for refusing to clean the toilet of a Dalit convert to Christianity. All his non-violent principles were threatened to be consumed by the all enveloping hate and anger against the action of his wife that had no logic but the fact that Ba was his wife and therefore subject to his direction and controi.

His anger and anguish at the actions of his estranged elder son, Harilal, were also similarly motivated. Would his reaction have been the same if Ba had not been his wife and Harilal not his son? Most decidedly no. But then it was Gandhi's greatness or call it luck if you like — that he could get out of this mould as well and reach the summit of greatness that destiny had decreed for him.

I have not made a systematic study either of charisma or of charismatic personalities. I'm sure if that is done, one would find that there is no sure way of achieving it; all the people who have attained it have done it in their different ways. But one thing is also sure: none who have attained charisma in their lives had it written over them when they were born. We all have the sparks of divinity in us. Some of us recognise that fact and become divine; others who don't let that be consigned with their bodies to the funeral pyre. It is for each one of us to decide as to in which category we wish to fall.

PART 2

IN POLITICAL TERMS

7

LET'S RETAIN OUR IDENTITY

For Gandhi Daridranarayan was the only and true face of God. For him the test for a policy or a decision was whether it helped the poorest of the poor. Whenever he was in doubts he brought before his mind the face of the poorest of the poor and then asked himself whether this decision would benefit him.

Now it seems that before taking a decision we have in our mind the face of the manager of the World Bank; how would he react to this issue?

What if we apply Gandhiji's test to our decision making process? What about the new economic policy? Do we allow Harvard and LSE trained economists and management whiz-kids sitting in the board rooms of MNCs and the World Bank to dictate to us what is right or should we try to find out the Gandhian way?

There are many who would question the very locus standi of the issue in the sense that it is not for us to answer since we have no choice anyway. According to these thinkers the downfall of the international socialist movement has left us with no choice.

According to these people the bipolar world that rose from the ashes of the Second World War gave us a choice between two systems; now that one of them lies shattered and exposed where is the choice? There is only one way left and that is the golden way of capitalism.

Partly they are right; there were two alternative ways available to us when we won our freedom. But what is questionable is the thesis that only one of them is available now. What has happened to the other? According to these thinkers that way also lies shattered and discredited along with the breakup of the Soviet Union.

I personally do not concur with this view. The breakup of the Soviet Union does no doubt represent the failure of the system of internationalization that Stalin and some of his forebearers had launched but that this means a failure of the thesis on which a certain philosophy was based is by no means established.

Just as the breakup of the British Empire did not mean the failure of a certain system of democracy that was evolved in UK; so the failure of the Soviet Union (read Empire) need not necessarily mean the failure of the philosophy on which the great Russian Revolution was based. Just as the defeat of democracy at the hands of emperor Napoleon Bonaparte did not prove that the French Revolution was wrong!

I am not saying that the philosophy is right for us; all I am saying is that recent events have no bearing on the subject at all.

The fact that the system of communism was not suitable for us was the cornerstone of Nehru's philosophy. And this has been the basis for our internal and foreign policy for the last five decades or so.

Nehru had two competing, and in their own ways successful, models of development available to him: communism and capitalism. It was easy for him to see that none of the two ways satisfied the aspirations of our own freedom struggle. While one took away liberties and freedoms from the individual the other denied social justice and economic equality.

The Indian freedom struggle, shaped by the likes of Gandhi, Nehru and Bose, fought not merely against foreign rule but also against economic and political exploitation. International leaders of the time, leaders of the stature of Attlee, Roosevelt and Khrushchew, appreciated the aspirations of Indians and their leaders and allowed us to develop within our own genius.

Thus the path adopted by us in the last five decades was not dictated by the choice of playing one power against the other but by the dictates of our own freedom struggle and the aspirations of our people and leaders.

Does the failure of the Soviet experiment have anything to do with the failure of our own aspirations and goals? Does the face of Daridranarayan change merely because Yeltsin has taken over the ruins of power in Russia in place of the Bulgarin and Khushchev?

Does Gandhiji's decision making test (about imagining of the face of the poorest of the poor before taking any decision) fails to apply now merely because international communism lies in ruins?

Let us remember that the Indians had rejected international communism even when it was at the zenith of its glory and prestige in the twenties and thirties of the twentieth century. The demonstration of its failure has come out only now.

The Middle Path that Nehru advocated has been the cornerstone of our international and foreign policies for the last five decades and that is the result of a deep and abiding understanding of our own philosophical ethos by our founding fathers and not the aping of any foreign system. This path has been advocated by a long line of Indian leaders right through from Buddha to Gandhi and can be discarded only at our peril. India selected the Middle Path at a time when most other countries around us were plumping in for the capitalist system. This includes most South Asian countries notably Pakistan, most countries in the Middle East and almost all countries in Latin America. Have we lost anything that these countries have gained?

Most people see the shining example of Japan, Korea and Taiwan but fail to see the condition of the debt ridden economies of Mexico, Brazil and other countries of Latin America.

What about the countries of Africa which have followed the capitalist path? For every Singapore there are three

Somalias; and for every Korea there are umpteen Argentinas and Mexicos.

Remember that if Korean and Taiwanese economies have achieved miracles under the capitalist systems, the Chinese have done the worse under the capitalist systems.

And when all is said and done, we haven't done too bad either under our home spun socialist system.

Let the international pendulum swing whichever way it like but let us stick to our own Gandhian, Nehruvian model of development. Change we must; especially in the bureaucratic mess that we have inherited from our foreign masters.

Maybe the permit-licence raj has to go too so also many other practices and rules. But much of the past policy must survive, especially the one about social justice and welfare of the poor.

Let us keep the windows of our house open for the winds to blow in from all directions; but let us refuse to be blown off our feet.

From all the systems that come to us from outside-including the one that is dictated by the World Bank and the like-let us evolve one that is suited to our own genius and one that is in keeping with the aspirations of our people and reflect in true measure the spirit of our freedom struggle and wishes of our founding fathers.

8

GLOBALIZATION Panacea or Farce

There was an item in the paper the other day that second hand Rolls Royce cars would be imported into the country soon. Another company announced that it would bring pillows (yes, the same pillows on which you sleep!). Are these fruits of globalization that we were told to look out for?

I am one of the implacable foes of globalization and of the economic policies that it decrees because of these reasons. But it's supporters come up with a killing argument in favour—'What is the option anyway'?

They argue that with the proved failure of international communism we have no option but to go in for the other option, that is now not called by the 'dirty word' capitalism but packaged more attractively as globalization.

My argument against such an approach is simple. If one of the two has been proved to be wrong, what is the guarantee that the other will prove to be right?

We have already seen two approaches of internationalizing politics after the earlier ones of imperialism became unpopular: one, 'the sun never setting' British Empire of Commonwealth, if you like, and the other the Soviet international communism.

Against the first of these we have struggled for the best part of a century and a half, and the ruins of the second can still be viewed in Russia and East Europe. Now we are in the midst of the third approach, cleverly called globalization.

The cornerstone of this policy revolve around free trade, the accent being on the word 'free'. It is argued that since communications and new technologies have already made the whole world a village, all protectionist policies should be given a go by and so should policies which restrict the free movement of commodities from one part of the world to another.

So far so good. Freedom is a lovely word and it remains lovely whether it is attached to individuals or to activities and there is no way that anyone can disagree. But in this context I am reminded of a story.

A chap was travelling along a road waving his umbrella all around him. Another chap who was passing by accosted him. "Please do not wave your umbrella like this, sir," he protested, "It may hurt somebody." "Why should not I?" said he, "I am a free man, am I not? I will do as I please".

Not to be undone by this facetious argument our passer-by was quick on the up. "Your freedom, sir", he remarked, "Ends where my nose begins."

That is true. Even an open concept like freedom is circumscribed, it cannot be taken as absolute. One is free to be 'free' so long as this does not mean lack of freedom for somebody else. Is this not true of norms like those that would be laid out for implementing concepts like that of free trade?

We would not like freedom for the rich to mean bondage and slavery for the vast majority of the poor. So can some people not be made to benefit at the cost of the rest.

Remember the opium wars? China of that period had imposed restrictions on the movement into China of opium and other drugs. This restriction was resented by the then votaries of free trade, companies like the East India Company. The extent to which they were willing to go to enforce their dictat is now history.

Are the enunciators of the globalization concept willing to accept the free trade law laid down by their ancestor companies? Are they willing to allow free trade even in commodities like opium and hashish?

There will be howls of protest if such an idea is even spelt out. How can we allow such contraband to enter our country? It's against our laws!

How short our memory can be? Do they forget that when the opium wars were fought, bringing in opium into China was also banned by Chinese Law? Or, is it that laws of the occident are superior to the laws of oriental nations?

If trade in opium, hashish and carpets allegedly made with child labour, oil drilled in Iraq and ivory and animal skins is banned in the US or Western Europe and such ban does not violate the principles of free trade, why should India's ban on trade in gold be such a bad thing?

In Hindi there is a proverb—*jiski lathi uski bhens* (the buffalo belongs to the person who wields the stick). It is that the right to define 'freedom' also belongs to the person who wields the stick?

We have been in the globalization process for the last four or five years and what one has seen in this period is the freedom enjoyed by foreign companies to bring in items like aerated drinks and potato chips from outside. Or consumption items like motor cars and colour TVs, all for use by the elite and the rich.

But this is not the end, we are told. Large multinationals are all queuing up for bringing in a large number of other commodities as well, all a result of the hi-tech revolution that has taken place.

What like? The four stroke engine to replace the two stroke one on the scooters? Yes, comes the reply, this and many more items to give us environmentally clean vehicles for our roads.

I'd like to ask: If the four stroke engine is clean for the two wheelers why are we using precipitators for the motor cars which have had four stroke engines for ages?

No sir, the four stroke on the scooter means technology that is not with us and would have to be imported from the West whereas the two stroke engine technology is with us for export. Because free trade here would mean a technological advantage for us, the West declares the two stroke engine environmentally unclean and thus tipped for banning in their countries.

This is the age of instant solutions. During the beginning of the century it was international communism that was the panacea for all that ailed society and now, towards the end, it is globalization and all that it implies. But very rarely have such instant solutions turned out to be panaceas: if there is any lesson in history it is this.

Before we commit ourselves irretrievably on the path to globalization, let us ponder and think. Our hard won freedom is not a commodity that can be bartered away so easily.

9

WHAT A BORING ELECTION ?

It's election day again. Who says? where are the buntings, the posters, the wall writings? Where are the processions, the blaring loud speakers, the thundering applauses of jampacked public meetings? Where is the excitement, the thrill, the applause?

Even in the recently held union elections of the university all this and more was there; how can I accept that the nation is going to the poll without any of these?

But it's true: despite the absence of all these external facades that traditionally follow the declaration of elections there is no doubt that the elections are on and also that today is voting day for those of us who have the good fortune of being registered as voters.

If you don't believe me, take a walk and you are sure to find one of the 10,000 polling booths pretty near your house. Each polling booth will be manned by a Presiding Officer and some 6 or so polling officers, apart from about 3 or 4 policemen. In addition, the main political parties will have their men there, both inside the booth and outside on the main roads. At a fair guess there will be about 20 people in each of these booths, making a total of 200,000 people assisting in their own way to ensure a free and fair poll, more than half of them are government servants.

So it is an election. But then why are the other parapharnelia missing? Why no buntings, posters, hoardings?

Where are the processions, the speeches, the public meetings? Some people say it's Sheshan, others Supreme Court.

Be as it may it all makes for a most boring election. But need it be so?

When the democratic process was first launched in the country in the late forties and early fifties, it was not clear if the masses were prepared for it. In fact, the British had assumed that they were not. That is the main reason why only a few of the elite and the landed gentry were allowed to vote in the limited local body elections that they had allowed under the Montagu Chelmsford reforms and the Government of India Act, 1935. The underlying assumption in disallowing the vote to a large majority of the people was that they could not be relied upon to choose their representatives.

Apart from the various other disabilities from which he suffered in this regard, was the fact that the common man was illiterate and poor and thus open to inducements of all sorts, especially monetary ones. Since he could be manipulated so easily, so went the argument, we should let others, especially those who were educated and rich, to take decisions on their behalf.

1947 changed all this. One of the sacred principles for which Gandhiji fought for freedom was that Indians have a right to determine their own fate. Thus the first step that Nehru took after the departure of the British was to hold the general elections on the basis of the principle of adult franchise. Children were denied the vote on the ground of maturity; but no one else was.

Everybody has one vote, be he a bachelor of arts or an illiterate, a car owner or a rickshaw puller, a Hindu or Muslim, a scavenger or a priest. This was the sacred mandate of the freedom fighters and history is witness how well this was discharged.

Giving the poor and illiterate man the right to vote is one thing but trusting him to cast it in a responsible manner is quite another matter. That such a trust was missing is amply borne out by every single clause of the election law and the code of conduct that was later framed.

The use of money power was what worried our leaders like Nehru the most. Probably because this is the commodity that they themselves lacked. (How things have changed now!) Many clauses were added to the election law to prevent the moneyed man to swing the course of the election. The restriction on the amount spent by a candidate is only one of them; there are many others, including carting voters to the booths.

I question the very assumption behind these restrictions. It is assumed that a man who spends more money prima facie enjoys an advantage over the person who cannot. It also assumes that the common man, who is allowed the vote for the first time, is less in position to resist monetary inducements than the rich and literate voter.

My own experience shows that the more you have the more you want. That only a poor man can be bribed is ridiculous; the rich and the educated have shown that they are not above inducements of this type. It is a personality type that can be corrupted; and this does not depend on his economic status or his level of education.

If this is true, the restriction on spending of money does not make any sense. I remember, Oberoi, of Oberoi Hotels fame, was a candidate from the New Delhi constituency in the first elections and opposed to him was a socialist leader. It is history now, how badly he lost, despite all the display of money power. There have been umpteen instances since.

In election after election our electorate has shown how mature it is and how wrong have been the assumptions to the contrary. There is widespread feeling that our election system has been tainted by corrupt practices, including display of money and muscle power. While the display may be there, I will give a simple example to prove that such a display has hardly any effect on the eventual outcome.

We have come to realise how accurate the opinion polls prove to be, especially the so called exit polls. These polls are conducted by impartial and disinterested non-governmental organisations. The mere fact that their findings so closely cohere with the actual results should be conclusive proof that elections really represent, at least at the macro level, the will of the people. This is despite all the use of muscle and money power.

We can't cut the head to get rid of the headache. No doubt, the strong arm of the law will effectively kill the campaign but do we realise what incalculable harm we are doing to the system?

Many polls have suggested that as many as 20 per cent of the voters may be undecided even a couple of weeks before the polls. To make up their minds they need to be told of the personalities and programmes of the competing parties and of many other facts. Many of us come to know of this from the print and the electronic media but what about vast majority of the people who cannot afford access to it? By blocking out the campaign we are effectively taking the right of choice from these people.

There is need to drastically change the election laws. Instead of more rules putting more restrictions we need simpler laws imposing less restrictions. Surely, our people have proved themselves deserving of this by always voting in a mature and responsible manner.

10

MOVE OVER MBA, THE FINANCIAL WIZARD IS HERE

When my son left a lucrative assignment in a top notch Tata Computer Company to join the MFC (Master in Financial Control) course in Delhi University, I was quite a bit surprised. In my time it was unimaginable for an engineer to quit the profession and go for something as mundane and dull as finance.

For the IAS, yes; maybe even for business administration. But never for joining something as esoteric as finance.

But, it seems, Yogesh is more in tune with the times and its needs and aspirations. Today it is not the administrator or the engineer who runs the country but the finance man.

In a way that was always true. In the governmental set ups in India the finance man is government's way of ensuring that the top man, to whom a lot of power may have been delegated, does not become a parallel center of power and influence. So finance department is given surprising amount of power.

There is a story of Liaqat Ali, finance minister in the interim government of 1946, who refused to sanction a post in the PM's house for one of the oldest of Nehru's servants!

It is true that the finance man has a lot of power but much of that power is of a negative nature. A finance minister can force the PM not to engage a servant but there is no way that he can force a certain action on the government, like sending a battalion of troops to his constituency where a law and order situation may have taken place!

It is for this reason that people who value visible symbols of power traditionally shy away from finance jobs; and that is why such jobs generally lack glamour.

But Yogesh's decision tends to indicate that things may be changing. The first signs of change was the larger visibility of MBAs from the IIMs in the cocktail circuits of the capital. These bright young men, more often than not, sporting IIT B Techs as well, while looking after marketing aspects had a total appreciation of the inputs that finance provided to oil the wheels of modern business and commerce.

But despite this appreciation, they believed in keeping the finance man on tap, keeping the top position reserved for themselves. After all, the finance man, is basically a taxation expert, and he comes in only if there is a profit! But without marketing how the hell would there be a profit?

It is true that the marketing people bring in the rupees. But Harshad Mehta changed all this. Overnight people realized that profit was to be had not merely by production or even by effective marketing of the product but also by managing your available funds.

And more often than not there is more money to be had by wise investments than by painful efforts in upgrading technology or by expensive and risky marketing.

More and more entrepreneurs wanting to start long gestation period projects, are realizing that crores are to be had not just by rubbing the feet of millionaire uncles or by taking rich people as sleeping (but interfering) partners or even by courting senior bankers but also by engaging share market experts to float issues and bonds.

Sometimes not only is the money from the share market more easily available it is also cheaper making the project more viable; this brings in the rich uncles and bankers rushing with their gold, all of them vying with each other to get onto the investment bandwagon!

I can see a number of eyebrows being raised especially on the mention of Harshad Mehta. These people will assert that Harshad Mehta, with his questionable methods, did for sometime overheat the stock exchange; but with what result? The crash in the stock markets ruined a number of middle class investors and left a permanent scar on the working of the institution from which probably it will never recover.

There is no doubt that Harshad Mehta and his likes manipulated the system; there is also no doubt that the system itself makes such manipulation possible. But do not forget that these people merely exploited a potential, they did not create it. The potential is there and it is for the right man with the right knowledge to use it.

And this is where the future masters of financial control, who are now doing these newly started course in Delhi University under the well-known economist and commerce Prof. M.Y. Khan, come in.

I can already see Prof. Khan and his team as the precursors of a new economic revolution in the country. But I can see skeptics raise their brows. This course is only eight years old and may have so far produced only a couple of hundred people; how can so few create a revolution of the type that I am talking about?

While I do not agree that a couple of hundred people cannot start a revolution (how many ended the long march with Mao? How many started the Dandi March with Gandhi?) I see these two hundred people as merely the vanguard of a movement.

In the beginning more and more such people will come out and provide their valuable inputs. Then there will be a redefinition of the role of the controller of finance. At the end of this movement I can see the financial controller emerging out of the shadows as a negative control mechanism of the top management and becoming an important input in his own right, a powerful tool and magnet.

Just as the IAS is making way for the MBA in the new era of privatization and market run economy, the MBA will have to make way for the MFC.

This trend will get accentuated as the intricacies of the

stock market and the money market dominate business and international finance.

Very soon both lucre and the complexities of the money market will attract the brightest and the most enterprising to the latest the courses, the MFC.

And it is then that the MBA will head battle cry.

PART 3

OFFICERS IN SEARCH OF DUTY

11

HOW THE BUREAUCRACY COPES WITH TECHNOLOGY

The other day I was in a seminar in which the great achievements of our bureaucracy were being eulogised in very glowing terms. Many achievements were mentioned and all of them by the members of this tribe. Some of them were such that they made me pat my back in appreciation.

Now almost at the end of a long road that began in 1964, the year I got into the IAS, I felt proud that I belonged to this select group of people who had the rare opportunity to serve the people and at the same time remain professional.

Some of the achievements are easy to recount: giving stability to the administration at the time of political turmoil, bringing oneness of administrative approach in this vast and diverse country, taking administration to the grass roots, and so on. But was this all?

I found that this was an occasion to run my mind back to see if I too could recall and eulogise the achievements of our great bureaucracy. But, I am disturbed to find that now that I really apply my mind to the issue, thoughts of a slightly different tenor come to the mind. Especially when we see how the bureaucracy has managed to cope up with the challenges of change, particularly one brought about by technological innovation.

There have been challenges aplenty in this age of technological achievements. Let us take just three of the major ones and see how the bureaucracy has coped up with them. Take the telegraph, the telephone and, now, the computer. There is no doubt that these three inventions, taken singly or together, have changed the face of the earth. Not just in how it looks but also in the way that we look at it.

Let us first take the telegraph. Remember, this invention came at a time when the fastest way of communicating was either through harkaras, or runners, or by running relay of horses, if fast communication was what was needed. The telegraph was truly revolutionary: all you needed to know was the Morse code and how to tap it on a key. And in moments your message reached the other corner of the globe, a feat that had evaded the fastest of horses that the rulers of that age could muster.

This technological innovation must have been particularly useful to the bureaucrats of the day because this was the time when they were busy colonising the world and the quickest way of reaching one part of the globe to the other was by slow steam-driven ships. The telegraph took messages fast and made administration that much more effective.

How did Indian bureaucracy cope up with this challenge (to its slothness, shall I add)? By making a rule that no telegram can be acted upon unless the 'post copy in confirmation'had been received! Since the 'post copy in confirmation' had to come by ship, the very advantage of speed that the telegraph offered was effectively negated.

Then came the innovation of the telephone, again a very revolutionary one. Against the telegram there was the objection that since it was not signed anybody could have sent it and there was no immediate way of the verifying its authenticity. But in the telephone, surely, the same objection could not apply since the order issuing authority was itself on the line!

But no! Immediately an order was issued saying that oral orders must only be obeyed only if they were confirmed in writing. And since the person on the phone had no way of doing it, he had to wait for the orders to be carded out till he had dictated the order and got it delivered by the quickest possible means. Can you blame if he now uses the telephone only for communicating instructions to his wife about the dal that he would have for dinner?

Don't imagine that the fax changed the position much: after all it's the original signed communication that is important, not the photocopy that the fax brings!

Now, finally, we are in the age of IT, the age of the computer, the super highway, web sties and what not. How will you think the bureaucracy will cope up with this challenge?

Whatever you may think, I have no doubt that we will emerge out of this too unscathed, with our red-taped file and the car-dickey sized file carriers intact. Don't believe me? Then listen.

The greatest strength of the computer is its computational skill, its ability to calculate fast. Accounts which take months to compile will be completed in hours. Government accounts are notoriously complicated and tedious with hundreds of heads and millions of entries. One would tend to imagine that the computer will be ideally suited to handle these and that is indeed the case. But would this happen?

There is a rule which says that at the end of the accounts the accountant has to certify that he has personally checked the calculations and found them to be correct. In the case of the accounts prepared by the computer, the calculations would have been checked by the computer; how then will the accountant be able to give this certificate?

You have guessed it: he will not be able to. That is the reason why accounts will now be prepared in two ways: one by the computer and the other manually by the accountant. After the computer has given the figures, the accountant will compile the accounts manually to enable the accountant to truthfully sign the certificate at the end of the accounts.

The same will apply to the other applications of the computer, whether it is in office automation or in maintenance of files. No doubt, the computer will be used more and more; we must give the outer semblance of modernisation. But the old system, more important, the old ways, will continue. The file is so sacred that no matter what happens it cannot be given up. Does it really matter that most important decisions are really taken outside the file, many times in lavish cocktail parties given by the legion of BMW driving agents and middle men? Hats off to the bureaucratic tribe not just for the achievements for which they are eulogised in seminars and discussions and also for which they often part themselves on the back but also for the brilliant way they cope with innovative technology.

12

THE NOTE THAT GETS A DECISION

It is impossible to forget the classic punch cartoon on the day Mussolini came to power in Italy. It showed Mussolini, dressed like a traffic policeman, regulating the chaotic traffic; but instead of the usual posture of allowing one side of the traffic to go and blocking the other, he had stopped both.

The punch line was: But the trains are running on time.

And that too is the line for our own administration: At least we are keeping the country going. And how!

One remembers the classic remedy decreed for the recession of the thirties in Europe and the States: make some people dig holes while others fill them up. It sometimes makes me feel that Indian administration may be doing exactly that.

One man spends the whole day writing a learned note on why a certain policy must be followed; he knows that another person somewhere is spending double the time to prove why the same policy is not to be followed. Since there are differences of opinion on the issue, both of them are now placed in a group, with a third person as a moderator, and asked to suggest a policy.

It is interesting that the group comes out with a entirely different tack: it rejects both the policies and comes out with a third option. But this is not the end of the issue: this option too is found unworkable, unviable, unacceptable or whatever; so the issue is referred to a larger special group.

This group is more representative and more specialized; therefore, naturally, they spend more time and generate more heat while debating the issue. One generally thinks that there could be one or two ways of doing a job; but interestingly such committees come out with a fourth or sometimes even a fifth option.

Such groups rarely, if ever, can unanimously agree to anything; and interestingly, it is these dissenting notes that are picked up by the media for highlighting. This sets the ground for a healthy and lively debate; and in a functioning democracy such healthy debate and participation by the people cannot but be welcomed.

An item in the newspaper is usually followed by a Parliament question: Has the government's attention been drawn to the item in *The Indian* so and so dated so and so and if so what is the government's response to it?

Government's response! That's not so easy to formulate. And who's government anyway? For the average suffering citizen government is whoever has the capacity to sit on his file and hold up his case, be it the DM or the Sales Tax Officer or even the humble *patwari* or the peon. But in bureaucratic government it could be anybody from under secretary to the Cabinet. Or indeed none of them.

Since it is even difficult to determine who government is, how can one determine its response! So Parliament is informed; the government's response is being formulated.

And this becomes, in Parliamentary parlance, an assurance. And for fulfilling such assurance a whole structure, with an assurance committee at the apex, has been set up.

An assurance has to be fulfilled in three months; but it is a rare assurance that can be fulfilled in the time allowed; if it could have been, why the hell it would have been allowed to become an assurance, in the first place!

In any case it is not easy to determine government's response. One would have thought that it should be easy; all that one had to do was to browse the election manifesto of whichever party was in power and determine 'government's response'. But if all the matters of governance of a past country like ours was as simple as all this, why would any government have such a huge apparatus for its bureaucracy?

No, the government's response is determined not by the promises made by the party in power but by the humble clerk and the peon and the *patwari*. So the matter is referred back to the select group, the special group and ultimately to the officer who had initiated the case in the first place.

Naturally, this gentleman repeats what he had said in the first place and sends the file to the second officer who does the same and pushes the file posthaste to the head of department. Since what has come to him is not only two different set of opinions but also contrary to what the various groups and committees had proposed, he is quite peeved.

After a series of 'please speaks' and asking for self-contained notes, this worthy gentleman is forced to pass an order. One would think that at least now this chap has been trapped; he'll be forced to be something that he has been trained all his life not to do; take a decision.

If all this were a scene in a movie, suspense music would be playing as he picked up his 'mightier than the sword' pen. What he writes is an anti-climax of sorts: In a grave and important matter like this it is better to seek government's orders before we determine our response.

For him determining government is not a problem; he merely addresses the letter to the under secretary concerned and keeps his worthy pen aside in the happy thought that he had taken a momentous and correct decision: in the history of Indian administration how many people had been questioned for not taking a decision? Contrast it with the legion who were put in the block house for taking wrong decisions!

The beauty of the whole exercise is that for the next couple of years nobody would remember what the original issue is: pens would be wielded and typewriter keys tapped on the issue of the fulfilment of the assurance.

Assurances are rarely, if ever, fulfilled: happily before the axe finally falls Parliament would have been dissolved and the new Parliament in place; who would then bother about the earlier assurances?

One would think that in this game of the bureaucrats, the officer who originated the note in the first place would be aggrieved; but then he has not reckoned with Indian bureaucracy, he had not written the note with the intention of getting a decision; he had done it because he did not want a decision to be taken anyway. And what better way that to push a note?

I do not think that you have still got the point. You'll never get a decision by making the legion of *babus* and secretaries to write notes and push them through. It's a note that gets a decision but it is the green one so ably produced and printed by the governor of the Reserve Bank of India. Got it now?

13

MAKING TENSION AN INPUT TO CREATIVITY

Tension is such a terrible fact of life that always one wishes that it were not to come. But it is also a fact that without tension life would be so boring and uncreative. At least it so seems to me, especially since I have managed to convert all the tense periods of my life into the most creative periods.

The life of a top bureaucrat seems so strait-jacketed and staid that to look for excitement in it seems a futile exercise. But tension is never in short supply when it is time for preparation of the panel.

I can still picture a colleague guzzling away from a foaming glass of beer and ever so often absenting himself from the table for taking a quick smoke (like the life of a bureaucrat, the dining hall of the Delhi Gymkhana is dull enough not to allow any smoke to pollute its atmosphere). The reason for his odd behaviour: a news item naming him as one of the new Secretaries to the Government of India. Needless to say the item was essentially incorrect since no such orders had been issued but became the cause of tension only because it gave hints at the names which had been included in the panel which, everybody knows, is currently under preparation.

It is easy to guess why the rest of us, whose names didn't figure in the item, were tense but what could be the reason for this particular gentleman's tension? The reason was the catch in the news item: instead of simply naming him and the others it said: 'the likes of...'. What was eating away my friend was this: if his name is on the panel why the appellation 'the likes of'?

It is a measure of the dullness that percolates the life of a top bureaucrat that one has to find excitement in a news item or in some other non-descript happening or event. You can find reason to be tense if the news is happy; and naturally if the tidings are not that happy. This does require some sort of expertise or intelligence to find tension (read excitement) where none exists.

Everyday it's the same dull routine. The office is 9 to 5:30, take a couple of hours this way or that. Saturdays and Sundays are holidays; and that is that: there is no way that you can make anyone, even yourself, come to the office if you can help it. Month after month, then year after year you get the same penurious wage with nothing but a small annual increment of Rs. 30 or Rs. 50 to distinguish one year from the other.

It is not that changing offices brings any variety. Not just the file covers are the same and printed at the same press; the red tapes that are used to tie up the file are also alike. The rules and regulations are the same; so are the problems and the issues.

No. Nothing much is different for the bureaucrat for the best part of the three and a half odd decades that he spends in service. Even the promotions are quite predictable: if you have outstanding or very good CRs (confidential reports are never as confidential as the name seems to imply) seniority pretty well decides your fate in the DPCs.

Can you really blame my friend for finding cause for tension even in a news item that puts him in the promotion list? Frankly speaking if this particular item had not appeared in the press he would have found some other excuse for the tension!

Tension is as important to life as salt and pepper are to the fried egg. Or as change and variety are to an unchanging routine. But howsoever important it may be, tension has to be coped up with when it comes.

The friend mentioned above is lucky that he can cope up with tension merely by guzzling bear and smoking cigarettes. Another friend, who was present in this particular party, said that he kept tossing in his bed the whole night. Needless to say that his name was not in the particular news item even though the names of many juniors appeared there.

Everybody has his own way of coping up with tension; over the years I have evolved my own way. I let the tension build up within me; in fact, I help it to grow by bringing in all sorts of irrational fears and frightful thoughts. Once it has been built up to a gigantic level, I channelise it into a fictional character and pick up a pen. Then I let the tension flow out through this pen onto a piece of paper.

At the end of it, I have a poem, a short story or an idea for a novel or a screen play. By the time the pen leaves paper, almost always the cause for the tension has ended, by either the fears materialising or being proved to have been without any foundation.

Even where the fears materialise it is not often that the tension continues because more often than not fears are proved to be without any foundation. It is only once that I have found tension to continue over a period of time; and this eight-month period was, literary output wise, the most productive period of my life.

In this particular period, I managed to write as many as three novels plus complete two research projects, one on cosmology and the other on Mahatma Gandhi.

I know that the present period of tension will also end. I am only hoping that while it lasts I will have penned a couple of screenplays and stories, if not a couple of poems as well.

This will be the last panel for those who make it this time. For the rest there will be a prolonged period of tension as the process of review begins. I have to be in one of the two categories: those who make it or those who don't. I'm not sure in which one I would like to be.

I'll be a liar if I say that I do not want to be amongst those who make it. And I'll not be true to my own creative faculties if I said that I'd like all my creative tensions to disappear by making it to the last possible panel of my career. My dilemma is typically Hamletion: 'to be or not to be'. On the panel, that is.

I do not wish to add to the tensions of the moment by trying to resolve this particularly tough dilemma. I can only pray that it is resolved in the best possible manner. Not just for me but for all of us as well.

Will you pray for us please?

14

ENGLISH AS SHE IS WROTE IN GOVERNMENT OFFICES

Powerful is the hand which wields the pen. But despite the power it is blind without mastery over bureaucratese.

Not so long ago, 'bade babu' Chatterjee peered over his horn rimmed glasses as his Collector, Mr John, read through his draft demi official letter. As the smooth-faced Englishman dipped his pen in ink, to make some changes in the draft, our babu's eyes almost popped out of their sockets.

'Wat you do, Sar?' cried Chatterjee babu in horror and disbelief. 'Wat you do?'

'Make changes, Man...correct your spellings and grammar.' Then, almost as an after-thought, smilingly added: 'English's my mother tongue, you know?'

The humour was lost on our venerable and graying Chatterjee babu.

'True, Sar, true. But wat you write not read Mr Jack, Collector saab...but...Me Chatterjee write and he Banerjee read...'

History does not record the reaction of Mr John; but he must surely have got the point. As have countless generations of bureaucrats since then.

One bureaucrat writes and another reads. Nobody else is made privy to the innermost secrets of their special language.

"For all Group 'C', Group 'B' and Group 'A' posts up to (and excluding) the level of Rs. 3700-5000 excepting promotions for induction to Group 'A' posts or Services from lower groups, the bench mark would be 'Good'."

There is an Indian English. There is an English English. And there is an American English.

And there is the bureaucrat's English—bureaucratese, the language of the worthy successors of 'Me Chatterjee and He Banerjee'.

When Macaulay first introduced English as a medium of instruction in Indian schools, his intention was to produce a babu who, though Indian by birth and breed, would be English in behaviour and actions. And in this he was remarkably successful; but could he have imagined of the monster that he had unleashed in the shape of bureaucratese?

The language of the bureaucrat is long winded and pompous. "The Government servant himself should, without delay, communicate a copy to the officer who audits his pay, and take his instructions as the officer to whom he is to account for the contributions, report to the latter officer the time and the date of all transfers of charge to which he is a party when proceeding on, while in, and on return from foreign service, and furnish from time to time particulars regarding his pay in foreign service, leave taken by him, his postal address and any other information which that officer may require."

By the time one reaches the end of this example of the worthy language of the bureaucrat, one has lost count of the number of officers that the sentence refers to; even of the fact whether the 'foreign service' that if refers to is 'service within India' or 'service outside'!

The word 'and' is used five times and as many as three times it follows a comma. Which one of these is dispensable—the comma or 'and'—is difficult to say; but one thing is sure: try removing any one of them and you will have hive-loads of babus after you crying 'foul!'

By the time the end of the sentence is reached, it is difficult to say whether the 'contributions' that are referred to are literary or more material ones! And, then, does one really care?

'Bureaucratese' has since taken deep roots in the milieu of the Indian bureaucracy; it has become a way of life to millions of people, ranging from the humble postman to the mighty Secretary to the Government of India.

And most of them know no better.

For all of them the messiah is Swamy, the latest edition of whose compilation is as eagerly awaited as the up-dated interpretation of the Bible was by the early carriers of the Cross!

One point for the bureaucrat: he has succeeded where others have failed. He has crossed the barriers of caste, creed and language. 'Bureaucratese' is bureaucratese irrespective of whether it is English or Hindi. Delhi or Mumbai. Scientist or saint.

The bureaucrat has succeeded in uniting the whole of this diverse country by this brilliant innovation.

Two negatives or sometimes even three and words like 'excluding' followed by 'excepting' is the 'grammar' of this new language. Also the almost never ending sentence!

Anybody who can decipher this code is deserving of a big prize: and the reward that beats all is to flower into a mighty pen-pushing clerk, occupying a ramshackle table in a dingy room next to the corridors of power.

Swamy is the messiah to the votaries of 'bureaucratese' and his compilation is a money spinning best seller.

As is to be expected, bureaucracy has its own high priests who interpret the sacred meaning behind the long meandering sentences; and woe to the babu who crosses sword with them! And double woe to him who cannot follow it!

'Show me the man and I'll show you the rule!'

This is the *mantra* of these pundits whose hallmark, apart from horn rimmed glasses, is their access to a dog-eared and well thumbed 'Assistant's diary' which contains notes of every circular giving the latest interpretation of the umpteenth clarificatory letter.

It is not that everybody accepts their interpretation; witness the large number of cases that go up to the courts every year. In fact so huge is this number that a couple of years ago CATs and RATs were specially set up to settle such matters!

But even here the most learned of judges discuss in awed whispers the subtle shades of meaning of a word or line of a Rule framed in the best literary traditions of bureaucratese. Remember Nehru getting up in the Lok Sabha during the discussions on the Official Languages Bill to argue how 'may' means 'shall' in bureaucratese?

The attraction of bureaucratese is that it ensures that its practitioners will never be without a job. If you need one man to write, you need dozens to interpret and clarify.

And it is remarkably infectious. Scientists and academicians pride themselves on the fact that they are precise and analytic and exact. But when it comes to writing their circulars and notes, they resort to bureaucratese; how else can you say nothing while appearing to say a lot? How else can you confuse a simple issue?

And in any case it is fashionable.

Simply, there is no better way to sound profound than bureaucratese when really, like the Emperor, you have nothing on!

15

THREE CHEERS FOR THE STEEL FRAME

How trustworthy is our administrative structure? How trusting is it? The answer on both counts is 'a'. Even if some diehard supporters of the 'steel frame' do not agree with this, they will not violently disagree, especially with the trusting part of the statement.

Any votary or practitioner of the art of administration in India will vouch for the fact that 'trust' is not one of its important ingredients; in fact, if it were to be seen that way, it is 'mistrust' which is such an essential ingredient of the heady concoction with which the administrative structure has been brewed.

One of the essential elements of our administrative system is the 'inbuilt systems of checks and balances'. Let us see how they operate. Government at the highest level operates through various departments, viz., law, finance, works, social welfare, police, defence, and so on. These departments are not just the instruments of framing and implementation of policy but also, more importantly, watchdog bodies to keep an eye on each other.

No proposal having financial implications can be cleared without getting clearance from the finance; and no legislation can be drafted by any ministry without referring it to the law people. If any proposal or policy has foreign implications, the external affairs people must be consulted and if there is any apprehension of a law and order or police angle, the home department must be kept in the picture. So far so good.

It is often very difficult to say which proposal has which implication. For example, the decision to import (or export) onions or potatoes could effect the prospects of some farmer in some corner of Maharashtra or Karnataka; so somebody could point out later that there was need to consult the ministry of states (called 'home') and the state governments.

Similarly, a decision to introduce a story on Indian writers (making a mention of, let us say, Rushdie) in the curriculum of a class eight textbook may have unimagined implications with our relations with a foreign power (Iran, in this case) and could, conceivably, lead to communal tensions in some corner of Kerala. Lest he be faulted, the experienced bureaucrat feels it fit to consult the home and external affairs ministry and maybe some of the state governments as well.

Anybody who has practised the art of administration in India knows how easy it is to be wiser after the event. And there are any number of bodies that are supposed to show their wisdom only after the decision has been taken and implemented. These include such respected and wisdom tainted bodies like the CAG, CBI, Parliamentary Committees, Enquiry Commissions, CVC, audit bureaus and what have you.

Wise bureaucrats who are well aware of this syndrome are very careful on this score before they clear a case: not only do they refer to each and every conceivable department, minis or commission who could conceivably be concerned with it but also to every possible tier in the hierarchy who could possibly get an opportunity to question the decision at some stage in the future.

Talking of hierarchy, let me share another secret about the strength of the 'steel frame': it is the hierarchical system, in which responsibility is collective and so is the ability to take decisions. Starting with the lowly babu to the all mighty Secretary, there must be at least 12 hierarchical levels: the LDC, UDC, Assistant, Superintendent, Section Officer, Under

Secretary, Deputy Secretary, Director, Joint Secretary, Additional Secretary, Special Secretary, Secretary.

The principle of collective responsibility implies that the file must go to all these levels before a decision is taken. When one talks of a decision in 'bureaucratese' all it means a decision within the competence of a particular functionary. More often than not, a decision involves consultation with many other departments or ministries; in such cases this process has to be repeated many times over.

If you think that a decision has now been taken, you have another thought coming: a Secretary can only decide within his competence and if the matter is required to go to the Minister or to a Group of Ministers, or to the EFC or PIB or even to the Cabinet, there it has to go. The principle of collective responsibility does not end with the babus, it embraces the political hierarchy as well.

The principle of collective responsibility may have been formed with the thought that it would involve the 'pooling of wisdom and experience' but the way it is operated it is now more in the nature of sharing of responsibility and pooling of the vast reservoir of mistrust that we have accumulated over the years that we have operated the system.

If it were not for mistrust, there would be one note emanating from the office and one single order reflecting the decision that has been taken. Such decisions could be taken in committee meetings or could be in the form a 'yes-no' memos from the various ministries and departments and intra department authorities.

The mistrust that emanates from the system naturally doesn't end there; it goes out of the system as well. It effects all those who are required to file returns (IT, Sales Tax, excise) or get ration cards, passports or the like from government. The government servant behind the counter will not believe anything you say. Sometimes even your name has to be proved. Certainly your parentage, address, birth date and so on has to be proved.

When even such basic facts are challenged how can other more important facts, relating to your income, business turnover, tax payable, etc., be accepted? A substantial hierarchy of the dozen or so babus that were mentioned before setting your return or application and scrutinize it with a glass magnified with their mistrust.

If trust begets trust it is equally true that mistrust begets mistrust. No citizen is willing to believe that the system will work on its own. Over the years of 'mistrust begetting mistrust' they have mastered ways of getting around to system. With the help of a legion of touts, agents and middle men they find it very easy to get over the system. This is the raison d'etre of the infamous Inspector Raj.

The system of 'mistrust begets mistrust' has now found a very comfortable niche in our administrative system leading to the greatest happiness of the greatest number. In this jungle of satisfaction there are a few unhappy people who have not been able to reconcile with this steel frame of touts and middle men but who cares for them? At least the system works!

Three cheers for the Steel frame.

16

BUREAUCRATS PLAY THE GAME OF NUMBERS

All of us play games. So it is no surprise that so do the bureaucrats. And the game that they play is the game of numbers. That is the number on the plate of our cars. I discovered this when I got delivery of my new car.

My old car had the number DBK2. The new one went something like this: DL1CH5374. Quite a mouthful this; should really have been the numbers of two cars not one! Had it been so at least one could remembered the two numbers: DL 1 and CH 5374. But when we make it a 'khichri' the way it is, memorizing becomes a difficult exercise.

It was exasperating trying to memorize this number; I found it a task much beyond my capabilities. By the time I reached home, I had forgotten it. I have always been a bit dense in remembering numbers; so I checked up with a friend. It was music to my ear to be told that he didn't remember the number of his car either!

I now faced the dreary prospect of going back to the office of the transport authority to check up. As it is I rushed to the telephone and was immediately on the line to a senior officer of the Delhi Government's transport department. (It's nice to know people in the right places.) She was good enough to solve my problem by giving me a number from one of the old series: DEM 12. Nice and sweet to read and easy to remember. And a VIP number of sorts, to boot!

I have been wondering since; where have the authors of the new numbering system gone wrong? When the answer struck me, it really is so simple. Instead of writing DL1CH5374 let us write it as: 1 DLCH 5374. The second of these, while giving the same amount of information, is much easier to memorize.

While in the present method we have mixed the numerical with the alphabets, in the second we have kept the two groups separate. We now merely have to memorize the two groups separately, which is so much easier.

I always wonder how we make blunders like this. After all we are a country where the Indian Evidence Act has been in existence for all of more than 100 years with not a single one of its 60 odd clauses having to be modified. And remember the political vicissitudes the country has undergone since then.

The 1911 Montague Chelmsford Reforms, the 1935 Government of India Act, the 1947 Independence Act and finally the 1950 Constitution of India. All these have not necessitated any changes in the Evidence Act nor the fact that it has faced judicial scrutiny many times during this period not merely from the lower courts but quite often from the highest judicial authorities of the land.

Compared to the drafting of the Indian Evidence Act, the framing of a number system for motor cars should really have been child's play. But the mess that we have made of it should have been more befitting to a more onerous task. Like the laws for preventive detention.

The British were a foreign (and for that reason a hated) power. Their administrative machinery was small in numbers and thinly spread over the ground. There was many police stations, especially the rural ones, where the strength of the police rarely exceeded a dozen or so. In most villages of the country the only person with police authority they would probably ever know in their lifetimes was the 'chowkidar', an honorary figure rarely ever paid upwards of Rs. 5.

Almost the only powers of detention that the officers in charge of law and order had in those days were the four famous sections of the Criminal Procedure Code (CrPC) 107, 108, 109 and 110. With these sections they not merely controlled the normal law and order situation but also the serious political agitations launched by the freedom fighters, including the ones who believed in violence and terrorism.

It was only during the extraordinary situation created by the Second World War that the DIR (Defence of India Rules) was brought into effect. Otherwise, the preventive detention powers given by these four sections of the CrPC we found good enough to face even extraordinary law and order situations that arose.

Immediately after Independence when, normally, threats to law and order should have subsided, we brought in the Preventive Detention Act. This continued for sometime but then had to be replaced by the infamous MISA and the now well known (Sanjay fame) TADA. Despite all these draconian pieces of legislation has the law and order situation improved?

I wonder what the wonderful number system now introduced is expected to achieve, except the wonderful thing called 'computerisation'? DL, I know, stands for Delhi. The 1 stands for something and so do the C and the D or H. So what? What does it mean to me anyway?

I will be told that it is not meant for me but for the policeman on the beat. It is probably supposed to tell him whether the vehicle he is about to challan is a car, scooter, motor cycle or a taxi. Poor fellow! How else is he to know?

I find the government luminary to make this system look at me sternly: 'Stupid! This information is for the computer. The one about the registration office is for the policeman on duty!'

I wonder if the computer has to be told the sex of the vehicle (excuse my ignorance of the progeny) through the number, how the hell will he discover my sex? Or my address. Or any of the large number of details that are required to be meticulously filled in the form before one is allowed to drive the vehicle home.

I admit it, in the age of computers I am a huge ignoramus compared to the powerful bureaucrat in his horn rimmed glasses but what I still would like to understand is the following: If the number is 9 why do we insist that it be written as 0009?

I am stupid. But still I do happen to know that the difference in the number 9 and the number 0009 (let me admit that till the recent amendment of the motor vehicles act I was not aware that such a number existed) is between a VIP and a very ordinary person (VOP). Frankly, given the choice I'd rather be a VIP than a VOP.

17

CAN YOU REALLY UNMASK THE IAS?

It was a most pleasant surprise when I received a book some time ago and found the name of the writer to be M.K. Kaw.

Kaw! The name took me 29 years back to Mussoorie. He was a remarkably good looking man those days (he still is; in fact, his silver grey hair add a touch of nobility to his physical beauty) and remarkably transparent in his mannerisms; there was no way you could forget him.

'I'm Kaw —spelt K A W but pronounced like C O W—cow.' This small remembrance brought a smile to my lips: the 'male cow' had his 'female bull' counterpart in Asha whose surname Bahl sounded very much like the Hindi word for bull.

I had read some of his works earlier, especially the one about the 'Art of Spoonery' and was keen to catch up on him. I was particularly keen to know if age and experience had taken its toll on his writings as surely they had on his social dealings.

The title of the book is typically Kaw: BUREAUCRAZY—IAS UNMASKED. Having myself been a part of the masked world all these years, I was less interested in finding out what the mask hid than in the way the unmasking was carried out by Kaw. The least one expected of him was that he would handle it with subtlety and tact.

Tact is the bugbear for all the younger officers: even a mention that a particular officer lacks it could result in loss of promotion or even worse. As expected, Kaw has taken it up in the unmasking process. He describes how it works. 'The home secretary's car is stopped by rioters. The cops look at the scene with unruffled calm. The tyres are deflated. The home secretary is forced out of the car. His face is blackened with tar. He is seated on a donkey. The rioters perform a ritual dance around him, mouthing obscenities.' And all this time 'there is a tactful smile on the home secretary's face. And responding to it are the tactful half-smiles on the face of the force.'

But I was in for a surprise: if Kaw has sacrificed anything in writing this book it is tact. I hope for his sake that his ACR writing officer does not get hold of it.

Well, this is the book for you: blunt and telling, shorn of all tact and subtleties. Irreverent, biting and sarcastic.

In this unmasking of the IAS, he spares none: no, not even his political bosses. He describes how during a CM's visit he had allotted rooms in the circuit house to the entourage, all according to the pecking order. In this process a particular lady doctor got a room near the kitchen, far away from the room of the CM. The young collector was surprised when all this resulted in a tongue lashing. How was poor Kaw to know that for reasons unconnected to her pay scale this lady was always given a room next to the CM and that too, one with a connecting door!

Problem solving and resolving of situations is one of the special preserves of the IAS. Kaw recounts a number of instances where situations have been tackled by 'presence of mind and absence of body'. He recalls how, when he faced a particularly difficult law and order situation, he was assured by his boss that he was rushing to the spot with force. When six hours later the chap had not arrived, Kaw rang him up. 'Don't worry, my boy,' assured the experienced personage, 'I am watching the situation....from the police station'.

The strongest of the weapons in the hand of the IAS is the meeting: it is used for all practical purposes, including putting off unwanted visitors, avoiding taking decisions and throwing one's weight around. Let's see what Kaw says about them. 'A really successful meeting is one for which the convener has drafted the minutes in advance. The only changes required are in the list of participants. No one need fear that there would be voluble protests from members. For, just as the agenda is never read, so never are the minutes.'

Kaw is as blunt as he is irreverent: Just hear what he says about Kang, a senior colleague, one who never said 'No' to asinine superior orders, but somehow refrained from compliance while displaying an outwardly obedient manner.

'It was soon evident to me that Kang was not the nincompoop he seemed to be. It was an affectation. Since then, I have come across a host of Kangs in the Service, all absurd half-wits but supremely successful. Naturally, there is a sprouting suspicion in my mind that there must be some preponderant advantage in playing the fool.'

Thanks Kaw, I know now why all the top chaps in the Service happen to be fools!

Kaw sees his book as a textbook for IAS probationers; I find it to be a must reading for those who are preparing for the Civil Services exams. Apart from preparation in Literature and General Knowledge, let them be prepared for the disillusionment to follow.

Looking back, Kaw, whose children are now pursuing courses in medicine and management, feels that his choice of career was not well directed; he would have been better off in economics. I could have said the same thing for myself, being one of the earlier IIT engineers to enter the IAS. Young IIT and IIM students now engaged in studying for the Civil Services exams, are you listening?

Kaw feels that the biggest failure of the IAS has been its inability to change the age old feudalistic systems in the bureaucracy that have prevented creative people in other fields from achieving their potential.

Kaw has only pointed out the ills without giving the solutions: he feels that analysis of a problem means half the solution. If this is true, then let all of us in the service examine at what stage our 'nation building' ideals got transformed to 'career building' aims. Maybe in this realization we may get the spark to reform and upgrade both ourselves and the service.

It has to start with some sort of a redefining of our relationship with the politician. Here I think Kaw deserves to have the last word. 'The politician feels out the spinal chord of the bureaucrat. It is this innocuous organ that can give the most trouble. If lacking in flexibility, it makes the civil servant rigid, unbending, obdurate, stubborn— everything he should not be. An ideal bureaucrat should be soft as butter, yielding as wax, pliant, flexible, sensitive to the compulsions of his political master.'

For the bureaucrat who fails to take the advice, Kaw lists out the Armageddon. 'As the political war rages fiercer, the allegiances will become stronger and the reprisals more brutal. Transfers will no longer satisfy. Cruel caucuses will demand the guillotine. Suspension, arrests, CBI raids, forced resignations will become the daily diet of scandal-hungry tabloids.'

Some diet that!

18

PANEL TIME IS TENSION TIME FOR IAS

Have you recently met a senior officer of the IAS who seems to you to be tense and under pressure? Before you go off speculating on the causes of his tension, be sure that the preparation of the panel is not the reason. Believe me, the panel is the one single reason for tension in members of this heaven-born service.

So inscrutable, mysterious and anonymous is the way of the IAS bureaucracy, it is difficult to understand, leave alone appreciate, its functioning. And nowhere is this mystique more in evidence than in the formation of the so called 'panels' for postings in the central secretariat.

A panel for a particular post is exactly what the word says: a list of names cleared for appointment to that post. For the IAS this list is purely an internal list, prepared after an internal scrutiny, neither made public nor as a recent supreme court ruling seems to imply, justiciable.

But still for people who do not make it to the panel, it is a disaster unequalled by anything that could have happened, mitigated neither by a promotion in their state cadres nor by a horizontal movement to the so-called 'equivalent posts'.

What is funny is that finding a place in the all important panel implies neither any special expertise nor is it a promotion list; more often than not most of the people seeking places on the panel are already cleared for that pay scale in the state cadres; many of them are working in those scales, some of them for many years at a stretch. But still for most members of the service, not making the panel is one of the particularly distressing nightmares that haunts them most of their service careers.

To understand the importance of the panel, one has to realise that the IAS is an All India Service, which means that its members can serve both at the Centre and in the States. Unlike the state service officers who serve only the particular state that recruits them and the central services officers only the centre.

But despite this all India character, basically every member of the service belongs to the cadre of the State to which he is originally allocated. For all practical purposes, especially for service matters like promotions, he is really an employee of that state.

For deciding which of the officers will serve the centre and for how long, a long list of rules, traditions and practices have been evolved. And formation of the panel is one of these practices.

While deciding the strength of the officers to be allocated to a particular state, a figure called the 'deputation reserve' is added on to the posts that the state needs. It is this reserve that provides the numbers who move to the centre.

The posts for the IAS at the centre are really of the Deputy Secretaries and above in the central secretariat; and for each one of these the appointments have to be cleared by the Appointments Committee of the Cabinet, chaired by the Prime Minister himself.

It is a long standing tradition that only those officers are considered for the central deputation whom the state governments are willing to spare. But there has been another tradition that if a particular officer's name is on the approved panel of the central government, the states generally don't hold back his name. In fact coming on the panel is one way of putting the states in some sort of a bind; and in a way this highlights one of the reasons for the importance of the panel.

The panel is used in two different ways for determining individual postings. There is one system for the juniors and another for the seniors.

In the case of postings up to Joint Secretary level, being on the panel does not imply any sort of assurance of getting a posting though it is a sort of essential condition for such a posting. Names out of the panel are circulated to various ministries; and it is to them that the final decision is left on which officer to pick. It thus happens that an officer way down in the panel may be picked up before an officer who may be many notches above him in the seniority.

For postings of Additional Secretaries and Secretaries, are usually centralised in the Cabinet Secretariat, though the selection may be preceded with some sort of informal consultations. In these postings seniority in the panel becomes the by-word.

The importance which is attached to postings in the centre by members of the service far exceeds the importance and content of many of the jobs that the central government offers. No doubt, some of the jobs are very high profile and sensitive; but these are only a few per cent of the total jobs. Many jobs are so decrepit that the general public, and sometimes even the officers themselves, have not heard of them.

On the contrary, most of the senior jobs in the states are very high profile and with high job content. Such jobs, including those of Chief Secretaries and Principal Secretaries, give much greater scope for satisfaction than most of their counterparts in Delhi. But still the dream of each officer is to quickly get to the centre and stay there as long as possible.

One of the reasons for such a fascination is obvious: it is the posting to both the centre and the state that makes an IAS officer distinct and more important than his counterparts elsewhere. Another reason for many of the officers could be the fact that more frequent changes of government in the state makes the job a little more 'dicey'. There could possibly be other reasons as well but do all these still account for the terrible fascination that the panel has for the members of the service.

I have been analysing it for the last three decades; both within myself and with my colleagues but have not been able to come to any satisfactory conclusion. I think it may be that merely because there is a panel, everybody would like to be on it irrespective of the fact whether it brings any substantial gains in job prospects or not.

If anybody can find any better reasons, I'd like to hear from him.

19

SUPPORTIVE ADMINISTRATIVE STRUCTURE NEEDED

We have seen how flimsy and superficial is the relationship between the 'policeman without uniform' (citizen) and the one in uniform, with the one expected to do the chores as the other enjoys the power, perks and privileges. This same relationship exists in other areas of administration as well, especially in areas where there is power to be exercised.

The deep fissures that have been exposed in the steel frame of the bureaucracy in the wake of the Uphaar tragedy calls our attention to the urgent need for reforms. In any reform environment, we have to find a way of substituting the present assertive model of functioning with a supportive one. How this is to be done is what poses a major challenge to the functioning administrators as well as reformers.

Many of us have faced such challenges in the past and have evolved our own structures and systems. I had worked out a similar system when I was called upon to deal with the massive problem of housing, clothing and feeding over a million Bengali refugees in Tripura in the early 70s. In this system, we had a small group of regular government employees (exactly 5 in fact) supporting the activities of a large number of civil servants, doctors and other personnel drawn from amongst the refugees themselves.

This system was remarkably successful but it may not be possible to duplicate it elsewhere since the same number of talented and experienced people as the refugees had may not be so easy to find. But there is at least one area in which a similar system can be duplicated and that is the field of social welfare and defence.

Let us take the vast problems that cities face from the growing army of beggars, juvenile delinquents, wife beaters, dowry hungry mothers-in-law, paedophiles and other similar social delinquents like those who commit crimes against woman and the like. How are these problems to be dealt with?

Our present approach is a legalistic one which usually starts and ends with the framing of a law which makes many of the undesirable activities cognisable offences, i.e., offences which the police can investigate without obtaining the orders of a magistrate. When we find that the approach does not yield any results, we constitute special cells and task forces for the purpose.

While the success or failure of such cells and task forces may depend upon the persons chosen to head them, the fact remains that their successful functioning remains circumscribed because of the very limitations of such an approach. Take wife beating: is there any way that even a Kiran Bedi can make any impact here? The relationship between husband and wife is such that there is no way that any outside force can have any impact on it, leave alone intervention by a member of a uniformed force.

The same applies to juvenile crimes, drug addictions, dowry related crimes, crimes against women, and the like. What we see as the crime is actually the end of a long and complicated process which must have begun either within the family or within a certain social circle. To tackle such crimes it is not the end that has to be controlled or checked but it is the cause that has to be identified and tackled. There is no way that Kiran Bedis and their ilk can do that and that is simply for the reason that there is no easy way for them to reach the family.

What competent police officers find so difficult to control and check becomes easy for members of the community. Let us take the case of the school boy who continually gets poor marks; the poor teacher has tried everything but finds that he is unable to help. The real reason for the poor performance of the child may not be what the teacher thinks it is (poor application, etc.) but may lie in the home where the child is made to suffer from a sense of deprivation because of the attention that the mother has been devoting to her newly born child. Had the teacher known this maybe he could have helped the child overcome this but, poor thing!, how is he to know?

Let us accept it: most social crimes result from some problem that has started from the home and cannot be tackled unless the basic problem in the home can be tackled. And this cannot be done unless the home can be reached and this the legal and quasi legal authorities, operating in the police station or out of it, find it well near impossible.

The assertive system fails; let us see how the supportive system can be made to work. Let us open Social Assistance Stations (I call them SAFE stations) where the teacher from the school, the mother from the home and the social worker from the street can all come for help. If these stations are bureaucratically manned, they will face the same problem that police stations face; let us, therefore, man them with members of the community, somewhat like the paid volunteers who run the refugee camps.

The members of the community who man these stations are not just ordinary people; they are the ones with special expertise, training and aptitude to tackle such problems. The only requirement is that they should be public spirited and should have time to spare for the community.

Being volunteers, they are more acceptable to the community and to the family. Witness the acceptability of people like Mother Teresa and Baba Amte. But unlike such personages, these people will enjoy a legal status and as such their findings will not be again put to test through a bureaucratic rigmarole of station house officers and the like.

SAFE stations will not register complaints with a view to ascertain guilt and give punishment as the police stations will normally do but will do so with a view to provide assistance and support. This may vary from case to case. While for an orphan they will try to find a suitable foster home, for the drug addict they will try to identify a suitable support system.

SAFE stations are not just manned by members of the community but their support system is also centred there. The support provided is not just physical but emotional and mental as well, something that no bureaucratic system can provide. Not being punitive in character they should be able to win social and community support in a big way.

The idea of giving an example of such stations is not to say that this may be the only or even the best solution to social problems but to assert that not only are support systems of administration possible but that they may even be better than the alternate models of assertive authoritarian administration. Any scheme of administrative reforms will have to keep this in view.

20

THE LONG LEASH OF BUREAUCRATIC LIFE

Bow out the old. Ring in the new.

Happy new year. Though these greetings have been repeated many times over, there is something special this year. This is the hundredth and last time that we are doing in this century. This completes a century of greetings this century: that alone is enough to make the greetings this year very special. But for me there is another more personal, even though fortuitous, reason.

As we arrive here, finally, in the last year of the 20th century this thought comes to me. In just a few months from now I would have retired from service. I don't know if that had enabled me to try to relocate the strings left behind when I joined the bureaucracy and try to build afresh. Or, take to the cynical old way of pontificating to my younger colleagues to do what I myself could never have the guts or gumption to do. Or, hesitatingly prepare to take the last few steps to the graveyard.

But no longer need the thought of immediate retirement trouble me. One of the first steps that the present government took was to take out the rejected recommendations of the Pay Commission and extend the retirement age to 60. This gives many of us a new lease (or is it leash?) of bureaucratic life. The inevitability of retirement still lurks in the distance, but who is thinking of that?

1999 would have been the last year of my service and

2000 the first of my retirement. That was my mental make-up for the last so many years. I now have to adjust to the fact that these two years are just two years in my bureaucratic life, no more. The crucial years would now be 2001 and 2002 but by then we will be firmly entrenched into the 21st century and well, who knows, one may be able to extend the lease even further into that century.

Lease, did I call it? Only a few months back it seemed to be a leash. A leash made of silk and gold, maybe but a leash none the less that imprisons and enslaves not just the body but also the mind and the soul. But now that I prepare for the new year, it is this thought that is far away from my mind which is engaged furiously in locating new and greener pastures.

The possibilities are immense and so are the grapes that are so enticingly entangling there. So attractive are these that one would tend to forget all the plans one had made not so long ago for this century and cling furiously to the bureaucratic leash, now extended a bit more, well into the next century.

I always thought that leashes really were for dogs but didn't realise that even bureaucrats didn't mind them too much. Ever so often they became so attractive that it is really difficult to let go. It is almost too painful to be reminded how only a few months ago how eagerly one was looking forward to the time when the unleashing (that's how I saw retirement) would be completed. I wouldn't exactly describe a bureaucrat's life to be 'dog's life' even though, I must admit, there have been times when it has seemed no better. But still retirement (many have preferred the 'resignation' route) did seem to be attractive in many ways, even if not exactly the dawn of a period of freedom. Many times I have dreamt of a scenario if I was young again but in none of these I have joined the civil service. Many a times I have become a writer and a poet; a :film maker or a creative artist, even an NRI. But never, never a bureaucrat.

Maybe it's being wiser after the event. Maybe better sense has prevailed. Or maybe it's the syndrome of the 'other side of the fence' being greener. But the fact is that the promises that a civil service career offered at the time were not fulfilled.

Creature comforts were there aplenty. So were the other perks and rewards. Big houses. Foreign travel. Fairly decent salary. Public recognition. Social acceptance and respect. Yes, all of it is there in a civil service career. Still something very critical is missing. What is it? I'm sure that much of the year 1999 I'm going to spend musing into this question: What is it that I expected to get from a civil service career that I failed to get?

Let us see what the other careers give; this might give a clue to the riddle that I'm trying to solve. Let's see the satisfactions of an acting career. Glamour? Sex? Money? Popularity? Yes, probably most good actors get it but it is especially reserved for those who are real hits.

Civil servants? Do these come with success or failure?

Failure for a civil servant comes when he gets charge sheeted or fails to get a promotion or is taken to a court in some sort of prosecution tangle under the Prevention of Corruption Act. As I throw my mind back to civil servants who have been in these tangles; those who have even lost their jobs as a result of these. Do they lack any of these satisfactions? Glamour, sex, popularity and money? They have so much of it that many of them later have managed to get into other fields where they have managed to even multiply manifold these satisfactions!

The success for the honest, hard working civil servant comes from a more sedate manner. Creative satisfaction, sense of achievement, pride in his work, and such like feelings. But none of these easily translate into terms that define success in the other professions.

Let's take money, easily the best indicator for success in any of the other career options for any young man, be it acting, business or profession of architecture and law. In the civil service it has a negative correlation with success. No matter what you do and how well, there is no way that success will translate into more money. Money by and large will only come if professional ethics are sold down the drain.

The sordid and ironic fact of life in the civil service is that what is failure in the other professions and career options is the prime indicator of success here. That is, if you wish to be successful in the sense that success is viewed by others, you have to be a failure.

For being successful, be not afraid of courting with failure. Is this a sobering thought for the new year or is it a wonderful new year resolution? I'll let the reader decide.

21
THE BACK SCRATCHING SYNDROME

The back scratching syndrome is well known; but what is not so well known is its relationship with that currency of Biblical times called 'talent' and that very special currency of Kalyug called *sifarish*.

The point now is, are these two commodities mutually tradable? If so, how many talents are equal to one *sifarish*?

We know that a dollar is thirty-seven rupees; we also know that, that talents of one R. Basu are worth a crore and a half. But what about the value of a *sifarish*?

Try meeting an important functionary in Delhi and then you will know what the value of *sifarish* is. Frankly, if you do not know a *sifarishee* there is no way that you can meet anybody who counts. But this still begs the issue: How do you get to meet a *sifarishee*?

Scams give us some idea but still the issue is not resolved with a finality. But there is no doubt that there must be an exchange rate though that rate may depend on various factors, which need to be systematically studied. But howsoever difficult it may be to determine it, its effect is not so difficult to uncover. Remember the story of the one way ticket to the moon? Here, it is said, that when the Bengali was offered this ticket, he asked for Rs. 10,000. After all, he exclaimed, I have to leave something for my family. The Punjabi wanted Rs. 20,000, Rs. 10,000 for himself to enjoy before he embarked on the one way journey and the remaining amount for the family. But the Marwari wanted Rs. 30,000. Like the Punjabi, he too wanted to enjoy life and like the Bengali he wanted to leave something for his family. But why another Rs. 10,000? I'll pay this to the Bengali, he explained frankly, 'so that he goes to the moon'.

The same applies to *sifarish*. When I have work with you and you with me, we merely exchange the *sifarish*. But, sometimes, clever people take advantage of this situation. X wants Y to do something for him and in return is willing to return a *sifarish* to him. Z, coming to know of this situation, brings the two together to exchange their respective sifarish. But in this process Z earns two for himself, one from X and the other from Y.

Incidentally, this is what all middle men and so-called contact men in Delhi are doing these days.

Apart from these effects, this exchange of talent for *sifarish* also gives rise to various syndromes. One such syndrome can be called the 'you scratch my back and I'll scratch your' syndrome.

The scratch my back syndrome triggers a chain reaction similar to the one that leads to the nuclear explosion. One *sifarish* leads to two; and these in turn to two each, that is, a total of four.

Though the process is not as fast as a nuclear reaction, it is fast enough to catch on. Now the only criteria left for judging whether a person deserves a job or not is not whether he has talent, but whether ones back will get scratched at the end of it.

This can be called the 'back scratching explosion'. Everybody is scratching everybody's back.

The result of the explosion is that, in due course of time, all of us are doing nothing but scratching each others back, just like monkeys. It does seem that in the ultimate analysis, it is back to square one.

But, as in all aspects of our life, there are two sides to the *sifarish* coin too. If on one side our simian behaviour leads to the destruction of 'talent raj', on the other hand it has the merit of at least helping us overcome some of the more baneful influences of the bureaucratic system.

In the system that we see today, the file is king; and it is almost impossible to make the babu look. Often we at our wits end when we deal with a government clerk or a minor functionary. Making him change dates of birth on the basis of statements of people who were present at the time of your birth is no doubt difficult in the light of what the certificate in the file says; but even making him change the spellings of your name is almost impossible. It's not only that he won't change the spellings; he would even refuse to put up the case to his boss for his superior consideration.

It is here that *sifarish raj* comes in handy. All you have to do is to locate a person who is deep in the 'scratch my back' syndrome: this may not make the learned *babu* to change his mind but it would at least force him to put up the case to the 'appropriate authority'!

It is true that the system of *sifarish*, to a large extent discounts merit. But it does seem that many of the system's evil effects flow only when the system is not widespread. The problem comes only when the chairman of the board receives only one telephone. But what if he received a call on behalf of every candidate that he is interviewing?

Of course, he will go for the stronger of the *sifarish*; but there are limits to this. These are not issues that can be decided so easily. A chap who is taken as weak now (a bureaucrat temporarily out of job or a politician out of power), can easily be strong at some other time and vice versa. One can only ignore some of these pulls at ones peril. A through going system of *sifarish* cannot be weighted down by these considerations.

I asked this question from one of the strong proponents of this system. He looked puzzled at first but soon the mist cleared from his eyes. That's the beauty.

The problems in the system come only when it is not amply widespread. Once the syndrome of *sifarish* is the rule, meritocracy can prevail again.

In other words, to solve the problem of *sifarish* vs *talent*, all we have to do is to abolish talent altogether. Ironically, this may be the only way to restore talent to its original glory.

22

ENGINEERS IN THE IAS, ALL SET FOR USA

'As soon as a student passes the IIT Joint Entrance Examination, he has arrived—arrived in the USA'!

This was Dr Arunachalam, in an address to scientists at the National Aeronautical Laboratory, Bangalore.

He could well have added the words—Or, in the IAS.

The highlight of the fortieth report of the UPSC: of the 85 toppers in the IAS/IFS more than 50 are engineers and medical doctors. And more than half of them from the elite IITs.

This goes on endlessly, year after year. Boy or girl be sure it its a topper, the must be an engineer and that too from one of the elite IITs. And just as expectedly, it is greeted with the usual cries which match the fervour of a Indo-Pak crowed booing the opposite team in a cricket match.

The arguments are endless–the best of the technical brains in the country are being wasted in jobs anybody else I can do! Moreover, how can people trained as specialists carry out tasks designed to be done by generalists? In any case if they were to join the IAS why were they allowed to waste seats at expensive medical or engineering institutions? And so on .

As I hear the arguments my mind goes back 30 years; in this period only times have changed almost nothing else. Certainly not attitudes.

I was just out of IIT and not yet fully 23 years of age as I found myself standing nervously before the then chairman of the UPSC, B.N. Jha waiting to be told to take my seat. Suddenly the venerable Jha sahib took his eyes off the table to where presumably, my form stood and stared at me. As if he was looking not at an IAS aspirant but a strange bird.

'You're an engineer, eh?' His voice was biting and sharp as he went on to repeat the now familiar arguments against engineers in the civil service.

At first I was too aware of the sweat on my collar, but then, stung by the abuse, I hit back; the reply flowed easy and smooth like, excuse the cliche, knife through butter. I enjoyed every moment of it then as I do not whenever I recall the moment.

"If I have wasted a seat, what about the student who specialized in international law or in economics or in commerce? An engineer is not a machine—the habits of quantitative thought which characterize undergraduate training in engineering is a superb preparation for other professional fields. If my IIT education, which taught me as many as 70 subjects including humanities, science and pure mathematics, has given me a single track mind—what about the person who has never gone beyond specialization in European history between the wars?"

I got the job—that too with flying colours, having come close to toping the list. But I wonder how many others were successfully blocked because of this prejudice. And the sad part is that this prejudice refuses to die.

I wonder if what motivates people like the infamous UPSC member Banerjee, who in the fifties blocked the prospects of a whole generation of engineers, is the possible waste of technical people; if an engineer in the IAS is wasted what about the engineer in any of the state PWDs? Or in the public sector for that matter what about those who become salesmen in multinational soap peddling companies?

What about an engineer who decides to make films? Or one who wishes to write novels take to politics or paint or even spend his life in singing hymns to God!

Raj Kumar Barjatya, an executive producer of 41 films ranging from the classic *Dosti* to the greatest money spinner of them all *Mainye Pyar Kiya,* is a mining engineer from IIT Kharagpur.

Ajit Singh, the youthful ex-Industries Central minister, is similarly from Kharagpur. Manager-owners of all the top computer software companies of Delhi are from that institute. As are the joint heads of the largest construction company of the capital. And the list endless.

Dr A. P. Mitra, the ex-DG of CSIR was very fond of saying that of the 250 odd winners of the Bhatnagar Prize, the Nobel Prize equivalent for young Indian scientists, only one has settled abroad.

Similarly the high class technical personnel who have exercised their freedom to join the IAS or other similar jobs at least have continued to make available their expertise to the country of their birth.

Have all these people been wasted? Can it be argued that they should have rather been engineers in the state PWDs? Or chief machinists and engineers in factories?

Well, even if one was allowed this argument there is another against which really no argument is possible. And that has to do with that elusive concept called freedom.

And freedom is not divisible. You either have it or you do not. We all know what happened when the erstwhile state or GDR made the infamous wall. Could it keep East Germans captive? Maybe for sometime; but then it led to the end of the whole system, the destruction of the state of East Germany. Can you keep people captive, be they poor landless farmers or bright young engineer as from our elite institutions including the IITs? May be you can; but this will be at the cost of the most precious of our legacies—freedom. And is there any difference between a chained genius and a chained idiot?

An engineer or a doctor who chooses to exercise his freedom and joins the civil services, he certainly cannot be motivated by financial consideration, in his profession he'll certainly earn many times more especially if he chooses to go abroad. In fact, the difference is so vast that it does surprise why anybody would choose the IAS!

It cannot be status because these days money can buy it. Then what is it?

I think it is basically the fact that one does not want to be taken as a non-achiever and there is no doubt that getting through the civil services exam today is taken as the measure of achievement. And to be accepted as an achiever is a most effective way of self-actualization.

If you want to keep the bright professionals out of the civil series, the most effective way would be to introduce a *sifarish raj* in the selections!

The Bhatnager Prize winners and the IIT engineers in the IAS prove only one thing—that people are willing to stay on here—not for money or even for status. But they will stay only if they are given opportunities for self-actualization.

Let us not delude ourselves: we cannot keep our engineers and scientists here just by offering them money or good jobs, certainly not through coercion and force. If we have to keep them here it will have to be by allowing them freedom, by giving them opportunities for self-actualization and expression.

It is only by giving them freedom to go out if they wish that we can induce at least some of them to stay on to serve their motherland.

23

A TIMELY WARNING

While roaming on the lakeside in Nainital recently I first saw the poster. It had the youthful first citizen of our biggest state at the top with one of her quotations printed at the bottom. I was so impressed that I immediately clicked my camera and imprisoned both her face as also those golden words on celluloid.

It is only the other day, as I received the developed film, that I felt the real impact of the words. After mentioning how she had now been converted from the service of the 'bahujan' (many) to the service of 'sarvajan' (all), she goes on to declare that in her regime 'decisions will not be taken on the basis of caste or creed but on the requirements of time and justice. In her words, *samay aur insaaf ka takaza kya hai* (what is the demand of justice and time?).

It seems fine enough till you realize that till now justice has always been pictured as a blind woman, keeping the scales steady irrespective of any extraneous considerations whatsoever. Yes, one did talk of justice being tempered with mercy; but 'justice tempered with time' is being talked about in responsible circles for the first time.

I wonder if the lady was being frank or the statement just slipped out; but the fact remains that what she said is the true state of justice in the country today. No, no longer it is acceptable to the dispensers of justice to be blind; nor do they agree that justice should be confined to the law courts: they feel that it should be taken to the streets and dispensed as per the needs of the hour.

Needless to say, the needs of the hour vary, literally, by the hour. If justice has one face at the time of the elections, it has quite another face at the time of the vote of no confidence in the Assembly. And then quite another altogether when it comes to collecting the loaves of office.

Facing the oppressors of our dowry harassed daughter justice looks quite different from what it does when one looks down the throat of the parents of one's own daughter in law!

If justice looks different in different situations, it acts different too. Let us take the justice that the legislators do to the constituents who elect them. They approach them with a certain party label with a distinct manifesto and programme. At the earliest opportunity they convert themselves from Aya Ram to Gaya Ram, changing not merely party labels but also their programmes and promises.

Let's see how the young medical graduate who grows up to be a crooked doctor dispenses justice to the institution that educated him and to the oath of Hippocrates he took at the graduation ceremony. More often than not he prescribes medicines not for the patient but for the drug company or medical agent. So is the case with the blood and clinical tests that he prescribes.

The same is true of the IIT graduate. Or the IAS officer. In fact, of anyone who decides to deviate from the straight path. There is only one way for such people to justify their behaviour: Yeh to samay ka takaza hai!' (It is the demand of time) The need of the hour!

Justice has an old and checkered history. But one thing about it has been unchanged: the fact that it is blind. It is blind to everything but the fact that it has to be dispensed irrespective of not merely caste or creed but also the need of the hour. And this lesson is often forgotten not merely by the politician or the bureaucrat but also by the judge and the law maker.

In violation of orders of the apex court a certain building is still demolished and a top politician assumes full responsibility. Along with him lakhs of other persons, sensing political gains, also take the responsibility and demand punishment. The important politician is tried in absentia, even though he was prepared to attend the court, and given one day's imprisonment.

An IAS officer disobeys the orders of the same court though not with impunity and not with a view to commit contempt, probably as a result of a mistaken belief about the interpretation of the court's orders. Despite entreaties and appeals for justice he is locked up for a month.

A humble policeman, taking a prisoner in handcuffs outside this very same court behaves in a brash and illegal manner. Poor fellow, this is the only way he knows of dealing with criminals in handcuffs and it was his misfortune that he happened to be in the temple of justice at that time. He is ordered to be arrested and, if found guilty, will probably have to face harsher penalties.

Even if justice is blind, let us remember that it is not divisible. As one goes up the ladder the punishment should be harsh and strict; down the ladder it should be tempered with mercy and compassion. It is unfortunate that it is the other way around.

What is the quality that differentiates the ruler from the ruled? Or the great ruler from the ordinary one? From time immemorial there is only one way and that is the way that he handles the scales of justice.

Not every ruler can be a Harun Al Rashid and not every leader a Mahatma Gandhi; but that is no reason why he should not strive. Ideals are unattainable and serve no purpose except to serve as norms and standards. But it is only those who are aware of the summit who have any chance of reaching it.

Let us rescue justice from the clutches of those who serve the needs of the hour. Let us restore to it its great timeless blindness. Let justice not be ornament of the time serving ruling clans but the shield of the weak and the oppressed.

24

THE 'DOHATHAD': TWO HANDED APPROACH

At a time when corruption was not as widespread and as respectable as it is today, my father would often refer disparagingly to the corrupt officer as 'dohathad', meaning 'the two handed'.

Every officer gets a salary which he takes with one hand; it is only the corrupt fellow who gets a second and thus has to use the second hand as well. So the name.

There are interesting sidelights to this as my father often pointed out jocularly. It seems that in many departments, I remember that the irrigation department was one of them, the second hand remained so busy, that these officers had no use for their main hand. In such departments the tradition was to pass on the regular salary to the clerk who makes the salary bill!

My first brush with corruption was when I was posted to Hamirpur as an Assistant Magistrate (under training). Since I did not have a regular charge there was no regular house for me. The DM (M.P. Pandey later became the Chief Secretary of UP) asked the local Tahsildar to organize something. Till that was done, I was asked to put up in the PWD dak bungalow.

I was there only a few days when the PWD Minister decided to make a visit to Hamirpur. Since the tradition is to give the dak bungalows exclusively to Ministers if they choose to stay there, I was forced to find some other accommodation. In the absence of other arrangements the SDO PWD, whose bungalow was in the compound of the guest house, was kind enough to invite me to spend a night or two with him.

It happened in the morning. We were having a lazy cup of tea in the lawn outside when this gentleman in *dhoti* came to meet the youthful SDO. In those days I was quite inquisitive about the ways of the government; so I paid heed to all that was being said.

Apparently the issue that had brought the *dhoti* clad gentleman, who, it didn't take me long to discover, was a PWD contractor, to meet our youthful SDO was a bill, payment of which was apparently pending in the office. No discussion could have been briefer: after the minimum of formalities and introductions, the contractor brought out a bundle wrapped in cloth from out of the folds of his *dhoti* and respectfully put it on the table.

My host barely looked at it as he offered a cup of tea to the guest who, it seemed, was barely in a mood to partake of it. His interest was more in wanting to hear about his pending bill than to take a cup of the refreshing brew.

Realizing this my youthful host gave him the most warm of assurances. 'Don't worry sethji...you will get your bill today itself'. Satisfied, the contractor was off.

I was as dumb those days as I am now. And probably as outspoken. After the contractor had gone, I found myself inquiring about the contents of the packet that he had left behind. The venerable SDO unpacked the packet and showed it to me. It was a couple of bundles of currency notes.

"Why," I asked surprised at the contents, "did this chap owe you some money?"

His reply was disarming. "This is my fees." Seeing my understanding gaze, he went on to clarify. "Like a lawyer or a doctor an engineer is too a professional and has a right to get a fee".

I was not convinced. "But what did you give him?"

The reply was ingenuous. "Advice. Why do you stare at

me thus? Would you stare at the doctor who demands a fee when all that he does is to look at the pulse and tell you what medicine to take? What about the lawyer who hears your case and gives you nothing but advice?"

"But what advice did you give him?"

"Why the hell do you think he came here for? He has a bill pending in the office; I advised him how to get it cleared quickly".

I have seen many faces of corruption since then and had many brushes—unfortunately not all of them as pleasant as the one described above—with corrupt people. But I haven't seen a single one who is repentant or who feels that he does wrong. In fact, the justification that they have for the same is more than the justification that I can find for remaining honest. The attitude of each one of these fellows, be they in business, government or any of the professions, is straight faced and honest to goodness.

But the frankness that beats all is the demand for linking pay scales of tax collectors to the amounts of tax revenue collected by them. Their argument is simple: pay us legally otherwise we'll get it all the same illegally. In other words, if you don't increase the money you put in our right hand, we will grab it with our left hand!

Superficially viewed it makes sense. Since they are going to make it anyway, why not give it to them. This way at least they will do their job more efficiently and honestly and more than make up the cost to the exchequer of the higher payment.

All this is fine except that such payments smack of the spoils system in which civil servants are not paid any salary but are allowed to collect it from use of their office. It was this system that prevailed before the British came here.

In this system the tax collector was paid a part of what he collected. But lest our present generation of tax collectors plump in for this system in their memorandum to the pay commission let them remember that the system was 'one handed' and that the percentage that they got did not depend on the money they actually collected but what was actually due. It worked like this. Let us say the percentage was 10 per cent and the tax due was Rs 100,000. The tax collectors were paid Rs. 10,000.

But what if they collected only Rs. 80,000? In the Mughal spoils system this would mean that he would have to pay the difference to the government. In other words, instead of getting Rs. 10,000, they would have to pay this amount to the treasury!

Before rushing to the pay commission let the tax collectors remember that in its prisine purity the spoils system is essentially one handed. It is only the present one that allows them use of both the hands: the right hand for collecting the revenue and the left one for failure to do so.

25
FLAG FLYING SUITCASE OFFICERS

It was amusing to read the other day about the protest of certain North-Eastern Chief Ministers against, what they chose to describe as, 'suitcase officers'.

These officers have earned this nickname because during their postings there they left their families behind in Delhi. They thus go there with only a suitcase. The Chief Ministers' complaint is that this affects their commitment to the states of their posting.

While going through this complaint, I am reminded of an officer of yore who had earned the ire of politicians for a similar reason.

'Phantom' is the name though I'm not sure if this is the way he spelt it. I've borrowed the spelling of the well-known comic character for the simple reason that I know no other and, moreover, the true life Phantom was no less a comic figure!

At the time I joined service in the sixties, Phantom was already a legend in UP. An officer of the Provincial Service, Phantom was known far beyond the borders of that state. And amongst the various reasons for his fame was the fact that he always kept his belongings packed in a suitcase.

Transfers and threats of transfers have now become the normal hazard of a civil service career. They are favoured weapons employed by politicians to keep civil servants, ordinarily surrounded by a vast and almost impregnable fence of protective rules and precedents, under control. Phantom was aware of this and had devised his own way of defeating it.

The easiest way of nullifying any threat is to succumb to it. Or so Phantom believed. So to nullify the menace of a transfer order he was ready to obey it at any time, day or night.

And that is where the suitcase came in. Whenever he went to bed, he packed all his belongings in it and placed it in the dicky of his weather-beaten car. He was, thus, ready to move, literally, at a moment's notice and just as soon as the midnight caller brought in the normally much dreaded transfer order, Phantom was up and away.

The suitcase ensured that a most potent weapon had lost its power. Not a very pleasant prospect for the wielder of the weapon.

As I went tnrough the item in the Indian Express about the protest of the North-East Governments, I wondered if here too this is the provocation.

To be sure this is not the cited reason. The upholders of good administration feel that this results in loss of efficiency and commitment. But is this the real worry of these worthies? Is it really fear of loss of efficiency?

My thought goes back to the time when the RAF, after having failed to penetrate the almost impregnable defence of the German wartime factories, decided to bombard the much more lightly defended workers' housing complexes. The idea was that the destruction of their homes would lead to demoralization amongst the workers and result in lack of productivity.

But just the opposite happened: deprived of the safety of their homes, German workers packed all their essential belongings into a suitcase and moved to the safety of the factories, many of them sleeping next to their machines; consequently production, far from suffering, increased since shifts could now be stretched much beyond the stipulated eight hours.

'Suitcase workers' were a god-send for the hard pressed

Nazi military machine; one wonders why suitcase officers should be any less important for the remote and far-flung area administrations and their political masters!

The North-Eastern Governments are reported to have argued that officers with only their suitcases (presumably what they mean is, without their families) are always looking for opportunities to come to Delhi to join their families.

While such a desire on the part of the officers is but natural, it is not understood how they can succeed in their undertaking but for the agreement of their political bosses. According to the rules, no officer can leave station without the prior approval of the competent authority; in almost all cases such an authority vests only in the political head, either in the territory or in Delhi.

It is clear that the problem is not in the fact of the suitcase but in the resultant independence that it breeds.

When the decision was taken in the early eighties to allow officers posted in the remote and far-flung areas of the country to retain their official residences in other towns, the idea was to make such postings less unattractive.

These places are not merely difficult and inaccessible; in most of these stations there are not even minimal facilities for schooling or health care. There are usually no schools or colleges; even where there are they teach in the language of the region. How does one expect the children of the officers posted there to continue their studies in such circumstances?

Tawang, Sela, Lungleh, Car Nicobar, Mokokchong or Agatti are all wonderful places to be posted in and they all present unique opportunities for the officer's talents to flower. They also all pose administrative challenges of a high order. But how does one expect his family to be there unless the children are less than three years old? And, moreover, they have to be in prime health.

Permitting an officer to keep his family in a place other than that of his posting is taken as a facility; but it is ignored that it places many difficult burdens on him. One has to live alone in these remote and far-flung places for some time to realize how difficult it is.

The difficulties are compounded because of the insular attitude of many of the locals who often surround themselves with a wall of resentment which often takes the shape of discrimination.

Millions of central government employees have to leave hearth and home and serve in these remote and inaccessible areas where, apart from the terrain and the poor facilities, they are not the 'sons of the soil' This results in numerous sociological and psychological burdens, which often makes life quite a hell. Instead of appreciating them we often add to their tension by giving them names, be they 'mayang', 'outsider' or 'suitcase officers' and deflect them from their difficult task.

Let us not forget that in many a remote and far-flung outpost the fact that the tricolor still flutters is a matter of tribute to the much maligned 'suitcase officers' and their families whom they have been forced to neglect.

26

POLICE-PUBLIC RELATIONS

It is only the other day that I was asked by one of my seniors or a police officer to check up from the computerised electoral rolls the percentage of population in Delhi that is in the age group 18-21. I was astonished with the result: it is about 20 per cent, i.e., a full one-fifth of the population is in the dangerous category of 'juveniles'. This is not all. In a normal distribution, what would the percentage of 18-21 population be? With the span of life being 60, the percentage should be 4160x100=7. What this means is that the actual population in this age group is three times what it should be.

One aspect of the Diana funeral that had struck me was the total rapport between the bobby of the London police and the citizens English Capital. There was a big crowd, almost approaching the standards that we are used to in this country; almost everywhere they were many rows deep, in places as many as 20 or 30 rows and in certain places even more.

It is not that the police was absent; in fact, if anything, it was everywhere, standing just a few metres apart almost along the entire route. But what caught the eye was the fact that though they were everywhere, they were more part of the event rather than being part of a law and order *bundobast*. None of them was armed; in fact, they carried nothing at all in their hands. They did not even have ropes to keep the crowds back; there were barricades, no doubt, but these were treated by the crowd as if there was a powerful wall.

As the procession started even more remarkable things

were to be seen. First of all, the VIPs who went to Westminster Abbey for the funeral service. All of them carried a small piece of paper which must have been the letter of authority. What seems remarkable is the fact that they just showed it to the man outside the Abbey and walked in without there being any intervention by the police, whether in plain clothes or in uniform.

The security aspect was also remarkable. Shortly before the cortege came in the royal family took a walk about just outside the Buckingham Palace. The Queen talked to the crowd as informally as she could, even shaking hands and helping them place their bouquets outside the gate. The Duke of Edinburgh, the Princes and others of the royal family just walked around the crowd in a most informal manner, without the overpowering and crowding presence of the police, whether in or out of uniform.

But the most remarkable of all was the cortege itself, consisting, as it was, of just three vehicles, out of which only one was a police vehicle. Just a few days later there was the funeral procession of Mother Teresa in Calcutta. What a contrast that was with dozens of vehicles joining the procession!

There were three points that formed the subject matter of discussion with the senior police officer. First of all, the security aspect. I, for one, cannot believe that with the royal family taking a stroll among the story there was no security man there; in fact, with my knowledge of security for VIPs worldwide I can say with assurance that there must have been more than a hundred people forming many rings around the royal family. What is remarkable is the fact that all of them were so well mingled with the crowd that there was no way of saying who was who.

My question was: why such a thing cannot happen here? Why does security have to be always conspicuous and gun-toting? If he did have an answer, the senior police officer in question did not give it.

The second point that stood out in the funeral was the perfect behaviour of the policemen on duty. There was no pushing or jostling of the crowd nor were they behaving in a lordly and bullying manner as their counterparts in India are loath to do. Even when a member of the crowd came out from behind the barricades to either throw a bouquet or to take a picture of the cortege, the police did not lose their cool. I shudder to think of how their counterparts in India would have behaved in such a situation.

The senior police officer had a very simplistic answer to this. The behaviour of the Indian police is conditioned by the behaviour of the crowds; if the crowds here behaved as well as they did in London on that day, the police would behave accordingly. In other words, if the police here was cruel or even brutal at time, the responsibility would have to be taken by the people.

I had another comment to make. Why is it that all through the day or so that the police was lined up on the London streets not one supervisory officer or one siren sounding vehicle came there to check up on the behaviour of the bobbies lining up on the route. In India such vehicles would have come every minute or two, sometimes with the inspector, sometime with the SP and other senior officers. Why did the Indian police constable need more supervising than his counterpart in London?

His answer was as frank as revealing. If every policeman in India he stated, was an IPS officer, there was no need of any supervising. But what about the bobby? Is he an IPS (or its British equivalent) officer? Yes, according to this senior officer because it was he who got promoted to the higher echelons of the London police. What didn't strike this worthy was the fact that this didn't make every bobby an IPS officer but made every senior officer there a promoted bobby!

Let us accept the statement of this officer that making every policeman an IPS officer will improve the situation here. What will that take? There is only one essential difference in the qualifications at the time of recruitment of a police constable and an IPS officer: the former is probably is a student at the school final level and the IPS man is a graduate. If we increase the essential qualifications of the constable to that of graduate, then the minimum conditions for good policing will have been met. At least that is what the worthy of the Delhi police seems to imply.

This is ludicrous to say the least. Even if every constable is a graduate, how will it make him a better policeman. What our worthy police officer forgot, perhaps, is the fact that what makes the London bobby different from his counterpart in Delhi is not that he is a graduate but that his superiors have all been bobbies in their time. The lesson of London for us is not that we make IPS officers of our constables but make our constables IPS officers in due course. I wonder if the worthy police officer who was advancing these arguments with such vehemence will buy this!

27

THE POLICEMAN WITHOUT UNIFORM

The goal of any good administrative system is to involve the public in the administration; that is the reason for the dream of any police structure to make all the citizens 'policemen without a uniform'. All steps taken in this direction so far have not met with much success but my feeling is that this has been so because all steps taken so far have been on the wrong track since by and large bureaucrats have been very reluctant to replace the power orientation of the administration with a service orientation.

I was really happy to read the statement of the Delhi Lieutenant Governor that henceforth cinema licences will be renewed after obtaining a certificate from the manager of the hall that his cinema complies with all the necessary requirements of the law and rules. I presume his certificate will be accompanied by a check list (prepared by the administration) of all the legal requirements which he will be required to tick mark as a token of having verified them. I hope that the renewal will be granted only on the basis of this certificate without any further checks by inspectors and their ilk.

This is a step in the right direction and in line with the suggestion made a couple of weeks back in this column of a 'service oriented' rather than a 'power run' administrative structure. To make the system completely effective, the LG will be required to take two more steps: 1. provide for stringent penalties for furnishing false certificates; and 2. make random checks on a percentage basis of these certificates by so called supervisory authorities. Naturally, the vast army of inspectors will be disbanded.

The Uphaar tragedy, like nothing else, has exposed the Indian Administrative structure to its very core. Till now the administration was found wanting if at all, it was on the development and the economic side but the steel frame held firm and strong on the regulatory side. It seems that the once powerful steel framework of the regulatory administration is corroded too. Otherwise, how could the licence system fail so miserably as it did in Uphaar?

There is no doubt that Patel and Nehru decided right when they decided to retain the administrative structure bequeathed to us by the British; it has served us well all these years. If nothing else, it has kept the country together and the democratic structure intact despite the turbulent period through which we have passed and all the external and internal pressures that we have faced. This itself is no mean achievement given the terrible consequences of failure on this front as witnessed in some of our neighbouring countries.

What was good for the first 50 years now seems to be rotting at the core. It's not just the failure of the licence system and the inspector raj that it has given rise to, it has its consequences in other areas as well. Witness the recent failure of the modified and improved PDS to take off. We must modify this system. And quickly.

One of the ways of reorienting the existing system is to move it away from the power based system; it is to make it more service oriented. And the LG has shown one way this can be done. One very great merit of the self-assessment system which LG has adapted is that it makes the citizen very much a part of administration. It thus makes the administration supportive rather than an independent and self-contained entity.

Let's see how the system would work in other areas. Police administrators and their training manuals are very fond of saying that a 'citizen is a policeman without a uniform'. I have always wondered what it means in practical terms.

The Criminal Procedure Code, framed more than a century and a half back, no doubt put a lot of responsibilities on the citizens, like reporting cognisable offences, co-operating with investigations and joining police raiding parties as witnesses. But what are the powers of the citizen? I have heard of a term called 'citizen arrest' but do not know how it operates. If there are any other powers that a citizen has under the various laws and police manuals, it must surely be a well kept secret.

It is not even clear if the citizen has the right to get any information except to a limited extent when it directly concerns him, as in the case of getting a copy of the FIR. Does the citizen have any right to see the *roznamcha* or the various *thana* registers? To the best of my knowledge, no. This power is reserved for the senior officers of the police and for the magistracy.

Without any powers, without even the power to get any information, how can the citizen be a policeman without a uniform? Police would love to have citizens as policemen with duties and responsibilities but when it comes to sharing power, they look blank and all their rules and manuals are ominously silent. No wonder the common man is not willing to accept this role and continues to be lethargic about their role as 'policemen without uniform'.

Can the police be made a service oriented organisation? Anybody who has seen the London bobby will have no hesitation in answering in the affirmative. But how is this to be made to work in the Indian context? Let us take just one aspect of police functioning, i.e., investigation. It so happens that this is the aspect that concerns the public the most.

The kingpin of the police administration is the police station, with the Station House Officer as the head. While above him is the hierarchy of superintendents and inspector-generals and director-generals, below him are a large number of supporting staff and assistants. How is the 'policeman without a uniform' to be involved?

Lately there has been a tendency to make more and more offences cognisable so that they can be investigated by the police. Now not just the usual heinous crimes, like murder, rape and mayhem, are cognisable offences, but also acts like unauthorised constructions, dowry related events, social and juvenile acts are also 'cognisable'. They are thus taken away from the purview of the public and added to the burden of the uniformed force.

One way of involving the public is to take such 'offences' out of the list of cognisable crimes and leave them for investigation to alternate forums, like panchayats, lok adalats, advisory councils and the like. These councils of public spirited individuals would be encouraged to investigate these cases to a point where they can be taken as complaint cases to the courts. The role of the police would be confined to providing technical and intelligence support to these organisations, who can also function under the aegis of an amended police act. The police would thus become a powerful support organisation for these 'policemen without uniform'.

There are many other ways that the citizens can be made effective policemen; I had once worked out a scheme for SAFE (social assistance for everybody) stations on the line of police stations functioning under the overall supervision and control of the superintendents of police.

PART 4

WORDS—WORTH

28

THE BUREAUCRAT AS A WRITER

It was only the other day that Dileep Rangachari of the Times of India asked me a pointed question: 'With the benefit of hindsight, would I still take the course I took?' His meaning was clear: Would I still, had I the choice, leave an engineering career after an HT degree and join the IAS?

With only a moment's hesitation I had said 'No' meaning thereby that I regretted leaving an engineering career for the glamour of the civil service. At the time I answered this, I was only thinking of that part of the service that consists of social climbers, seniority counters and the sycophants. But now, when I hold in my hand a book 'A tryst with the Mshmi Ffilis' by Dev Singh Negi, a colleague of my service, I'm not sure if my answer to Rangachari's query was correct.

If one part of the IAS consists of insufferable sycophants and climbers, there is another, probably by far the greater, part that, like Negi, there are creative and aware people whose creativity flows out in diverse ways, even when the stifling on-the-job environment does not provide any outlets. The IAS, as a group probably has the largest talent bank in the world: management and administration experts, media professionals, poets and writers, artists, actors, film directors: you name it, and it is there. In my own humble way, I too have contributed to this talent bank.

But the point is, someone may counter, a talented man will

remain talented no matter where he is. How can the IAS get the credit for something that the individuals have contributed? The point here is: has any being in the service contributed in any way to the talent, or latent talent, that an individual had? My answer to this is that but for the experience that the service has provided, none of us would have had the talent that one is now displaying.

Take R.K. Basu of Star TV and Bhargava of Maruti as examples. Both of them have made their mark in international companies in the face of tough international competition. But where would Basu had been if he had not been DG Doordarshan and Bhargava not headed Maruti as a government nominee? No doubt, the experience and opportunity that the service provided to these two made them what they are today.

The same holds true of most of us. I would never have made a foray into film making and direction had it not been for my experience as an Administrator in Lakshadweep and all my novels are about subjects that came to me in the course of my official postings. Let's accept it: the IAS puts its members in situations and places that would otherwise simply not be possible. And gives an experience that would otherwise take an age to accumulate.

Take Negi's book as an example. After just a few years of service, he was appointed the Deputy Commissioner of Lohit in Arunachal Pradesh. He was here for 3 years, before this he was in a similar capacity in Siang district of the same state. For most of us even a few days travel in that state would be a prize: Verrier Elwin had to forsake hearth and home to spend a longer time there; but then his experience of that state was at the cost of many other things.

But not for Negi. After 5 long years in that state, he spent a few years in the lovely island territory of Andamans and Nicobar and is now looking after environment in the capital of the country. If all this diversity of experience does not make an artist and writer of you, the discredit is on you and not on the service!

Negi's book is a mix of a travelogue, an aide de memoire, a

diary and a treatise on the area in which he spent a very good part of his early life. It is replete with funny incidents including the well known one about how the Knister of Home turned out to be a Meat on Hoof (MOH)! Another not very well known one is of the tribal chief who queried of Nehru as to how many niithuns he would have to pay for the right to marry Indira Gandhi!

Sometime back I had read a novel by another service mate, Upamanyu Chatterjee in which the protagonist picks up hashish from the Deputy Commissioner's office and smokes it. Unlike this fellow, Negi spent most of his time doing his 'best to curb poppy cultivation by destroying poppy fields, en masse and also by enlightening them about the ill-effects of opium, not only on their health, but also on the fragile economy'. This is a much better depiction of the idealistic bureaucracy than Upamanyu projects in his novels.

Negi brings out the stone-headedness of our rule-bound bureaucracy very poignantly by mentioning the ordeal of the hard working tribal pharmacist who insisted on billing government for such items as porter charges, non-vegetarian meal and rum. What did the poor fellow know that everybody, veg non-veg, drinkers teetotallers, light travellers heavy travellers, all get the same daily allowance on tour! The lack of logic in our rules not only befuddles the poor tribal pharmacist but also people like me who once was told to plant 4 lac trees in Lakshadweep essentially in areas that have at least three metres of sea water flooding them!

In one part of the book Negi talks of the 'common practice to pull strings, prostrate in front of powers that be' to get cushy postings. He may be talking of the north-east but what he says applies equally to the capital. I know of an officer whose wife went to the extent of even combing the hair of the boss's wife to get posted as the Chief Secretary. If you think he succeeded, you would be absolutely right!

If Negi's book had only been an account of his personal experiences, it would have had only a limited interest; but is told it is an interesting blend of his own experiences with that of the earlier administrators, which makes the book an important addition to the lore of the country. Since the book talks of the erstwhile NEFA, where the Indian army suffered its most humiliating defeat, there is bound to be references to the poignant memories of the heroic exploits of the underclothed and unprepared jawans. All this is punctuated by the foreword by none other than Lt General RS Dayal himself who commanded the 4 Corps in 1981-83, the period in which Negi was posted there. I wish there was a little more on the development front. We know that tribal areas are undeveloped, but what we don't know is that what little efforts have been made so far have been largely ineffectual. One would like to know the reason for this and it is here that people like Negi could have made a contribution. Negi does mention of the harmful effects of Jhum cultivation but, apart from repeating a few cliches like developing of horticulture with 'adequate marketing' facilities, he does not offer anything substantial. I wish he had because this is the key issue of the day: how to develop these areas without affecting the traditional way of life and culture of the tribal population.

I hope Negi's book goads other IAS officers to also take this way to express and give life to their creative urges. This will not only lead to better self-fulfilment for them, but will also go a long way to close the information gap that exists about these far-flung and remote areas.

29

DESTROYING HATE THROUGH PEN

Even engines have to let off steam occasionally, why not humans? But how?

There is a person who has caused immense harm to you; an enormous amount of anger and hate wells inside you against this fellow. So much so that you cannot sleep and most of the time you are tense and fidgety. What do you do?

In a typical Hindi film, the hero faces such a situation when the villain carries off his heroine, or his small son or sometimes even his mother. The script writer's task is tailor made: to quickly find a way of taking the hero to the hideout of the villain to enable him to let out his hate and anger by giving the crooks a good 'dishum dishum' thrashing.

In real life it is not so easy. For one, our fists are not as strong as those of our counterparts on the screen; for another, hideouts of crooks are seldom so easily traceable. But while in reel life big things have to happen to the hero to build up hate and anger, in real life often much smaller and more mundane things bring about the same amount of hate. Like a few insulting words or even a minor altercation.

Rishis and munis have always been telling us that hate is an ugly emotion and needs to be curbed; but despite all their preachings hate as an overpowering emotion has always been with us, always challenging and troubling us. How do we curb it?

One way is to let this emotion travel down from your mind into the trigger finger of your right hand, hurtling a lead bullet at more than 600 kms per hour at the heart of the hated one. But this means a whole lifetime in a small cell even if one can escape the hangman's noose.

Recently I faced such a situation; for an instant I too wanted to pick up a loaded gun and pull the trigger; but for one I did not have a gun and for another, the recipient of my hate is well guarded by security. All the better for me since my ambition is not to spend the rest of my life in solitary confinement in Tihar.

But the hate welled up inside me. I tried the method of the rishis but nothing worked. All my efforts only succeeded in increasing the intensity of hate and led to sleepless nights and very tense days. Soon it became unbearable; something had to break and I did not want it to be me.

Often when I am in such a situation, I pick up my pen. I decided to write a letter to the villain. I was not sure if it would achieve the purpose but there was no harm in trying. Would you like to see what I wrote? I do not have the letter with me now but I'll try to recollect.

Dear Evad,

It is said about your job that a chap who can survive for a year is good and for two years is very good; but those who manage to stay on for three must be duds. What does one say about you since you are now completing the fourth year? A personification of evil, a perpetrator of scams, and the king of corruption! Each one of these description fits you well.

As the grand lieutenant of the Duchy, you should be the upholder of noble virtues and high standards, but by your dealings, especially in the case of the utilization of the funds of the Great Chance, you have presented the ugliest face that a public servant can present: what makes your diseased and haggard face even more ugly is the fact that you have shrouded your crimes in a sheet of moral righteousness.

The ugliness of your personality should have been apparent when you dared not utter your warning regarding spoiling of my career to me directly but through K.L. Madan; but the way you used C.P. Prem, a person whose very fact of birth stinks, shows how similar your blood is with this *gandi nali ka keera*.

I do not know how much of the Rs. 10 crore or so that you distributed illegally went into your pocket but I do not care. The important thing is that you did this in complete violation of the rules and provisions of the law and the constitution, which you had sworn to protect. The worst facet of your personality came out when all this was pointed out to you and your response was: "I will spoil your career."

You used public funds as your own: whether it was the central air-conditioned luxury that you enjoyed in your house or the Rs. 30 lac Mercedes that you wanted to buy or the fact that you made government pay for the telephone of the house in which you did not even live, all these establish your criminal nature. Your response to anyone who pointed out this to you was: I will spoil your career.

When the press exposed this scam, you used your influence with the powers that were to keep the scam under cover; you successfully prevented and audit. In fact, you used this as an excuse to remove me from the job. This gave you freedom to organize your cover up operation as also to carry on your nefarious deeds without any let or hindrance.

The public may be blind; so their leadership. But, happily, god is not. You got your second heart attack shortly after you took, what you thought, the decisive step to harm me by writing a wishy-washy report a couple of days before my promotion committee was to meet.

Your *chamcha* P.C. Prem has similarly been punished by god. My prayer now is: let both of you worthies, once you go up, be relegated to the deepest and darkest depths of hell.

May both of you stink and rot in your tottering and diseased frames while alive and be roasted in the fires of hell after death.

By the time it was time to sign this letter, all the hate and anger had evaporated from my mind; left in their place was just a broad and understanding smile: how else would you expect rotters like them to behave?

Even the fictional situation portrayed in the letter had helped me to overcome my tension.

I picked up the letter, tore it to bits and allowed the pieces to be carried away by the wind.

There was now no need to post this letter; in fact, even hating such evil people seemed demeaning.

I hope the reader has got the message. Both I and the rishis are right. Hate cannot be dispelled with more hate, as the rishis say but then it cannot be left bottled inside to create tension and sleepless nights.

Let is flow out of your pen onto a piece of paper and then sleep over it.

30

THE WORD SCORES AGAIN

There will hardly be a Hindi-knowing Indian who has not read and been influenced by the short story written by Chandradhar Sharma Guleri. On the other hand one wonders how many have seen the movie of the same name and how many even know that there was a movie of this name!

One of the most touching and memorable scene of this story is when our hero meets the heroine and queries in colloquial Punjabi: *Teri mangni ho gayi*? (Are you engaged?) and she replies: *Dhat!* That's all to the love affair that will eventually make him sacrifice his life to save the life of her husband, merely to keep up the promise he had made to her before leaving for the front.

Just imagine this scene in film. It is obvious that without any other embellishment this will fall flat. For one, it is too summary; for another and far more important reason, it lacks any emotional overtones. Clearly, if it is to make an impact it has to be preceded by a more elaborate storyline.

This is the reason why even in ordinary Hindi movies, the hero spends many minutes of footage chasing the heroine in the park circling trees. It is only when the relationship is fully established that a sensitive scene, like the one written by Guleri, can be effectively portrayed.

Here one question is bound to arise; why is elaborate foreplay necessary in a movie when in the book or in the script nothing of this sort is needed?

The comment here is very pertinent and needs an answer. While Guleri could straightaway write a couple of lines and make the necessary impact, the film maker falls flat if he attempts the same. Why?

I think the reason lies in the nature of the two media. In the written word, the meaning that is communicated is not necessarily what the writer is trying to convey or depict; nor what the word 'ordinarily' depicts: it will depend on a number of factors, not least of which is the social and psychological background of the reader.

In the example that we have taken, the brief line that the man utters to the woman conveys to an average Indian audience, quite a bit of information, not only about the speaker but also about the person it is being addressed to. While it is clear that nobody will ask such a question till he is familiar with the other, it is equally clear that this person does not even have basic information about her.

In an Indian context a question, like the one asked, will be taken as impertinent, borderlng on eveteasing and would evoke an appropriately rude response. In fact, in a 'filmi' situation, the responses could vary from a resounding slap on the face to a screaming and scratching assault—depending on the kind of person she is.

That the response is none of these tells volumes not about the character of the lady but also about the sort of relationship that the two enjoy. To any Indian audience, nothing more needs to be told. The position, of course, would be different in the case of a foreign audience, who would fail to relate or even to understand any of these characters and probably the story would fall flat on its face.

Why does the same thing not happen in a film? It's quite obvious, is not it? A film does not leave much to the imagination. The lines uttered are not allowed to resound in the mind of the viewer in the same way that they do when read on a page. For one, the timing here is not in the hand of the viewer but determined entirely by the director and the actors. For another, viewers response gets conditioned by the fact the lines are coming to him from the mouth of an artiste.

No scope left for any imagination on this score. The age of the actor or actress, his or her background, appearances, and many other facts are all predetermined for the viewer. He is not allowed to give free play to his imagination to determine all or any of these facts. And because of this, he is not allowed to match this character with a person drawn from his own experience or knowledge. Therefore, his emotional response will have to be determined only by what this character does on the screen.

In Guleri's story the characters do nothing whatsoever till the crucial dialogue; and if the story is presented as it is on the screen, the emotional impact will be exactly nil. It is true, that a skilful and talented director will be able to reduce the foreplay to may be just a couple of characterizing incidents. But without a single one even he cannot hope to make any emotional impact whatsoever.

This difference in the two media—the print and the written one and the one enacted on the screen—is hardly appreciated and that is the reason that even the most touching and popular stories have not been converted into effective films, especially in India. On the other hand, 'bad' stories, like the ones by Gulshan Nanda and the like, are made into more effective films.

These writers are writing for the lowest common denominator and usually precede their emotional scenes with a lot of foreplay. Thus, when all these are translated to the film media these scenes can be more effectively portrayed.

Does it mean that only bad books can be made into good films? Certainly not and there are a host of examples of good books being made into good films. Take Satyajit Ray's Premchand classic 'Shatranj Kay Khilari' (the chessplayers) as an example.

I think we have to remember that these are two different media and requires effective translation from one to the other and not merely copying. And this 'translation' has it own rules.

31

WIELD THE PEN SENSIBLY

I firmly believe that the artists who make it big and good are not necessarily the best in their areas, but certainly the ones with a higher aptitude for PR and ability to charm and influence the gentlemen of the press.

But this is a belief not many successful artists will share with me. Especially the ones who make a comfortable living out of their art.

Artists traditionally command fees of thousands of dollars and are well known and much honoured. But is all this adulation and reward really justified on the basis of their merit or is it a mere reflection of some promoters views?

Recently an artist, generally very arogant and brash, admitted that while only a couple of thousand people saw his plays, many more read about them in the papers. It is clear that these people, who have read about an artist's work only in the daily papers, form their opinions about its artistic or literary merit from the views of the critics.

It is clear that for the vast majority of people, the artist would not even exist were it not for the critic.

Lest any artist should deny all this, let me remind him that any new tele serial, film, new book or even a painting exhibition is invariably launched with a grand and expensive party where not only liquor flows freely, but also expensive gifts and cash/ cheques are given to the critic-guests.

Some time ago, Amir Raza Hussain made allegations

against one particular critic and did not allow here to witness one of his shows. This lady, the venerable playwright charged, always wrote unfavourable reviews. It is because of this that he found her reviews to be prejudiced.

But what about the favourable reviews? Are these not prejudiced precisely because of this reason?

The cat is out of the bag: the critics are not invited to give the public an advance notice of the work of art that is about to be unfolded, but are invited to ensure that the 'ignorant public' is favourably informed.

This is not the least to say that all artists are like this. There must be quite a few who could not care less what this or that critic has to say. But such people will surely not be written about and thus would be in the company of the relatively lesser known ones.

It is this fact that raises a critic's stature to almost being a god to just anyone with little pretensions to art. Struggling actors, new movie makers and stars, fresh painters and writers—all spend their spare time not in the libraries and the art galleries, but in the newspaper offices and critics homes and eating places.

And this is what gives power to the critic. Power is not necessarily a quality that is condemnable; and not also a quality that will necessarily be misused. Take the 'power' that a man like Mahatma Gandhi enjoyed, or the power that is given to the head of the family. This power is used for the good of all.

While determining the use to which power can be put, two factors have to be borne in mind the source of power and the person who has the power.

If the source of the power is true knowledge and not merely the fact that one wields the pen, the use of such power can be responsible and controlled. On the other hand, if power is combined with a lack of knowledge and ignorance, its use is more often than not misdirected and misapplied.

Even when power flows out of knowledge, it is important who wields it. In wrong and irresponsible hands, it again spells danger. All this is true of the knowledge that flows out of the critic's pen. All too often the critic tends to forget that power should flow out of knowledge and that its use should be accompanied with responsibility.

I am in the unique position of being both an artist (at least with pretensions to be one) and a critic at the same time. I know how the biting and unfair comments of critics hurt the sensibilities of the artist. At the same time I know how wrong a critic can be!

I am a long standing friend and admirer of Raj Barjatya, the maker of such immortal hits like *Dosti* and *Maine Pyar Kiya*. And not the least of the reasons is the fact that we are class fellows of that wonderful institution called IIT Kharagpur, where every minute spent is etched in my memory. Each one of his movies becomes an event for me.

Thus when *Hum Apke Hain Kaun...!* was released in Delhi few years back, I was among the first ones to see it. And review it in this column.

As a critic, I held a pen in my hand and thus enjoyed power. While reviewing this movie, I had predicted a dire fate for this movie: I had confidently asserted that this would be a flop at the box office.

I had made many predictions before, and had been proved right despite assertions to the contrary by other critics. This made me believe in the power of my pen!

I am not ashamed to admit how desperately wrong I was. Where I had predicted a commercial disaster of the highest order, was heady success that even the successful father-son team of Raj and Sooraj had not even dreamed of before! For me this has been a sobering influence. I hope other critics also have similar experiences. There is nothing wrong with being powerful, but effective power has to be wielded with responsibility.

32

HAS LITERATURE PASSED?

In this highly commercial age it is natural to measure success and failure in terms of commerce; so it is with literature. It is true that while the success of an individual writer can be measured in terms of money, this cannot be the criteria for literature as a whole. How are we then to answer the question: has literature passed?

The writer has many crosses to carry: apart from his own he carries the cross of his generation. He suffers not his sorrow alone but shares the sorrows of an entire suffering humanity. His failure, therefore, is not his alone; it is the failure of an entire generation of an entire civilization.

And thus the answer to the question involves all of us intimately. And when that failure comes through 'the intervention of power', as Alexander Solzhenitsyn called it, woe indeed to the nation!

It not merely violates the freedom to print, it 'is the closing down of the heart of the nation, a slashing to pieces of its memory'!

A few years back the Sahitya Academy addressed itself to this question 'Has Literature Failed' and called upon the staid and urbane professor, critic and writer (happily not in that order) A.A. Soroor to attempt an answer.

'Literature has not failed', said the staid Professor. 'There is some kind of conspiracy going on all the time against literature, in the name of attention to literature or attention to social needs... The powers that be, knowing that in the last analysis, literature is the conscience of the people, pay lip service to literature, but as literature poses some inconvenient questions and exposes many skeletons in the cupboard its voice has to be drowned, its arrows blunted, in several ways'.

But negative or not, is it not necessary to probe the question further? What had literature set out to do? It is only in relation to set objectives and tasks that one can talk of failure or successes; what were the tasks set for literature?

The absurdity of the question stands exposed: can literature ever be set a task? If not, how can it fail or pass? The question needs reframing: Has literature fulfilled? Presumably in the face of challenges from 'television and the other technological marvels of today.'

Has literature fulfilled itself by making us to see and perceive the world around us with the imagination in the face of the challenge of the cold reason of the understanding?

Has it been able to apply 'the language of a whisper, a whimper and a bang, the language of love, passion, anger, the language of stirring and rippling emotion, the language of heroic thoughts and fleeting ideas, the language of converse with man and god' to the articulation of our primordial yearnings and urges?

What are the ghouls that plague literature? We can find many. For sure government and bureaucracy head the list. But media and the educational system are not far behind. So is science and technology. But what about the literati themselves?

It is a fact that more is being written and published today than ever before. And presumably read too. It is also not untrue that much of what is being printed and read is 'trash'. Why? Why is good literature being squeezed out of the market place and being forced to yield its rightful place to the 'literature of fashion and formula, literature of sex and violence, mindless affirmation.....the portrayal of boredom'?

A key issue here is about government patronage to literature and art as also to the issues that plague the educational system, especially the medium of instruction.

It is almost a truism that government support helps a little but not much, but it can harm a great deal. But still we ask for it.

Savoor had said: 'With the mother tongues and or regional language as the medium at the primary and secondary stage, along with familiarity in one other Indian language and fair knowledge of English as the window to the world, at the secondary stage, the genius of the people can blossom'.

The three-language formula was introduced over three decades back and if the genius of the people has blossomed, it must be a well kept secret at the libraries of our Academies!

One wonders why we say resoundingly: 'No government please!' and 'Instruction in the mother tongue!' The literati could do well to remember that pithy one liners with which their lectures abound, make good slogans for our bureaucrats and politicians but reflect our failure to come to grips with the problem.

It is easy to blame science and technology for the battering that culture and language are getting. The chief culprits are also easy to identify: politicians, bureaucrats, business leaders. But the challenge for the writers is to go around them and reach the readers.

Readers are by and large seeking affirmations to their established norms or escape; literature seeks to shock them out of their dream world to an awareness of what happens around. It is the abyss created by this dichotomy that we have to bridge.

Science and scientists are allies in this quest. Not for nothing is the best prose of the twentieth century penned by Bertrand Russel!

The soul searching has to be done as much by the reading public as by the literati. Unless we do this in earnestness and with expedition, we may soon see the fulfilment of the prophecy of Norman Podhonetz, the well-known editor, that we may already be tuned into a future 'in which literature will cease to exist'.

And in such a system can we exist?

33

POETRY IN VERSES

It was a pleasure to hear from Shekhar Malhotra, in the bookish sense of the term. You see, Shekhar belongs to a family of publishers, his bookish roots taking him right back through the partition. What makes the latest contact doubly pleasant is that the missive he sent is actually a beautifully produced and bound copy of the 'The Holy Vedas', published by Shekhar's own Clarion Books.

I have never ever read the Vedas, letting the derived knowledge about them from secondary sources satisfy the student in me. Now, thanks to Shekhar, I read them. Let me admit that the experience was exhilarating.

It is not the philosophy or the so-called revelations that I am particularly referring to; nor is it the interpretations of Pandit Satyakam Vidyalankar, great may be the pains that he has taken to prove that our sages knew intuitively what modern scientists have learnt through a great deal of effort. No, all this does not impress me at all. What particularly strikes me is the sheer poetry in the verses.

The bright dawn heralds a new day/Its rosy lances have opened/the golden gates of the Sun/and lit up the path of action./Awake, O man, the slumber/and darkness of the night are over./May each dawn lead us from/triumph to triumph in the long journey of life! (Rig, 1.113.16)

The translators, Pandit Satyakam and Swami Satyaprakash Saraswati, taken great pains to give us details of the Vedic texts they have translated and now Shekhar has published.

The four Vedas have together 20,416 verses with half of them (10,589 verses) being in the Rig Samhita. From this, they have selected 1000 verses for the present publication.

They believe it to be first literature that man wrote from the earliest time of his appearance on the globe, though many believe it to be divine revelation. There are many beliefs of when the revelation took place or, in other words, when these works were actually written. There is little doubt, though, that it was many millennia back. It must first have been passed from generation to generation in the oral tradition and then put down in writing in the present form.

What is remarkable is how the early man chose to describe the beauty that he found in nature. We ourselves, with all the sophistication in language, could not have articulated it better. The verses draw your attention to the glory of the rising sun, the vast luminary that enlightens us through the day and then takes us to the thrilling evenings and the calmness of night, cool and refreshing. The sky and the firmament have their own beauty with stars set like pearls and diamonds on a blue background.

O Sun, on thy coming./All living beings are awakened./ And the winged birds flock around/From the boundaries/of skies to greet Thee. (Rig. 1.49.3) Soothing be our nights./ And inspiring the dawns/Tender be the dust of earth/May heaven be kind to us! (Rig. 1.90.7)

Most interesting is the concept of the creator. It moves, it moves not/It is far, and it is near,/it is within all this,/and it is outside all this./(Yajur 22.5) In the verses of the Vedas, we invoke the Supreme Lord, the sole Master of Creation and the living beings. Man is the creator himself, but he creates only outside; but the Supreme Being creates everything within Him, for there is nothing that exists outside Him and He is within all.

The Vedas always saw the Supreme being, or God, tied intimately to the beauty of nature.

Nature's beauty is an art of God./Let us feel the touch of God's invisible/hands, in everything beautiful./By the first touch of His hand rivers/throb and ripple./When he smiles the sun shines, the....dawn is the dream of God's/creative fancy. (Rig, 1.6.3)

From here to the evolution of a personal god was not a very long leap. By identifying god with his creation, it was clear that the idea of such a personal god was germinating. It needs just a little bit of advancement to make it the way we know it.

While he is near, He leave it not; though it is near, it sees Him not. Behold the Art of God, His poetry that shall not die and shall never grow old. (Atharva, 10.8.32)

Such a god could be found everywhere and in everything, particularly in nature. The authors of the Vedas find them even in the gentle rain that falls from the sky above.

God is just behind us when we cry for help/We feel our prayers might not reach Him/In our panic we seek the assurance of safety/In a moment the clouds of gloomy fears are swept away/My soul, bathed in celestial joy./The heavens laid bare their blue abyss/The choicest gifts are showered upon me from all directions/and I am lost in complete bliss. (Atharva, 19.52.3)

The Vedas are wonderful for more reasons than one. First, they are the earliest source of knowledge. Second, they are in a language prior to which there was no language; in a way in a language in which man must have first articulated. Third, the Vedic God is monotheistic, but purely ethical. That is the reason why Vedic verses uphold high moral values. Lastly, Vedic verses refer to man as a type of co-ordinated being, not just an individual. He is a social organism and God loves only those creatures who serve other beings. The immortal soul assuming a human form may be regarded as a purposeful benevolent bondage and it is through a series of such bondages that man is expected his fullness.

Series of bondages. What a wonderful idea! Bondage is what we are afraid of, what we are fighting against. And here we have a philosophy which talks not of one such bondage but a series of them. And when you spare a moment to think about it, this is what life is all about. Ask not how you can free your bondages; ask how you can add to them. This seems to me to be the substance of the teachings of the Vedas.

Thanks, Shekhar, thanks for reintroducing me to my roots. From tomorrow, I will give up the quest for freedom for the 'series of bondages' that the Vedas are talking about. Just imagine what will happen if all of us did the same!

PART 5
BEYOND THE HEADLINES

34

SOME EDITORS DO HAVE'EM!

It was only the other day that I was having dinner at the India International Center when I saw John Dayal at another table. I realized that it would be most imprudent of me not to acknowledge his presence; after all he's the editor of the paper in which I have now been writing for the best part of 5 years! So I got up to say hello. Imagine my surprise when he told me that he had just been released from jail.

Jail going has had a very hallowed tradition in our country, with most of our earlier leaders having spent the best part of their lives in jail. If I remember rightly, the world record in this regard too is held by a fellow sub-continent leader, the great Khan Abdul Ghaffar Khan, though our own Sheikh Abdullah may not be too far behind! In fact, but for the time spent in jail, Nehru might never have been the great writer that he is and Gandhi not the Mahatma that we know!

But recent events have removed the halo from jail going somewhat, what with some scam or the other facing every other day. I know John well to be sure that he is not a scamster, but one cannot be sure these days. And considering the delicacy of the relationship that a column writer enjoys with his editor, it was only wise to be prudent. But I well knew that I would have to react to this earth shaking announcement. Remember, I was at his table, which was quite a few metres away from my own; there was no way of escaping or pretending not to have heard.

Well, how do you react when somebody tells you that he has just returned from jail, especially when that somebody is the editor of the paper in which you have been writing a column for as many as 154 weeks! There could have been many possible reactions especially if the history of our relationship had been other than what it has been.

I know how I would have reacted if John had been always tampering with my column, changing the structure of the sentences or shortening the climax or even inserting an opening by himself. Or even if he or his sub-editors had not given my piece a proper display or troubled me unnecessarily about the deadlines. In any of these eventualities, all I had to do was to order a bottle of wine (fortunately, the Center permits that in the dining hall) and celebrate.

But he and his sub-editors have all been very nice. It's all a matter of relationships.

The human condition is all about relationships: the *guru-shishya:* master-servant; boss-subordinate; father-son; et al. The beauty of these relationships is that it needs two to make it; alone they have no meaning. Moreover, we all, in relation to some person or the other, fit into any of these slots. I can be a father in relation to one person and a son in relation to another; while continuing in this relationship. I can be *guru-shishya*, a master and a servant, a boss and a subordinate, all at the same time. Remember the movie *Sass bhi kabhi bahu thi?* It was timely reminder to the harassing mother-in-law that after all she too had been a daughter-in-law at one time.

But the editor-column writer relationship is unique; you are either one or the other. At least that is true in my case, though a man like Khushwant Singh, whose column is on the left, once wore the other hat too. So, that's the dilemma, how does a man like me react to the statement that his perfectly nice editor was just a few moments ago in the cooler?

I started thinking of situations in which going to jail is not such a bad thing after all. I remember, there was a time when people in whose homes there had been income tax raids, proudly narrated the event in parties and cocktails. They knew that to invite an income tax raid, one's economic position had to be above a certain threshold. It is difficult to tell anybody directly how well off you are; the mere fact of the tax raid established it anyway.

If John's going to jail was in the same bracket, the response was easy; there was no need to sympathize or feel sorry; you could merely acknowledge the greatness of the man and go back to your seat. But, I knew, that journalists and bureaucrats were birds of a feather as far as economic condition was concerned; both were, if not exactly paupers, quite not in the same class as the millionaire businessmen who have the good fortune at being singled out by the become tax people.

John Dayal is not a scamster; he's neither a millionaire tax dodger; nor is he a dyed-in-the wool, head-in-the air intellectual: so why was he in the cooler? In my ability to answer this question lay the future of my column and all my journalistic pretensions and ambitions.

Though not exactly a computer, my mind works fast in such situations. Since a man is known by the company he keeps, may be I could get some idea of the deeds which landed my editor in the cooler by finding out more about his companions. I found that one of them; a fair and handsome man was a Supreme Court lawyer.

A very ominous discovery it seemed, considering the spate of public interest litigations that are taking place before the Apex Court. An editor cutting his bread with a lawyer does not seem a very happy omen.

But it was the identity of the other that alarmed me the most; this gentleman was a priest. My god, what was my editor doing with a man of god? Could he be making confessions or something of the sort?

Things were now going too far; the computer in my mind was working feverishly, working out the various options. A stage comes, even in a mechanical computer, when it becomes so confused that it is in danger of getting fused out; I was about to reach a situation. If I didn't take the bull by the horn, things might go totally out of control.

I rushed in where angels fear to tread: I asked Dayal about

the arrest, "It's reservations for the Dalit Christians"! he explained. "We courted arrest". The sweep of his arm took his two companions in his description. And then, almost as an afterthought, he added: "We were released since the Prime Minister invited us for talks".

Three cheers for the editor! Three cheers for John! It's the time honoured, old fashioned motives that took him to the cooler. The same that inspired the founding fathers of our freedom, the same that have inspired patriots in which ever time or place they lived.

I ordered the bottle of wine anyway. But this time it was to cheer and not to jeer. Cheers to you, John!

35

THE MECHANICS OF OPINION POLLS

It has become a habit with some people, even our national newspapers, to ask astrologers and charlatans to predict the results of an election. There is no need to do so now, when psephology had almost become a science.

Over the years the opinion poll had become the most effective weapon to solicit the opinions of a group of people, even predict their behavioural pattern. But a number of people pooh pooh such polls, especially their accuracy and impartiality. Their stock reaction to such polls is: I have never been questioned; how can my voting behaviour be determined by questioning a person who may be as distant from me as a personality as an ant from an elephant?

Their basic objection is to the fact that such polls are based on the opinions of a minuscule minority of people. To determine the voting pattern of 60 odd crore people, the psephologists will question not more than, hold your breath, 5000 people!

Before we rush to any conclusions let us see what these polls are all about. What opinion polls determine is not how you, as a single unique entity, will vote; there is no way of doing that except by questioning you. But what they try to determine how a group, of which you are a member, will vote.

Let's take an example. Toss a coin; will it be head or tail? Experience tells us that it will one of the two: but there is no way to tell which one will come with certainty, except by actually tossing the coin.

Mathematicians call it probability. Since there are only two ways that the coin can possibly 'behave', the chances that it will behave in one particular way is exactly half or 50 per cent. Now let us suppose instead of one coin we toss two; what are the chances now for the result that we are looking for? The chances that it will not behave so are reduced by half, that is half of 50 per cent, that is 25 per cent.

This figure will continue to be halved as we increase the number of coins. In other words, the more the coins, the less the chances that our event will not happen. Please note, that with 5 coins the uncertainty comes down to 3 per cent or so. Please also note that even if we increase the number of coins indefinitely, still the uncertainty will continue; even though the margin of error of any one predicting any particular, even in such cases, will be reduced to a very minuscule figure indeed.

What we are saying here is that if you want to be sure of getting heads or tails you will have to toss a very large number of coins indeed. But if you want to be right 97 out of hundred times about the outcome, five coins are good enough.

This is exactly what opinion polls do. There are two contesting candidates and only one can win. Without doing anything we can assert that one particular chap will win; the only problem is that half the time we will be wrong. Now let us question 5 people and answer our question as per the majority opinion; we will be right 97 times out of hundred.

That's what such polls are all about. To find out the winner amongst a million voters we don't have to question a million people; 5 are enough to give us the answer with a reasonable certainty. That seems easy enough: but before you rush onto the street to conduct your own private poll, remember these 5 people are not just any 5 people; they must be representative of the whole group.

Let us say that the group is divided into upper income, middle income and the low income groups; we also assume that income is the sole factor that influences voting patterns. Is it enough to take 2 from each of these groups and decide on the basis of the majority opinion of the sample? Yes, if the size of these groups is approximately equal. But if we know that the first group comprises of only 1 per cent, the second 20 per cent and the third the remaining, our prediction will surely be wrong because when the votes are actually cast, the weights of the respective groups will be dependent on their percentage composition. In this case the candidate getting the support of only 2 of the sample, if they belong to the third category, will win hands down over the chap who gets the entire vote of the upper and middle income groups.

There can be other factors too. Like the propensity of a voter from a particular group to exercise its franchise. Let us say that only 20 per cent of the upper class actually exercise their franchise as compared to 70 per cent of the voters of the lower group. This means that the votes of the upper group lose further weight as compared to the votes of the lower income bracket.

The complications can go on. There may be more than two candidates: apart from income, social and religious backgrounds could influence voting factors. There could be other factors. All these can be determined by a study of the past trends; or by carrying out special surveys. But remember, none of them influence very materially the size of the sample. Of course, the number 5 was only illustrative; if Muslims constitute only 5 per cent of the population and that is a factor to reckon with, any sample that doesn't have a couple of Muslims in it would give a wrong picture.

This is the reason why we have to sample thousands; but no way that we need to question crores of people to determine how they will behave as a group. All we need to keep in mind is that what we are predicting has a margin of error, which comes in not just from the size of the sample but also from other factors which could make the sample not truly representative.

We also need to remember that we are trying to determine the voting behaviour of the people in one constituency and on the basis of the opinion of people in; quite another constituency.

There are many riders here like the swings and the dependent relationship in the voting patterns of the two areas; but still there is an element of inaccuracy that could creep in.

Whatever the uncertainties and errors of a sample survey, the small size of the sample is not what should worry us unduly. If the sample has been randomly and correctly selected, even a sample of a couple of hundreds could correctly tell us how the millions whom they represent are going to behave. Let us say goodbye to astrologers and charlatans and go to psephologists for our forecasts.

36

COMPENSATION FOR THE 'COMPLETE MEN'

The latest example of the hypocrisy that has come to prevail in our country came to my notice during my last visit to the commercial capital of India, Mumbai. As my son Yogesh drove me to downtown on his second hand Maruti, my attention was arrested by a hoarding carrying the photographs of the two most towering personalities that India has produced in this century, Gandhi and Nehru. But what was remarkable about these photographs was not about the fact of their being there, remarkable as the fact may be, but about the caption underneath that read 'The complete men'.

In this age of media dominance it was difficult to miss the significance of this message. 'The complete men' is the ad slogan of a leading fabric producer and the underlying message in the hoarding is clearly to identify the product of the company with these two personages.

While designing this ad campaign the copywriter blatantly ignored the fact that both the personalities, Gandhi and Nehru, pictured on the hoarding, wore only *khadi* almost all their life. The irony is that at least one of them was instrumental in arranging a nation-wide boycott of the sort of garments that this particular group is trying to promote through the impugned hoarding! That's hypocrisy for you.

It's not just that this company is tainted with the brush of hypocrisy; the others are not much better. When a leading cricket player or a film star endorses a particular product and his pictures are prominently displayed and publicised, it is not as if this particular gentleman has made any comparative study of the merits or demerits of the product displayed or being endorsed or even that the endorser is in any way a knowledgeable man on the subject: all it means is that the endorser has been paid a fat cheque for the same.

Unfortunately, in the instant case of 'the complete men' even this is not true. Not only are Gandhi and Nehru well known *khadi* and homespun wearers, one of them going to the extent of calling it the 'livery of freedom', and both in their lifetime displayed immense hostility to the sort of garment that they are now being asked to endorse, the users of their endorsement have not even tried to compensate them for the same. It is true that these two personalities have no use of money, at least of the variety that commercial firms can churn out, but it is also true that the trusts that are now working to perpetuate their memories could do with some cash.

This is especially the case with the Gandhi Smarak Nidhi and the other trusts associated with is his name. Being starved of funds by a particularly negligent and callous political system this trust is languishing and could do with some cash. It may be argued that these personalities would have refused or the trusts set up in honour of their memories may refuse. But has this company even bothered to find out?

Anyway, it is not so much a question of money as of ethics and principles. If the company that makes these garments really subscribes to the principles of whom it describes as 'the complete men', the least it can do is to stop manufacture of the products that they now make and shift to promotion of homespun and *khadi*; and if it does not, let it stop exploiting their names and memories for their own narrow and selfish ends.

It is not just that this particular company has found it particularly attractive to exploit the names and memories of these great Indians, almost everybody every day does the same and, probably, in a way that is even more destructive to their memory than this particular hoarding. The campaign for the elections is just over and almost every politician of almost every hue has been singing paeans of their praises and claiming to be the inheritors of their traditions.

Even politicians belonging to groups that have done their level best to destroy all that these two 'complete men' built, are now staking claim to their legacy. The criminals and the corrupt, the casteists and the communalists alike while doing their level best to destroy all that these two built, are loud in their claims to their legacy. In fact, people with nothing else in common except the Gandhi-Nehru name are now laying stake to the leadership of the system or parties that these two personalities have so thoughtfully and cleverly crafted.

Hypocrisy is the name of the game. And this game all people, whether political or criminal, commercial or NGO, are willing to play. And this is especially the case when it comes to any mention they may make of these two great men. Staking claim to the Gandhi-Nehru legacy is now fair game to politicians of all hues and even though their own actions may not match this legacy they have no compunctions whatever to making their claims.

I find the practice of getting paid endorsements bad enough but the ones like what the garments firm has done is particularly galling. In the case of the former, at least the money is benefiting some young talent even if it is misleading to the public but in the case of the latter while we deceive the public, we at the same time do insult and injury to the memory of these great people. Now that the 'crime' has been committed and damage done at least this company will think of doing damage repair, which in the instant case can only mean payment of a hefty compensation by the company.

I have no way of putting a figure to it but it must be adequate both as a deterrent for such misuse in the future as also provide some help to Gandhian bodies. Will Rs. 10 crore to the Gandhi Smarak Nidhi suffice?

PART 6
UNCLE SAM

37

CAN WE AFFORD TO GIVE THE AMERICAN AN UGLY IMAGE?

My generation was fed on the image of the ugly American, built up on their crass commercialization and brutal business tactics. And see how they lived up to it in Vietnam! Today again, when Enron et al are forcing their dirty bodies on us, we are tempted to paint them in the same brush. But is it the right thing to do?

Indo-American relations reached a nadir with the expulsion of the Coca-Cola and IBM in the late seventies, the two prototypes of the hated and feared Corporations. The image of the American was that of an ugly businessman with a rifle in one hand, a cheque book in the other and a crooked smile on his face.

Is it a surprise that the American lived up to his image too? Witness what happened in Vietnam and what could well have happened at the time of the Indo-Pak war of 1971 when the 7th Fleet was ordered to sail to the Bay of Bengal. Or the Bay or Pigs. Or Panama. Or wherever.

The lesson of the past is that whenever we have given the Americans a dirty image they have lived up to it. Can we afford, to repeat this experience?

Let us try just the opposite. Let us give him a beautiful image and see if he can afford not to live up to it. In any case the Americans have given us ample reasons for calling them beautiful. And Michael Jackson and Madonna are not the only ones. The six Nobel laureates out of the eight last year and their innumerable predecessors in the eternal Hall of Fame are reason enough.

Of course, some people, like the hag who writes for many newspapers, find reason enough in gazing at their bodies in serials like Baywatch. But that may be a result of their own lack of virility but it is this falsehood that masks the real beauty of the Americans.

Can we ever forget the picture of a Roosevelt standing out against the likes of Churchill for the freedom of our own country?

And the likes of Kennedy! or the American tourist in the bush shirt! I am one of the few here who love and admire the Americans for all the right reasons.

It was a pleasant experience last year to read the list of the Nobel laureates in Science? Seven of the eight winners got it for work done in the USA and out of these six are American citizens.

And these achievements came at a time when Science has been falling out of favour with, as it has been put by one commentator, 'young talented people who spurn it, press commentators who slam it and congressional budget makers who squeeze it'.

It is a surprise that in a country where everybody seems to be working against them, the talented community can still come out and make a mark. I wouldn't know if this is an achievement of the Americans or of the talented amongst them. Whatever it be, it must lead to changing of the image of the American.

And thank God for that! It would be terrible to be led by people—and like it or not, Americans are the leaders of the world now—who are perceived to be ugly.

Even in this unipolar world it is probably not important how the American really looks; what is important is how he is perceived to be. If he is perceived to be ugly that could lead to very important consequences for all of us. Because if he lives up to his image, and that becomes a psychological imperative sometimes, that could be terrible.

On the other hand, even if he is ugly, by giving him a beautiful image we may be forcing him to live up to his image, and thereby mould his behaviour.

And that is important now. No longer is the balancing act that Nehru, Nasser, Sukarno and Tito devised in Bandung possible now. For one, the hand has been over played; and for another even if the whole world were to unite against the Americans—and that must remain a pipe dream—it would still not be possible to balance their power and wealth.

It is no longer for governments to counter the growing power and influence of the one Single Power: it will be soon that they themselves will have to look for support for survival to them. The people of the world will have to take the task in their own hands. And in this they will have to draw upon the support of the most independent and talented community the world has ever seen—the Americans.

The Americans are not what their ugly American image would have us believe. It was the GI who first brought to the Indian scene a white man who was not a lord: and, what is more important it did not like to lord it. This image was buttressed by the image of the American package tourist, dressed as he was in the bush shirt and marked as he was with an air of informality and friendliness.

But unfortunately this image did not survive for long. Soon the ugly American was back, backed as he was with the fast growing— both in economic and political terms—Corporations and the MNCS. They led to the revival of the image of the East India Company which came with the ostensible purpose of trading but stay.

38

PROFILES IN COURAGE

It's election time in America and, as the time for the titanic Bush-Clinton clash approaches, there will be excitement aplenty. Much more than that generated by the cliff hanging Kennedy-Nixon contest of the sixties.

But the excitement, such as it may have been, was on which my generation was fed. And still I can feel the remnants of that period which, I find, have become a permanent part of my psyche.

The clash took place in the pre-Vietnam period of the USA, and it was a period that was dominated by many age old values; such as patriotism, for instance.

'Ask not what your country can do for you...ask what you can do for your country!' still rings in my mind, disturbed as it is by cries of strife from various parts of the country, be it extremist activities or threats from all sorts of people ranging from civil judges and lawyers to ordinary workers and blue-collar workers.

The new cry: 'To hell with what I can do for the country; tell me first what the heck it has done for me!'

Yes, the cry survives all these decades and all these strife-full decades. But what survives most of all is a fond memory of that wonderful Kennedy publication: 'Profiles in Courage'.

That it was written by a Kennedy scion was part of the mystique of that wonderful publication; but what struck most of all was the fact that it was the dissertation that he had presented for his graduation and that he had won the Pulitzer Prize for it!

The book was good; so were the impeccable credentials of the writer. But what made the book so memorable that it had been penned by somebody who was a 'politician' and that it was being presented as a part of his credentials for the job!

We have seen how the 'qualifications' for politicians have evolved in the first forty-five years of our democratic history. At first it was how many years a politician had spent in British jails. (In fact, it led to the common gag which said that while criminals first commit crimes and then go to jail, politicians do just the opposite!) The criteria became how many years one had spent in the service of such politicians or, which really means the same thing, how much confidence one enjoyed of such personages.

Soon the years spent became irrelevant if one enjoyed the important person's confidence; so the words politician and 'confidante' became synonymous.

It is difficult for us to believe that there was a time when writing a prize-winning book could actually be touted as a qualification! But such are the ways of the world!

I don't remember the personages whose examples of courage Kennedy had profiled; but I have no doubt that they were not a patch on the courage shown by Sidney Hawking, the British physicist.

39
THE AMERICAN VISA

The foreign travel bug has bit the Indian middle classes ever since the film 'Around the World' hit the silver screen and its theme song 'Around the world in eight dollars' disturbed the air waves in the late sixties. Since then almost everybody has wanted to go abroad. Even the paltry $8 allowance could not deter them.

Any country is good enough but the maximum demand has always been for the USA: its attractiveness was probably a hangover from the Roosevelt days when USA was seen as a staunch supporter of the Indian freedom struggle.

One would have expected with the passage of time for the attraction to weaken: but it has actually increased over the years. This could possibly be the result of the United State's growing power and influence. And at no time was that more than it is now.

The new found freedom to travel, despite the foreign exchange restrictions of $8, was great fun, at least at first. India, through years of a unique freedom struggle, had acquired many friends and admirers abroad. Moreover, many Indians had friends and relations there. So it was sunshine and roses all the way.

But soon it began to sour. For one, familiarity breeds contempt and that grew when the world came to learn that not all Indians were Mahatmas. But the worst came when the world realized that not all came with the sole intention of sight seeing and visiting relatives and friends; many had ulterior motives—like trying to emigrate and settle down in the foreign land.

So impediments came to be placed in the way of Indians going abroad: the most cumbersome of these was the visa.

A visa purports to be an endorsement by the embassy of the guest country permitting the traveller to enter its borders but mainly it is a description of his status. That is whether he is a tourist or a student or an emigre or has been allowed entry for business purposes.

But over the years it has become a bureaucratic weapon for a closed door policy. And this is especially the case with the USA.

Although it is difficult to get any visa but the most difficult of all—and the one most prized, probably for that reason—is the American visa.

Everybody seems to want it—but only a few lucky ones succeed. Trying to find out why some succeed when others fail is like trying to unravel some detective mystery.

Ever since my brother (a fellow engineer and a year my senior in IIT Kharagpur) emigrated to the States in 1964 I have never found myself confronted by any more compulsive situation for going to the States than when he rang up the other day to invite us for his daughter's marriage coming June.

It is important that at least one of us goes since he or one of his family members has been attending important family events all the time.

We are a family of five and I wasn't sure how many of us I could afford to send. But since one of us had to go the choice naturally fell on my younger son Devesh who is doing computer engineering in Moscow.

Devesh's selection fulfilled another important need: he has always been keen to go to the States, probably fascinated, like the Russians, with Hollywood movies of the James Bond genre; since I didn't want him to go there, being afraid of what the exposure could do to a 16-year old, I had put him in Moscow instead.

Devesh immediately applied for the visa at the US embassy in Moscow and was promptly advised to apply in Delhi. Recently he was here and we thought that this was the time to apply.

In the meantime bits of information started flowing in about the visa: the most heartening part of it was that the decision was quick: within hours of the application there was an interview and the result was out there and then. To Indians, used as we are to a system where it is almost impossible to get any decision from the bureaucracy, it was happy news.

But the other pointers were not too happy; it seemed that all applications by young people were summarily rejected. The US embassy assumed that all young people allowed to enter their country would settle down there.

"But he's going for his sister's wedding!" I said incredulously.

"So what? It's like the law on rape—if the girl is less than sixteen..."

"What the hell! There must be a way! My brother is an American national, a Professor..."

"That only makes it worse..."

It boiled down to one thing: the counsellor must be convinced that he would return; and there seemed to be no way of doing that since his age was against him.

Since I couldn't make him any older than 18½ next June I tried the next best: try to give convincing proof that he would return.

It is not easy to convince a bureaucrat, Indian or American. The reason is that he already knows everything. Remember the village school master in the famous Goldsmith poem who 'though vanquished could argue still'? Though the task was undeniably tough, there was no harm in trying.

Devesh carried two 'proofs' of his intention: one, that he was my son and I, though an IIT engineer for the last three decades, was still in India; and two, a sponsorship from my brother, an American citizen of two decades' standing and a computer engineer of renown.

To establish the first 'proof', he carried a letter from the Ministry of External Affairs; and for the second my brother sent him a notarized letter from his University in the States. Both were very impressive 'official' documents which, it seemed to me, could not but impress any bureaucrat, however imperious he may be.

Devesh's interview lasted but a few minutes, most of it spent on inquiring about the internal affairs of the Russian Federation. At the end of it the venerable representative of the President-Emperor shook his imperious head and said: "I'm not convinced". He then stamped his passport and called the next victim.

That's that. It's so final: no visa, so no going to the wedding in June. I wish it had been India: the decision would have been pending till a couple of days before the wedding; till then at least Devesh could have been basking in the happy thought of being best man in country.

PART 7

TRYST WITH LIFE

40

MISTRUST BEGETS 'MISTRUST'

Saigal's first law of administration, if there were one, will read something like this: if you mistrust a man, he will soon prove worthy of your mistrust. And the more you mistrust, the more worthy of it he will prove himself to be.

This law, which has been drafted in the light of the experience of the functioning of our administrative system, seems to work equally well in other spheres as well. Remember the story of the mistrusting man who went out on a long business trip abroad? To ensure that his wife stayed home all the time, he told her that he will be writing to her every day and she must receive each one of his letters and reply to them. The letters were duly written and replied but when the mistrusting businessman returned you know what he found? His wife had run away with the postman!

This is exactly what happens in government. We setup an elaborate inspector setup to maintain a system of license-permit system to check and counter-check the activities of the people but our distrust is such that it extends to our trust of our own system as well. This we maintain an audit-cum-vigilance network to keep a check on our own agencies. But do we trust them? Heavens, no! How can the sacred law of mistrust be violated?

We have a complex legal machinery to scrutinize what these agencies have done. A Special Judge now scrutinizes all these people have to say. But is his word final? No. There are appeals to every level on every single decision that this Judge might take: from the framing of charge top disallowing of witnesses. I do not have any authentic data but to the best of my knowledge only a few of the many thousands of audit paras finally lead to departmental or criminal action, of these few only 1 or 2 per cent actually end up in jail or with a less severe penalty like censure or demotion.

Even though the operation of the law of mistrust has its serious drawbacks at best and is self-defeating at worst, still almost the entire structure of laws and the functioning of government is based on it. You apply for a ration card and you realize how the principle operates in practice. You have to prove almost everything that you state in your application. Nothing can be accepted 'without due verification', not even the place and date of your birth, leave alone your name and place of residence.

The same is true when you apply for a passport or a voter's identity card or a simple thing like a bus all route pass or a *tatkal* railway ticket. It's not as if you were seeking a special favour from the government when you are questioned thus: it's just that the principle of mistrust on which the system functions is such that it does not seem strange to a bureaucrat that he makes such inquiries even when the voter is merely exercising his right, as in the case of the passport.

It is a matter of no concern whatsoever that such a principle leads sometimes to laughable situations as in the case of a man who turns up before the treasury officer for his 1999 pension, but has to give a certificate of being alive in 1998, if he wants the pension of that year as well.

The principal of mistrust not merely extends to members of the public but to other branches of the bureaucracy as well. This is the sole *raison d'etre* for the existence of a large number of agencies like the CBI, CVC, CAG and the like. And is certainly is responsible for the all of suspicion with which such agencies surround themselves.

If trust begets trust it is equally true that mistrust begets mistrust. No citizen is willing to believe that the system will work on its own. Over the years of 'mistrust begetting mistrust' they have mastered ways of getting around the system. With the help of a legion of touts, agents and middlemen they find it very easy to get over the system. This is the *raison d'etre* of the infamous Inspector Raj.

While thinking of the 'mistrust begets mistrust' syndrome, my mind goes to the 'I'm okay you're okay' precept. In our mistrust syndrome, this would be 'I'm okay you're not okay'. That is to say that my Inspector is okay but you, Mr. Citizen, are not. See the whole thing now from the citizen's point of view. Well, Mr Bureaucrat, he will say, I'm okay, you are not!

The same 'I'm okay you are not' precept will be operating between two bureaucrats as well. See how the IAS-IPS fight each other; or how the department of personnel ticks off the other departments or the suspicion with which CBI inspectors view almost everybody else. Of course, it is quite another matter that the suspicion is mutual.

There's another way to judge the principle of mistrust. Kant's categorical imperative is such that it can without any self-contradiction be universalised. The way, let us say, a dictum like 'Truth is good' can be. Where does a dictum like mistrust take us when universalised? We all end up mistrusting each other; the time will soon come when I will not be willing to trust even my own shadow. Can such a society be sustained?

No, mistrust cannot be sustained as a universal law; so it cannot be the basis of any long lasting rule or principle. On the other hand, trust can be such a law. Surely in 'Ram Rajya Trust' will be what will define our mutual relationships and not lack of it.

It is sad that the system of 'mistrust begets mistrust' has now found a very comfortable niche in our administrative system and to sustain it our administration is getting more and more insular and is getting more and more isolated from the community it is meant to serve. Mistrust feeds upon itself: the more we mistrust the other, the more untrustworthy he will be. This is the basis of my first law of administration.

41

TALES OF INVERTED TRIANGLE ON TELLY

Much has been said about the role of television as an agent of change but has anything substantial been done beyond shouting slogans and reiterating homilies? Television series have to be entertaining; so we can have nothing but episodes with canned laughter or the ones that give a glimpse of a never to be had lifestyle. What about a series on family planning that entertains as well?

An ancient culture like ours runs more on myths than on facts. And that is one of the main reasons why many of our problems become difficult to solve, even intractable. Take the problem relating to women as an example. These are crucial not merely as human rights issues but because interlinked with them are various social and national issues, family planning, for example.

There are many myths in connection with the place of women in the home and the position of the girl child. One of the key one is that she is the weak link in the home, the reason for this probably is the fact that she leaves the home after marriage while a joint family system ensures that the boy even after marriage remains with the parents.

This myth clouds judgment to the extent that the girl child is denied access to most of the amenities that the family can afford; sometimes even education and a nutritious diet. Sometimes this denial reaches an extreme: she is denied love and affection and is relegated to the role of a performer of menial task, a position similar to that given to animals.

This leads to ironic situation that the girl child, while having to share the burden of looking after the home with the mother is denied the wherewhithal which would make this task possible. What does it matter if this leads to incomplete and poor bringing up of the kids.

It is also ironic how these myths make us work against our better judgment and natural instinct. There is a natural bond of love and affection for the girl child: while realizing the existence of the loving bond, she is still taken as a burden, even a curse.

Apart from the implications there are many social implications too. One implication of this attitude is that unless a boy is born, couples tend to continue to produce children, no matter how weak they may become economically as a result.

It is felt that the removal of some myths, like the concept a boy being an insurance for old age, and the creation of some others, like the loving and caring nature of the girl child, could result in substantial changes in attitudes, leading not merely to solution of some of our social problems like population control but also to the welfare of the family as a unit.

There is little doubt that the single most important problem facing us is the problem of population control. With fast diminishing natural resources and increasing problems of poverty and threats to the environment, development in any case a tedious process but the unrestrained population increase further compounds it.

Many crores of rupees have been spent on population control measures but the results have been indifferent. This is so because the issue is a complicated one, being intimately linked to larger social, economic and even emotional issues and often it becomes interwoven with the sort of myths mentioned above.

We have already recognized that amongst the various issues involved, the key one is the role of the girl child and the place of women in the socio-economic fabric in the home. Apart from the fact that this requires definition but the key requirement is the removal of these myths.

How are myths to be removed? These myths have been created and built into our psyches over a period of many generations. These are now hardened; in many respects they are now part of our cultural and emotional make up. To change them mere interaction of them being wrong is not enough; many people know it to be wrong but still are unable to do anything because it is part of their emotional structure.

To change the setup we have to tackle the issue at the emotional level rather than at the intellectual level. What we need is not just an intellectual belief but the creation of an appropriate emotional response. And this response has to be in the individuals that make up the family.

As a first step we have to reach the home, where the family as such resides, that too in a way that we can make emotional sense to everybody who lives there. It is only when emotionally changes have been induced that we can work for inducing appropriate behavioural changes.

The short story and the novel are the ideal vehicles for inducing such attitudinal changes, especially when written by aware and creative writers. But the problem is that these can be accessed only by the educated, moreover, with paper prices rising and a dearth of libraries, even they find it difficult to get hold of them. How are we to reach them to the bulk of the people who individually form the family group?

The advantage of television as a communication media is that it is placed in the home itself and that too usually in a place where everybody has access to it. Moreover it is the ideal vehicle to convey messages which are designed to appeal to the emotions. To top it all, it has the largest possible reach, many times more than any other media.

The ideal situation would be to pick up stories by aware writers and adapt them for television. Just see what the impact of serials has been. For most people the truth of the stories told for centuries by epics like the 'Ramayana' and the 'Mahabharata' was brought home only when these epics were shown on the telly.

A creative work is by its very definition one that induces behavioural and attitudinal changes; all we have to do is to pick up appropriate stories and present them through the telly. At a very cursory running through some short stories by Indian and foreign writers I could pick up almost a dozen.

The key aim of a television series on family planning, would be on the whole to lead to the creation of a strong awareness on the true role of the girl child and lead to important attitudinal changes and the abolition of the myths that have given rise to discrimination and ill-treatment. Any takers?

42

FESTIVALS, THE UNITING FACTOR

The festival of 'Bhai-dooj' is the dat of the brother and sister. It is the day when sisters will get up early in the morning and go to their brothers house to apply sandal paste to their forehead and also to give them sweets. In turn, sisters will receive a memento or a gift the price of which will no doubt depend on the economic status of their brothers but which will be valuable nevertheless.

India is a country of ancient festivals and practices; hardly a day passes when one practice or the other is not on us. If today we have the 'practice' of washing the feet of little girls, tomorrow it is time for putting a copper coin and some oil in the bowl of the 'Saturday man'. If today it is the festival of throwing coloured water at all and sundry, tomorrow it is time for lighting lamps in front of your house and bursting crackers.

To many it seems that all this 'time pass' is really a waste of time and a reminder of medieval practices and times. But is this really true?

It is difficult to understand how these practices have survived all this time. Nowhere else in the world is the bond between brother and sister so strong that they should meet year after year on such an occasion! Why so here?

I think the answer is to be had in the nature of our festivals and practices. Maybe a study of these will help in understanding their logic and locus standii.

These festivals and practices are not just ways of 'time pass' nor are they merely to mark the passage of one day and the advent of the next. They invariably have a logic of their own. Sometimes this logic is apparent in the festival itself and sometimes it is not so; but logic there is.

Let us take the three most important festivals of Holi, Dussehra and Diwali. The first of these comes at a time when winter has either come to an end or is about to. It thus marks an important landmark in the year and it is appropriate that the advent of summer must be heralded by the throwing of cold water.

Holi has another important meaning. It comes at a time when the winter crop has just been harvested, presumably at a considerable physical effort and labour. It is, therefore, appropriate that one should celebrate and enjoy.

Dussehra is at the other end of the fulcrum: it comes at a time when the summer crop has been harvested and it is still time for the winter crop to be sown. The few weeks between Dussehra and Diwali represent a period when one is absolutely free to enjoy and celebrate.

Diwali comes at a time when again it is the change of season, this time of course from summer to winter. Is it then not appropriate that we should celebrate it with lighted lamps and bursting fire-crackers?

Apart from being linked to changes in season, all these festivals are linked with agricultural practices. In fact, since sowing and harvesting practices are themselves linked to season, it will be a truism to say that it is agricultural practices that determine the timing and importance of these most important festivals.

So far so good. It is easy to understand the importance of these festivals for the agriculturists; also the enthusiasm with which they celebrate them. But how do you explain the enthusiasm for these festivals among the town people?

In a way, town practices (especially trade) is linked to agriculture; but this is not all. Most town people are not connected at all with country practices. Why do they show so much verve and *joie de vivre* when celebrating these festivals?

It is clear that agriculture and season are not the logic and locus standii of these festivals; at least not the sole logic. We have to see the logic elsewhere, maybe in our cultural, if not genetic, make up. Let us see what links us with our brethren in the other parts of the country.

Nothing seems to be similar. Not the colour of the skin, not the language; not even religious practices. From geography and topography to dress and behaviour everything is different. But still there is a commonness. What is this? And how has this been fostered?

The second question is more important than the first. The commonness is there in the very nature of the human being; in fact, we share this commonness with the rest of the world. Out of the millions of factors that go into making of the genes, only a couple of hundred factors will distinguish the American from the Indian. But still the American is poles apart from us.

It is clear that it is these festivals that have fostered the commonness and has brought about so much secular unity that we see amidst the obvious diversity. What is true of these festivals is also true of the practices. Let us take practices like Bhai dooj, when sisters will apply sandal paste to their brothers and get gifts and assurances of affection in return. These festivals are also reminders to her 'by marriage adopted' family that she is not as lonely and alone that they might sometime tend to assume.

These practices have played another wonderful role. They are the sole guardians and reminders of the so-called old values and virtues. The fact that the relationship of brother and sister, as indeed many other relationships as well, are merely biological is lost in the multitiered relationship that these practices bring about.

Is a sister merely because she is born of the same parents? The question becomes irrelevant because we know that she is a sister because she has been applying sandal paste on every Bhai dooj day. Thus, even when biological relationships have been forgotten, other relationships continue. And this is the important contribution that these festivals and practices have played in evolving an Indian identity and culture.

43

LISTEN TO THE RHYTHM OF THE FALLING RAIN

The rains have come at last. Belatedly though, but still surely. As I look out of the windows of my office, I find the diffused sunlight pleasant as opposed to the harsh sun we had all this while. The scenery also gives a washed look with the trees a shimmering green and the air washed and clean. How wonderful, really? If the rains have come, can the mosquitoes and the flies be far behind? What about the waterlogged roads and the clogged drains? What about the floods? And all the sweating?

So short is our memory that with the first rains, the pain of the hot scorching days is forgotten. It will be the same when a short break in the rain will make it hot and sultry.

As one thinks of all those hot and sultry days ahead, the summer does not seem that bad after all. Remember this was the only time when the flies and mosquitoes were totally out of reckoning and you could sleep without the smell of the mosquito repellent filling up your nostrils.

Mosquito and fly free days were not the only boon of the hot season. Can you ever forget how your taste buds were activated as you bit into the sweet and juicy melon and as the cold glass of *lassi* cooled its way into the tummy? Or how wonderful it was when your teeth bit into that favourite ice-cream chocolate bar!

The hot season had another bonus for us. Most of the viruses and disease-causing germs were also forced to take a break. I suffer perpetually from a sore throat and flu (of the running nose variety). It must have been the heat because these two months my problem was sort of dormant. There is no doubt that with the onset of the monsoons (only a few days away) my running nose and sore throat cannot be far behind!

But the biggest thing that the summer did to me was that it killed my appetite to a large extent. My appetite for greasy food and *mithai*. And this helped me shed a good three kilos of useless flab from my body, much of it from the tummy. From a very unwieldy and ugly 75 kilos. I'm almost down to 71 or so. Had the hot summer lasted another month or so, I could have been down to a slim and trim 69 kilos!

With the first rain will return mosquitoes: and since my mosquito repellent devices are in a state of disuse, it will mean long and uncomfortable nights.

Moreover, I find it difficult to sit out in the lawn, despite the cool breeze and the green and clean surroundings. This is thanks to the mosquitoes who, it appears, are only waiting for the summer to end so that they can surface.

Now that the mosquitoes have come, can the housefly be far behind? As I pen these few lines, my mind goes to how terrible a nuisance the fly can be!

As one tries to read the day's headlines, the flies come in from all directions, taking all vantage points on the body which are not covered.

While folding the newspaper into some sort of a fly swatter, one has to stamp the foot into the ground or shoot the hand angrily into the air to scare them away. But still they'll come, angry and pestering.

It's not just the flies and the mosquitoes. The worst part of the rainy season is the failure of the clothes, especially the under garments, to dry. Sometimes the option is between reusing the previous day's sweat filled vest or putting on a half-dried one from the previous day's washing. More often than not you have to start the day with a body scrub with a towel that may be as wet as the body itself.

Add to the above the image of your son muddying the house with his wet shoes and that of the guest stepping on your favourite carpet without using the foot cleaner or taking off his shoes. What sort of a picture you get!

My god! It's going to be terrible in the days ahead. How much better were the days just gone by, howsoever hot and scorching. At least we did not have mosquitoes and flies. No running noses and debiliting sicknesses. Towels and undergarments were dry and clean; so were the shoes of your children and your guests. I almost wish to pray to god: please take me back to the scorching heat of May and June. Anything to keep away from the sweat and mud of the monsoons.

As I look up to pray, I find dark rain-filled clouds in the sky. There is a crash of thunder, and here comes the patter of the drops of water from the heavens. Soon it is a downpour.

I find a numbness descending upon the thinking part of me as I survey this wonderous scene. At this instant. I could do anything to shed my inhibitions and my clothes to be out in the pouring rain just as the urchins down the street are.

The monsoons come but once a year; let us enjoy them as heaven's own gift to our country. Do not let the mosquito and the fly, or even our running noses, spoil the moment. And for heaven's sake, do not even think of the June sun!

PART 8

TRYST WITH MIND

44

IS IMAGE BIGGER THAN THE MAN?

I have often seen my image in the mirror and have always felt that I am better looking than my image. I wonder why my entire scientific upbringing forces me to believe that the image is exactly the same as the man.

Science may be right as far as theories go; but our entire experience tells us that for most people we are not what we actually are but what our image is. Don't believe me? Let's take Hitler as an example.

'The best thing that has happened to Europe', declared Chamberlain, the then Prime Minister of England when Hitler became the chancellor of Germany. And now? 'The beast of Europe!'

Do we really know Hitler the Man? All we believe about Hitler is what his image is.

It's really so obvious, when you think about it: Man is nothing but his image. What seems so odd to me is that all this while I have believed to the contrary. Not only believed, but actually acted on this principle.

One of my friends, now a top political leader, advised me long back that what was lacking in me and many others was the ability to cultivate our image. He had warned me against this tendency.

I disregarded this advice not simply because I did not respect the judgement of this gentleman: in fact, I respected him on this account. But I ignored his advice as I felt that whatever the image the true man will come out in the end.

It is said that in the long run we are dead; so if the truth comes out after death what good it is to us or to anybody else?

It is said that you can fool some people for some time but you can't fool all the people all the time. But is it really necessary to fool all the people all the time? So long as we can fool some people for some time successfully what need is there to fool all the people?

Why do we need the support of people? Is it for big things of life? Maybe, once in a while. But on a day to day basis one needs support for the really small things: getting onto a bus, getting a cinema ticket when the 'House Full' board is displayed, sometime getting promotions or held-up increments.

It is the sum total of such benefits that make up the really big things of life. The denial of some of them can cause more worry and problems than missing out on the so called big things. And these small benefits can come out of factors connected with your image rather than the real you.

How does one make one's image? Frankly speaking, I don't know. This is a game that I have never played and even if I had I don't think I am equipped to win. But all my life I have seen people work to building up a good image. And I am now in a position to distil some of the principles of the approach they follow.

The first and foremost of these is to ignore the dictum 'don't blow your own trumpet'. In fact, one has to do just this. I remember a former boss, a great votary of the art of trumpet blowing, ticking me off when I protested to him that too much of self-praise was not good. He said: 'If I do not blow my trumpet will you do it for me?'

It's true: if you don't blow your own trumpet, no one else will do it for you. So, for all those who care for their image more than they do for themselves, the buzz word is: Blow your trumpet and blow it as many times and before as many people as you can.

The second principle is: don't waste any time in upgrading your skills or adding to your knowledge. All this will only add to the real you and not in any way enhance you image. If anything, it will affect your image adversely. This is so because all people who do not have the skills or the knowledge that you have now acquired, will start mistrusting you.

And mistrust is the real enemy of the image builder. If you want a good image the first and foremost thing to do is to spread the impression that you are a big dud and know nothing more than the other fellow does. In short never try to spread your image of one who knows more than the others.

Another important point to remember is that you should never come very close to people, especially those in whose mind you are trying to create a particular image. Remember, these people are to know you not for what you actually are but what you want them to believe. It is, therefore, a big mistake to be too social.

Well, for those who want to be social and want to cultivate a fine image too, there is a word of advice. Be social if you must; or cannot avoid it for other reasons. But, for heavens sake, do not mix the two companies. You will have to live in two different worlds: the world of people with whom you wish to cultivate an image; and those with whom you socialize. Please try to ensure that the two worlds do not mix under any circumstances.

There is one factor in which no formula can help: your own temperament. This you have to mould and how you do it depends on the sort of person you are, the sort of image you are trying to cultivate, and other such factors. The important thing is not what you do but the fact that you recognize that there is a problem and you have to do something to overcome it.

Now that I have completed my lecture I am wondering: is it always possible to cultivate an image? Or, is it at all desirable? And if at all one could answer these questions in the affirmative, is all the effort worth it?

While I make an attempt to answer these questions, dear reader, you could do the same. The least we can do for ourselves is to ensure that our image is not worse looking than we actually are.

45

DO HABITS DIE OR HAVE TO BE MURDERED?

If it is difficult to kill bad habits, its all the more difficult to kill habits which are worse. They have to be murdered and the murder has to be premeditated and totally ruthless.

That is how two of your fellow human beings got rid of a particularly bad habit. If you want to know more, please read on.

Getting up late in the morning, drinking a cup of a tea or coffee, telling lies or even talking on the telephone. All these habits die hard. But not as hard as it is to give up alcohol or drugs. Or even smoking. Especially smoking.

It is now well known that a heavy smoker over a lifetime stands to lose about 23 years of his life. Considering that the biblical ideal life span is three decades and ten, that is quite a substantial portion of one's life. And also not to forget that these lost years are those that come at a time when one has peaked in ones creative and intellectual faculties.

Would any man of forty or fifty like to die? Well, you can make up your mind yourself; I don't.

It is difficult to see what attracts one to smoking. And this statement is being made by a one time heavy and compulsive smoker like me. I passed through all of school and college without succumbing to the temptation of this dried leaf. It was in Mussoorie that I succumbed to its devilry.

One can question the contribution of the National Academy

of Administration (NAA) in Musssoorie to the making of administrators of our country, but there is no doubt about one of its achievements—that of introducing hudding administrators to drink and smoke.

In the Indian Administrative Service (IAS) there is a sort of divide today—those who went to Metcalf house in Delhi and those who went to Mussoorie. While the former rarely drink if ever, the reverse is the case with the Mussoorie goers. Why this is so is a digression I don't wish to take.

It is difficult to see what attracts an intelligent man to take up smoking. There is not a single doctor who will not warn you about its evils. (It's quite another matter than many of the gentlemen in white coats have themselves been seduced into its evil ways!)

It's not that smokers are not aware of the evils attached to their habit, in fact, I have yet to meet a person who is not aware of the effects of smoking. Every cigarette advertisement has an endorsement to this effect; so does every pack of cigarettes. But has this helped them to give up the habit? Or has it prevented others from picking it up? May be it has helped some; but as zooming sales of cigarette companies show the effect has not been very much.

It is said that we have no say in our birth but at least in the manner of our death we should be able to have some choice. To each on his own poison. It is true that there are many ways of dying but could there be worse ways of dying (or living) than of cancer induced by excessive smoking? Except maybe death of drugs and alcohol addition.

For most of the twenty years that I was a smoker. I was trying to give it up. And that was the case with most of the smokers that I know M. K. Kaw, the 'crazy bureaucrat' now in charge of civil aviation, through houts of smoking and drinking, used to say, "Who says it's difficult to give up smoking? I' we given it up twenty-seven times;" I'm sure he's hit a century by now! That is if he is still smoking.

And that gives an idea of the difficulties that confront the smoker who wants to quit. It is a constant effort and struggle. I remember how I once asked my thumb sucking son to give up his dirty habit. It's not difficult once you try! I added helpfully. It's surprising how intelligent little kids can be. His immediate retort was—"Why can't you give up your smoking habit, papa?"

His retort struck me between the eyes but it was still not provocation enough to quit smoking. That was to come later. It was a short story by a Nobel laureate. Again given to me by this very son.

The story goes something like this. A chap is dying of cancer. He has only five minutes to live, so the doctors remove all his tubes and free him from the oxygen cylinders and blood urea and the heart lung machines. His doctor stands before him and says, "Well Sir....we've done our best and it's time now for you to go. You have only five minutes left and probably in this period you can meet only one of your loved ones. Everybody is there outside—your dear wife, your doting daughter, your two sons, all your best friends, your boss and your subordinates—all of them there. There is the priest and there is the swami. All of them are waiting to see you. But we have decided to abide by your decision in the matter. Please tell us whom we should call."

There is a moment of hesitation on the part of the dying man. He finally says, "I want to be left alone, all by myself. For the last few moments of my life. I want to be all by myself!"

As is to be expected everyone abides by his decision and the closing the door behind him. As soon as he is out, there is a flurry of activity from the bed. In a flash the dying man removes the pillow and under a couple of folds of the sheet there is hidden the butt of the last cigarette that he must have smoked after evading the stare and glare of the doctors, nurses and the relatives.

I know what the effect this story had on me; but I could not have anticipated the effect it would have on Rakesh Kumar, the director of many Amitabh movies, when I sat narrating it to him in his Juhu flat as his little girl played on his knees.

Since. Not one single puff.

A habit that we couldn't kill, we murdered; ruthlessly and without any pity or remorse.

46

TRYST WITH SELF

It is difficult to realise it, but all of us have a tryst with ourselves. I discovered this truth as I accidentally chanced upon one of my old pictures.

Just a few days back while cleaning up some of my old papers I found a picture of a young man staring at me with a pair of bright, sensitive, penetrative eyes. These playful eyes were set under a wide and clear forehead, itself covered by a thick tuft of jet black hair. As I looked up I found that the hair, well combed and glistening with brylcream, took a Dev Anand like twirl on the forehead, almost merging with the bushy eyebrows. These bow like brows rounded into a well constructed and thick set nose, which stood guard on beautifully constructed lips like an *asura* guarding the portals of the gods about to embark on a love making duel with the consort.

The well rounded and protruding chin; sulking cheeks and the small but majestic ears served to complete the picture that could only have been of a 17-year old youth, with a winsome smile and godly demeanour.

I took some time to realise who it was but when I did I gave out a cry of alarm: is the man behind those playful and mischievous eyes really me? Could it really be true?

I wistfully walked to the mirror and there it was the stark truth: yes, the same features, the same sharp aquiline nose, the same eyes and wide forehead. No doubt, the thick tuft of black hair had vanished but it was unmistakable; the man in the photo is no doubt the same chap who stares out at me from the photograph but still in some important ways he is not the same.

For one he is tired and wan, with none of the exuberance and excitement of the younger self. For another, the age shows and not just in the colour of his hair and in the wrinkles of his forehead.

It is strangely disturbing to see yourself now and compare yourself to what you were. Even worse, when you compare yourself with what you wanted to be. Don't we now want to become young again?

Is it only the physical aspects that make us want to be young again? Well, in a way, yes. Now as we stand in front of the mirror and look at our protruding hair line, double chin, shadows under the eyes, tyres around the waist, it is natural to recall the time when we too were slim and trim. But it is not merely the physical aspects of youth that I miss.

What I miss most is the free, almost casual, mental attitude of the young.

For the advanced metaphysics paper for the IAS, I had to struggle through the very abstract concept of 'dasein' in the existentialist philosophies of thinkers like Jaspers. It is easy to grasp this concept if one sees the attitude of these young years.

If there are any 'dasein' years, they were these. What mattered was the moment and nothing else. Though well versed with the philosophical concept of 'dasein' now I still cannot live it; but in those days when there was no way that I could be induced to go through books of existentialist philosophers like Jaspers and Sartre, I still found it possible to 'live' their philosophy.

These were heady days, not a care in the world, not a worry. It is this aspect more than anything that makes those days look so attractive and wonderful and the present ones so painful and tension-ridden. It almost makes me fall in love with the past.

This love affair has all the makings of a tragedy. Love it is, but love that cannot be fulfilled. A tragedy of the like that would have done Shakespeare proud; or made a great novelist of me: but not what will make life any simpler to cope with.

But why is it that such a love cannot be fulfilled? Because of the gap of time? Because of the huge age bar? Because of any other reason?

Let me sit down and look in the eyes of my latest love, me as I was at the age of seventeen. Can I read anything there?

It comes as a torrent, a flood of thoughts and feelings. There are so many of them that I can fill up books and books. But what are these books written of?

These books are written in the ink of emotion and ambition and burning desire. Hopes, aspirations, dreams. Yes, dreams above all. Wonderful dreams, wonderful thoughts. Flying in the air, floating with the clouds...everything is there.

Now as I read these books, I find emptiness all around me as the words vanish before my very eyes. All my hopes, aspirations, burning desires, dreams...they have remained mere empty words.

At that time they were bundles of emotions and happy endings to be soon achieved; now they are frustrating failures, shattered dreams and devastated castles...all enveloped in the deafening silence of a graveyard-like past.

I wish it were only the physical part of me that I missed. In that case I could have rushed to the health club and the plastic surgeon. If that was all that I loved and craved for from the past, the task was not difficult.

But it is not only the return of the physical beauty that I crave. Nor merely the restoration of the physical me. Then what is it that I seek?

Well, as I look into the eyes of the photograph, I realize what it is. What I miss is the 'joy of life', the burning desire and ambition, the 'devil may care' and 'hell with you' attitude. The complete command over yourself and overriding desire to 'become'.

And what I miss is the fire of ambition that drives the mortal to struggle; and struggle to the extent of forgetting death and seeking immortality.

Yes, what I love in 'me that was' is the struggle and striving for immortality, the ambition to get what the gods have denied and what other men will surely resist.

It is this that the adult in me has effectively buried in the ground and it is for this reason that the bright young fellow in the photograph disturbs so much.

There is no way out. Sooner or later you have to face your maker; and that maker is none other than yourself. And that is why this picture of the boy of seventeen is so disturbing. The least I owe to myself is to pledge to this boy of seventeen, that this aging man will carry forward the struggle that you began and carry forward the torch of burning desire and ambition to the extent of striving for immortality. You have dreamed not in vain; nor have you strived and struggled for nothing.

No excuses, no empty words. The striving, the struggle and the toil...all of this and more...in fact anything that you had dreamed...will go on. This I pledge to do even if I have to dip my pen in my blood and tears.

47

DOES READING OF PHILOSOPHY HAVE ANY UTILITY?

A young postgraduate from Jamia Millia whose intelligence and understanding I have come to admire, asked me for a list of books which he should read during the forthcoming vacation. I thought for a moment; then without any further hesitation suggested to him Bertrand Russell's *History of Western Philosophy*.

Aslam Naved mulled over this for a moment; then pat came his response. 'Philosophy is fine,' said the bright eyed young man, 'but what is the utility?' Naved had probably wanted me to suggest books on management or accounts and was a bit nonplussed when I suggested philosophy instead.

This question made my own mind rush back to the days when I myself read books on philosophy. Two of my five papers for the IAS exam were Philosophy and Advanced Metaphysics and, since my IIT engineering background had hardly prepared me for these subjects, I had scarcely any option but to guzzle down one book after another, be it on existentialism or pragmatism or logic. The question of utility that Naved put to me never came to the fore simply because I read philosophy not for any 'love of wisdom' but for the pure and simple reason that it was 'part of the course'.

Now that I think of it, indeed, does philosophy have any utility or does one read it only for that elusive commodity called wisdom? Why indeed should one read Russell's book on the history of western philosophy or even Will Durant's book on the same subject? Is there any point in reading the very tough and obtuse 'Critique of Pure Reason' by Immanuel Kant or the book on dialectical Idealism by Hegel? Or Bradley's Appearance and Reality or Descartes 'Cogito Ergo Sum'? What about our own philosophy or books on logic and intuitive thought?

Reading these books seems even more incongruous when you realise that it is bread and butter issues that dominate us day in and day out and who has the time to just learn, or mug up, something just for the love of wisdom? Naved's question is not really as irrelevant as it may sound at first thought. If one does advise a young man to read a book by Immanuel Kant or Russell, he does have a right to know if there is any utility in the same.

Needless to say if one is appearing for the IAS and one has taken Philosophy as a subject one has to read it; that is utility per se. But if one in not required to take an exam why should one read it at all?

I have a very good answer at the superficial level to this question. Knowledge of philosophy helps one to impress listeners with the depth of knowledge that one has. If dropping names of people like Kant and Russell helps in cocktail circuits and kitty parties, surely displaying some sort of knowledge of what they have to say, howsoever hollow the understanding level may be, would doubly impress. How often have we not seen people with wine glasses in their hands impressing their listeners with their in depth knowledge of what Karl Jaspers or Heidegger has to say or what dasein of the existentialists really means? Imagine the impact on pretty girls of a statement on Ding An Sich of Kant!

For many people this is sufficient reason for rushing to read books on philosophy or by philosophers. But a little thought will convince that there are weightier reasons as well.

All people conversant with the scientific method know that any research or scientific quest begins with an hypothesis. The hypothesis can be anything: Is the earth flat or is it round are both equally acceptable examples and both can lead to the application of the scientific method. Is the moon made of cheese? Or is it made of water? Is the sun the centre of the solar system or is it the earth? One can go on endlessly.

We know that the hypothesis is the key to the scientific method but have we wondered how the hypothesis comes into being? How is it that a man like Newton can question why the apple falls downwards when millions before him just accepted this as a given fact of nature without really try to hypothesise it and question its veracity?

It is not difficult to answer this one. Well, Newton and for that matter Einstein or Descartes or Copernicus, were all more wise than the rest of us. There is no other way to explain their questioning spirit and their quest for new knowledge by rejecting strongly held beliefs than to note their wisdom and their love for it.

If you don't still accept this, then try explaining how hypotheses come into being. You cannot rationalise them; nor can you get them out of observation or belief. They generally come ready made and they come to certain individuals. Once the hypothesis comes into being, it is then simply a question of making observations and carrying out experiments.

Remember Edison's statement on genius being 1 per cent inspiration and 99 per cent perspiration? Well the hypothesis is the 1 per cent part and the observations and experimentation the 99 per cent part.

While talking of philosophy we are to confine ourselves to the 1 per cent part. Let's ask ourselves: from where does the inspiration come? And, more importantly, how? I think this is where philosophy, in its wider context of 'love of wisdom', comes in.

Now I think one can answer Naved's query of the utility of study of philosophy. While all the other subjects combined make up the 99 per cent perspiration part of genius, it is philosophy that gives it the 1 per cent inspiration. Needless to say, without this 1 per cent the entire 99 per cent perspiration will have been in vain.

If we want a world to be people solely by cutters of wood and carriers of water then philosophy is of no need whatsoever; but if we want the genius too then we can ignore it only at our peril.

If we want status qùo to continue to take us from one slothful slumber to another then, and only then, can we ignore the study of subjects like logic, philosophy and metaphysics. But if we want to wake into a new dawn every morning then let the teachings of the wise men of the past make us not only wiser but also alert to the cries of inspiration that may erupt any moment out of our subconscious into the sublime realities of our existence.

It is only through the bouts of wisdom that the labours of man can rightfully be adjudged as works of genius.

PART 9

TRYST WITH BODY

48

THE FOUNTAIN OF ETERNAL YOUTH

If there is a part in our brain in which dreams are made and stored, then surely it is here that there is a fountain in which flows the elixir of eternal youth. Dreams are horses that only fools ride but no longer, at least not as far as this particular dream is concerned. If ever science stood close to locating exactly such a fountain, it is now. Well, almost.

In theory there should be no problem in this. After all, the human body is a mechanism albeit an immensely complex one, subject to wear and tear and also breaking down. With proper care and replacement of the worn out parts, there is no reason why the life of the machine cannot be prolonged, even made indefinite.

Our past history has shown that this is possible. For the most part of his history, man has had an average span of life of less than 20; in fact, even five decades back in India the span was no more than 29 or so. Better medical care, more and better nutrition, and better techniques have already enhanced it to more than 60 or so now. In fact, in most of the Western world it is already closer to 80 or so, clearly indicating that we could increase it by another 25 per cent or so.

The landmark developments that have affected life spans in this century include the discovery of vitamins in 1906, Fleming's discovery of penicillin, the first of the antibiotics in 1928, the polio vaccine in 1955 and the knowledge of the hazards of smoking in 1964. In our own country, it is all this and better nutrition that has caused dramatic changes in this regard.

But despite all these dramatic changes, for researchers studying the aging rules have been fairly simple: organisms are born, they live a more or less prescribed number of years and they die. For those who watch their weight, eat right and get a lot of exercise, a bit more time could be squeezed out here or there but no more; the very idea of eliminating life-spans is not an option that is available.

But scientists are no longer talking in these terms. Already in the case of particular types of worms and fruit flies it has been demonstrated that a tripling or even a quadrupling of life spans is in the realm of possibilities; in laboratories around the world investigators are discovering that what works in the case of worms and flies may work in the case of humans too.

In different species the cellular mechanisms responsible for aging appear to be the same and that is the reason why researchers are now able to seek answers to questions like: Why do we age? and What can we do about it? The question before scientists today is not whether it is possible to increase life spans or even double or triple it, but it is the culmination of the very concept of life spans!

One of the issues that is engaging the attention of scientists is whether aging is a process that is genetically determined. If it is so, then by suitable genetic manipulation, it should be possible to increase these spans dramatically. Scientists could then treat aging by getting inside the body's engine room—the cells themselves—and rebuilding from genes up. There are indications that this could indeed be the case. But there are problems too.

The problem facing any scientist trying to find a genetic lever on the aging process is the sheer number of genes involved. It is believed that even if only a few master-clock genes directly guide aging in humans, up to 7000 more might be peripherally involved. Re-engineering even one of them is an exquisitively complex process, doing it to A the 700 would be almost impossible.

But this should not put us off. We should devote our efforts to goals that are more achievable. Even if the concerned genes can't yet be manipulated, is it possible to directly treat parts of the body they act? Many researchers think that is feasible. Others feel that the right approach would be to attack the diseases that afflict the old and this way keep the very old from becoming even older. For example, if heart diseases can be eliminated, as many as 3 years could be added to the national span of life. The detection of a gene that seems to confer protection against Alzeimer's disease may help treat yet another scourge of the aged.

While none of these therapies would take human beings anywhere near the tripled and quadrupled life-spans achieved in certain worms and flies, they could at least improve life expectancies. There is reason to believe that the figure of 80 could realistically be expected to improve to 120 or so, not a mean achievement when you consider that only a few decades back it was only a lucky man who survived beyond the age of 50 or so.

There is one way already known that can make us increase our span considerably. In the case of rats it has been proved that if they are fed 30 per cent lower calories than the normal requirement, their life span goes up by almost the same percentage. By the same yardstick, people who live on 1400 calories a day, i.e., 30 per cent lower than the average requirement of 2100 calories, will get 2-3 decades of life span.

Just how this business of swapping of food for life works is not entirely clear, but it has to do somewhat with the drop of body temperature that this entails. From a growth mode they go into a survival mode and this increases their spans. This makes sense: have you ever seen an old person who is fat?

For many people the prospect of living longer and longer, even if that were feasible, is not attractive. If you see the terrible conditions in which some of the old people live, death for many of them sometimes seems a saviour rather than a killer that it is. But what these people forget is that if life is prolonged by the doctors, it will be healthy life that will be prolonged. In fact, it is not just more years of life that we will get but a few more years of useful and healthy life.

I am well past my first five decades of life; had I been living in the early part of this century, I would have been well past my prime and afflicted by all sorts of diseases. But, as it is, I have at least another two decades of healthy and useful life ahead of me. And it is these two decades that can bring out the best in me, what with all the experience and knowledge that only age can give.

If doctors can extend this by another decade or two, so be it. As worst my usefulness to society and environment will be double of what it would otherwise be. At best, I may yet become an Einstein or a Tagore.

49

GOOD NEWS FOR THE GLUTTON DIETER

Are you on a diet and still want to eat your potato chips and fried fish? Yes? There's good news for you. But as you hear it, please ponder on the effects of that news on your underprivileged neighbour in the global village.

It is true that satellite communications have converted the world into a global village but in other respects it continues to be 'great divide' where never the twain shall meet. And nowhere is this more apparent than in what we eat.

I remember when I was administering the ICDS (Integrated Child Development Scheme) program, the key issue was how to make the gruel supplied more tasty and increase the calories at the same time. We tried various combinations and found that the most effective way was to put a couple of spoons of palm oil in the *khichri* supplied.

The problem in the more affluent part of the world is to make the food tasty but not to add calories. That is why there has been a lot of experimenting with fat free foods but none of the combinations worked out so far have succeeded on the taste front. But now there is news that something may be on the cards.

The other day, when I read about the invention of synthetic oil olestra by a US firm, I was struck by the difference in perceptions in the two parts of the same 'global village'. While we are talking here of finding ways of increasing calorie intake by adding oil, they are trying to invent oils which will actually reduce calorie intake!

Unlike natural oils, which are absorbed by the body's digestive system, olestras pass through the intestines undigested. But in the mouth its effect is the same. Oils have a strong chemical affinity for the aromatic compounds that give food its taste and smell; they extract these substances, spread them around the taste buds and waft them up to odour receptors in the nose.

Olestra has no distinctive flavour of its own, just like corn oil. Like natural oils, though, it has a creamy, tongue-pleasing texture. The fact that we get such pleasure from fat-filled food is believed to have its roots in evolutions. Having unpredictable food sources, the primitive hunters who had a taste for calorie rich taste buds were likely to survive than who did not have these buds.

The beauty with the new synthetic fat olestra is that while it tastes the same as the natural variety, it does not give to the body its calories. Thus while giving food the same taste and flavour and the palate the pleasure as those which are rich in fat, it does not contribute to the flab in the body.

There is a reason for this. Most dietary fat comes on the form of triglycerides, three fatty acids arrayed around a molecule of glycerol. In the intestines there are enzymes whose task it is to slice these triglycerides into manageable pieces so that they can be absorbed into the system. Olestra molecules, on the other hand, have six or eight fatty acids attached to a sugar molecule and are thus much bigger than triglycerides. They are packed so tight that the enzymes cannot cut them apart to enable their absorption by the system.

If you take *pakoras* deep fried in olestra what will happen is that while the taste buds in the mouth will get all the pleasure, the oil will pass unabsorbed through the intestines. Isn't it wonderful news for the glutton who would like to diet at the same time?

How many times have you wanted to take peach pie or a chocolate cake or a chocolate ice-cream but have not because of the high calories? Well, once the new oil comes out the number of such occasions can be literally cut down to half because that is what is going to happen to the calorie position of these foods.

Can you believe that a serving of chocolate ice-cream, now 270 calories, will come down to less than 110 calories? A slice of chocolate cake, now 235 calories, will give you less than 165; so with a whole lot of other mouth watering foods.

Well, where will all this leave our ICDS child? In a way exactly where he is now: struggling to find the money to buy two spoons of palm oil to put in his *khichri*. As for the chocolate cake or the ice-cream variety it was not in his repertoire anyway considering the money in his thin purse. But does the development leave him entirely untouched?

Well, maybe not. There may be light at the end of the tunnel for him. If and when this synthetic oil becomes popular in the affluent West, this should free natural oils which are now being consumed. These will then be available for the consumption of the underprivileged and poor.

Let us assume that the new synthetic oil will replace 200 calorie intake for about a billion people in the West and parts of the rest of the world. This would mean about 100 calorie extra availability for each of the remaining 2 billion people. Considering that the bulk of them are below the poverty line because they are not getting sufficient calories, this should enable most of them to move up the line provided a way can be found to funnel the surplus natural oils to them.

This should not be as difficult as it may seem. Olestra is a new product on whose development over Rs. 600 crore have been spent over the last two decades. The company which has developed it can be counted upon to recover this cost from the consumer. Considering the big advantage that it gives him, he will not be loathe to pay for this cost. Let them add a small surcharge to it; this will help the company finance the funneling of the calories to the world's deprived and downtrodden.

There is quite a bit of talk of the global village; let us

remember that a village comes about not merely by speaking to each other on the telephone or watching each other's television programmes: it needs a feeling of compassion and concern as well.

Is it too much to pay a couple of cents extra for the peach pie or for the box of potato chips if it finances an extra spoon of palm oil in the *khichri* of the ICDS child?

50

HEALTHY IS AS HEALTHY DOES

This week when I was invited to inaugurate the health mela of the Brahm Kumaris near Kidwai Nagar I wonders why Gandhi came back to me. I think it was because of the holistic approach he too had on the subject of health.

Asha Behn, who took me around, was at pains to describe that the WHO describes health 'as a state of complete physical, mental and social well being of a person and not merely the absence of disease or infirmity—to be physically healthy one needs to have sound sleep, balanced diet and health, promoting positive thoughts and action'.

Disease, according to Dr. Avdesh Sharma who was also with us, is as an iceberg, with only a small tip being visible on the outside and thus clinically detectable. It is in this context that importance is being given to the non-physical dimensions of health, especially the ones concerning the state of the mind. But just how holistically even mental health is being perceived.

During the last few decades it is being realized that health is immensely influenced by one's mental state. Research implies that disease first originates in one's mind and then only if affects the physiology systems.

Mental health is not merely the absence of psychological disease but also the balanced development of an individual's personality and emotional attitudes which enable him to live harmoniously with his fellow-beings.

See how nicely mental well being is being linked to social health. Let's see how a socially healthy person lives. After fulfilling his responsibilities to his parents and given proper attention to his wife and children, he makes lasting and satisfying friendships as well. He serves his fellow beings and prevents activities that adversely affect society.

Social health extends to occupational health as well. We spend many hours at our place of work, where numerous psycho-social factors operate. There are human relationships at work there, among workers themselves, with worker and boss and so on. Lack of job satisfaction, insecurity, poor human relationships, emotional tension, are some of the psycho-social factors which undermine the state of health of workers.

It is thus that health is not just an absence of disease but a more positive and holistic concept that includes mental, social and psychological factors as well. It was this thought that filled me as I stood to address the gathering assembled for the *mela*.

On one side I could see the snarl of traffic as it meandered its way on Aurobindo Marg and on the other was the *shamiana* put up for the health exhibitions. It come naturally to me as I said that while on the left is the disease, the cure is on the right.

The disease that afflicts us, or our age, is not just the fact of the pollution that the vehicles create, or of the noise or even of tension that the jostling and rushing creates—it is actually the accumulated sum total of all of this. The biggest disease of a big city is its depersonalized entity—the 'loneliness in a crowd' syndrome. What can be more debilitating is that despite the fact that there are more than a crore people in the city, it is difficult for any one of us to name, leave alone count them as friends, more than a couple of dozen people?

Imagine the discomfort caused by the fact that when we want some ice for ones chota peg or some curd for curdling our milk, there is not a single house where one can walk in an ask for the same. Or that your neighbour's father has died and you didn't even know that he lived there!

The real sickness of the city life is not merely in the noise and pollution of the road side or even in the gutters and slums: it is actually in the negative state of mind of the people and the depersonalized way of life that has developed. To become healthy we will have to become more a part of the life around us, and less a prisoner of our 'loneliness in the crowd.'

I think it is this wisdom that Gandhi had imbibed and was the secret of his good health, despite his very sparse diet and excessive fasting. One of the prime factors of his faith, or call it philosophy if you like, was reaching out to his fellow men by faith in himself.

Hindu philosophy talks of the *atman* striving to attain the Brahman—Christians talk of the individuals being the sparks of the divine. While we read all this in books, we don't really believe in its truth. If we did, we'd realize that all of us have the potentially to attain godhead.

Gandhi believed in this philosophy and proved it in his life. He proved that man can rise above his condition if only he believed in himself. This is what is called self-realisation. In a way we too have proven this adage. All of us, or at least most of us, have proved how easy it is to fall to the level of a Godse. All we have to prove now is that it is equally easy to rise to the level of Gandhi.

Gandhi was a healthy man because he could reach out to his fellow men. He was at peace with himself and had total control over his body and mind. His thinking was positive, so was his approach to others. Truly can it be said that he was healthy in what he did, how he thought and how he reached out.

If you really want to be healthy, remember the—*healthy is as healthy does, thinks and feels.*

PART 10

PRE-METAPHYSICS

51

TECHNOLOGICAL VISION INDIA-2020

Scientists as a class debunk astrologers and palmists; but did we know that there is a scientists' organisation which predicts the future? This is what an organisation called TIFAC does routinely. TIFAC (Technology Information, Forecasting & Assessment Council) and when I read in the papers recently that they were bringing out a publication called 'Technological Vision India: 2020' I was interested and tried to get a copy. Imagine my surprise when I discovered that it was priced at, hold your breath, Rs. 50,000!

Even the most greedy of the Bhrigu pundits would not have thought of that price; so I was keen to find what it contained. My appetite was whetted even more because I knew that the study had started way back in 1993 and involved more than 500 members from Industry, Government, R&D institutions & Academia. There were 17 task forces which employed various techniques like Brainstorming Sessions, Preparation of perspective and scenario reports, Workshops, Delphi techniques, etc. This is the reason why I am interested to know about their work. But all that I could lay my hand on was set of small monographs which summarised the study by the large number of groups that had been set up.

From one of these I learn that the areas in which these groups worked included socially and beneficial areas, major infrastructures, and advanced technologies. The groups actually covered more than 100 areas and sub areas. Each vision report runs into numerous pages having valuable information on current status, the forecasts, the assessment in the Indian context.

Each of these reports suggests various outcomes, from simple modification of policies and/or introduction of relatively simple technology practices to those involving mastery of new and emerging complex technologies. The beauty of these reports is that they all have a thread of interconnection. It is very difficult to choose one or the other; it is essential to orchestrate all of them in a systematic form and also with a reasonable time-synchronism.

Realising that it would be necessary to go through all of them, I still picked up one of them, that too in a brief summarised form; I hope this overview summary would be useful for highlighting a few illustrative major issues in a respective fields.

I picked up the summary on road transportation. It has something very interesting to say. First of all it finds a correlation between increase of GDP and demand for transportation: a 4 per cent increase in GDP leads to a 5 per cent increase in transportation needs. Projecting it to 2015, it finds that freight (by road transportation) that was 6 billion ton-km in 1951 and increased to 472 now is expected to further spurt to 1821 billion ton-km by 2015. Passenger traffic will increase even more dramatically: from 2382 billion passengers km now to 15174 by 2015.

Such massive increase calls for advance planning to meet the demand. Due to the impact of liberalisation the number of vehicles plying on the roads are likely to double compared to the present level by 2000 and increase 7-8 folds by 2015. This has important implications in various areas, especially in the road design and construction.

Most of the roads in the country are flexible pavements comprising either of bitumen bound or non-bitumen bound layers. The resources of fossil fuels and consequently the bitumen are likely to be exhausted in the near future; concrete and other composite materials will have to be popularised. Other new construction materials like stabilised road construction, lime concrete construction, cement fly-ash construction, additives to bitumen emulsions, etc. are to be tried.

Appropriate technologies have also to be developed for rural roads. More than 3 out of 4 villages with a population of more than 1000 have been connected with rural roads; even 1 in 3 of the small villages have been similarly connected. But still there is a big gap. The report notes that these roads are connected through manual methods, it is essential to detail work methods and manuals giving all precautions, etc.

The report also gives the demand for road construction machines. It predicts that the requirement for machinery like hydraulic excavators, front end and wheeled loaders, mobile cranes, etc. should go up more than four-fold in the next 20 years. So would the pollution from road transportation as road transport is a major consumer of energy and contributor to environmental pollution. The problem is further compounded due to poor state of road infrastructure and overaged and inefficient transport vehicles. It calls for modernization of the system by making it energy efficient and environment friendly.

Improvements in roads and their surfaces can lead to major energy savings. Bitumen surfacing saves 15 per cent, widening one lane to two lane 10 per cent and improving riding quality 5 per cent. Traffic management can also contribute to substantial savings.

The report also predicts substantial increases in highways and expressways which now constitute only 2 per cent of the total roads but carry most of the traffic.

The report goes on making predictions and suggestions: finding ways of modernising the system and making it more environment friendly and energy efficient. It also shows how the present rate at which cities are growing has enormous implications, both for safety and for the environment. The area of roads in Indian cities varies between 4-10 per cent as compared to 20-30 per cent in the developed countries. It finds that the inadequate road space and public transport facilities coupled with poor traffic management systems and poor quality of roads are responsible for the host of urban transport problems faced by the cities.

Knowing this much has whetted my appetite for knowing more about what the future has in store for us, especially in the areas of technology. But where will I find the money to buy the publication?

I hope one of the TIFAC big bosses reads this and gives me a copy gratis. Till then all I can do is to let my imagination run wild to imagine what is in store for us in the other sectors.

52

THE SCIENTIFIC REVOLUTION

Lately two golden jubilees have come and gone; both of them hardly diverted public attention, riveted as it is on more ominous and threatening political issues. But they were none the less important because of that.

We observed the golden jubilee of the Quit India Movement and the 50 years of the formation of the CSIR—the Council of Scientific and Industrial Research—in the same year, almost at the same time.

Is there any connection in the call to the *firangee* to quit and the indigenisation of science? Or were the two events really coincidental?

Well, in a way science is global and it is difficult to see how it can be indigenised; but then what about India? Is it possible to circumscribe it in artificial boundaries on man-made maps? How can we 'nationalize' an international concept like 'India'?

Well, I'm afraid not; as much as science cannot be confined. Then what is the significance of the two golden jubilees?

Golden Jubilees are generally meant to be events of celebration and joy; they are also meant to be memories of landmarks and achievements. And memories need not always be happy ones.

The two events—Quit India Movement and formation of the CSIR— are not important that they happened; they are significant because they were really assertions—assertions that India and Indians were no longer willing to be left behind, whether in politics or in science.

Both these were really declarations of intent. And promises excellence to the rest of the world.

Have our intentions and promises been fulfilled? Have we lived up to the expectations that we raised with these two events? As an honest Indian I would like to answer honestly; and I'm afraid the answer is a resounding 'No!'

Take science. We have a network of over 300 National Laboratories; and many hundreds more of regional and local centres besides the hundreds of state and central universities and institutes. We boast of the third largest technical and scientific manpower in the world and our industry has grown both in size and depth. But what are the results?

If a single Nobel Prize has been awarded to an Indian in the last five decades for work that he has done in India. Not a single patent has been taken in India or abroad by an Indian for any major invention which has made a substantial impact in any area.

The irony is that Indians not working in India have made a big mark. Apart from the Nobel Prize for Hargovind Khurana, Indians in the USA and other countries have made notable contributions to the development of science and technology.

And even more ironic is the fact that before 1947 large numbers of Indian Scientists working in India (Raman, Bose, Chandrasekhar) were very much a part of the world scene.

Scientists today have a counter to the charge that science in India has deteriorated since Independence: they say that other areas have not improved either!

Tagore could get a Nobel Prize in literature then; but why no Indian writer has not been able to get a Nobel Prize lately? What about administration? Politics? Public life?

They have a point: the deterioration in science cannot be singled out; it is part of the general malaise.

Though this explains a certain phenomenon, can it be taken as a complete excuse? As a complete explanation? Can it be explained as a cause and effect relationship?

I am bad because everybody is bad. We have done nothing in science because the administrator has failed to administer and the politician to rule! Is that enough? Is that true?

There is no causal relationship between the failure of one and the failure of the other. Unless, of course, one likes to argue that the failure of one has contributed to the deterioration of the environment as such.

Regrettable though that it is, such seems to be indeed the case. And this has become a vicious cycle: in the system of competition that prevails today it is not that the effort of one group goads the other to higher performance but the lower achievement of one becomes an excuse for even lower achievement of the other.

In this system of 'sink lower than the other' it is the higher performers who are the first casualties: they either give in to the 'sinking game' or quit the system altogether. Either way they contribute substantially to the downward slide and the lowering of the average.

Golden Jubilees are not merely occasions for celebrations; they provide golden opportunities for stock taking and introspection. And not merely for one group or the other. All of us should come out of our narrow compartments and see at ourselves as others see us.

Let the politician see himself as the scientist sees him; and the scientist as the administrator. Can the public servant, for a change, come out of his dehumanized cocoon and see himself as the suffering public sees him? And this is for the other groups too.

Too long have we sat in our water tight compartments; too long have we allowed the part to determine the whole. Too long have we seen the collective goals being overridden by our individual aims and aspirations; too often have we asked what the country has done for us.

It is time now that we face the fact: it is not what the group can do for us; it is what we can do for it.

53

THE LASER DIWALI

As I watched the spectacular laser (fireworks) show at the capital's Pragati Maidan, the first thought in my mind was that at last we are part of the international sub set; now Diwali in India will be celebrated with the same modern gaiety as Guy Fawkes day on the 4th of July 1998. No more the deeps with the danger of fires and the noisy fire crackers which only lead to more fires and personal injuries. The spirit of Diwali will remain but not the dangers.

But then other thoughts started coming in. Will it? Are the fire crackers and the mustard oil *diwas* just incidentally a part of the festival of Diwali or they are Diwali itself'? Is the spirit of Diwali satisfied with sitting back and enjoying a spectacle such as the one I witnessed in Pragati Maidan or is it participation by bursting crackers oneself, howsoever unsophisticated and uncomplicated they may be?

In short, will Diwali still be Diwali if all the oil lamps and candles are replaced with sophisticated lights invented by Phillips and if the fire crackers, rockets, laris, atom bombs are replaced with the sophistication of lasers and sophisticated and safe crackers? Will Diwali still be the same if it is laser Diwali?

My mind goes back to my childhood days when I had read the poem which said, 'The old order changeth yielding place to new'. Was I witness to a similar change and transformation? Or was I watching not the change itself but something which was a manifestation of change taking place in the city? Or, it wasn't change at all; it was merely a cosmetic cover up for the change!

Long after the half hour laser show is over, doubts continue to assail me. Disturb me. Is the old order really changing? How is the new going to be? There is something in the old that the new can never have. Howsoever detestable and stale, howsoever difficult and hard, the old is still known. And this fact is itself comforting.

New always comes with a lot of comforting thoughts and promises but the fact remains it is unknown and comes in with a bit of uncertainty laced with a lot of fears and dreads. But I had the uncomfortable thought that it was not just the uncertainty of the future that disturbed me; the dread was something which went much deeper and had a much greater significance.

Long back I had visited a place called Sivakasi; it was a dirty, poor little place hidden somewhere in the deep south. The place appeared totally ordinary and it was difficult to imagine that somehow it too had something that gave it a passport to fame. It was only when someone mentioned that this was the place from where the entire firecracker needs of the country were met that I realised why the place was so important.

Thousands and thousands of people there were busy day and night making all sorts of firecrackers and fireworks: the phirkis, the laris, the rockets, the bombs, and what have you. Some people were directly engaged in this activity, others indirectly. Whether engaged or not, there was no doubt that all of them were dependent on it. They worked 365 days in the year and all for that one day, the day of Diwali.

I had wondered at that time: what would happen to these people if somehow the day of Diwali did not dawn. Or if the festival got somehow wiped out of the psyche of the people of India. I saw into the eyes of one of the children there and dreamt this nightmare with him. I realised how terrible all this was.

As I looked at the laser display in Pragati Maidan I dreamt

that nightmare again. It was terrible and excruciatingly painful, full as it was with the tears of thousands and screams of countless infants and little kids. 365 days of labour and sweat cannot be allowed in a wisp of smoke, unless it is the wisp and smoke that the firecrackers of Diwali leave behind. Certainly not in the artificial smoke that the laser firecrackers leave behind.

A movie I had seen long back came back to me. *Naya Daur* was the name of the movie. The grand climax of the movie is when there is a race between a tonga and a commercial internal combustion engine run truck. What is the beauty in this climax was not the novelty of the idea of a race between a truck and a horse driven tonga but the pitting against each other of technology and tradition.

This is not the first time this has happened. If now it is traditional Diwali versus laser Diwali and Sivakasi vs Lancashire, earlier it was Gandhi vs Churchill, the Spinning Wheel vs the automatic wheel, ahimsa vs violence, the unarmed satyagraha vs the tank, Jesus vs Pontius Pilate, David vs Goliath.

The image of the lone Chinese citizen stopping a whole column of red tanks will remain forever etched in our minds. The identity will forever remain anonymous but his spirit will always find expression in the cries of countless Gandhis, Christs and Davids. If he is the symbol of the weak vs strong, his is also the epitome of this eternal struggle between the two mutually opposing forces.

As the MBA run army of MNCs invades the country, countless unorganised, weak citizens watch with awe as they march to threaten the very fabric of their existence. The laser Diwali threatens not just to destroy its traditional version but threatens tradition itself. Just as the laser versions of fireworks threaten the very existence of the people of Sivakasi, the power that these forces of change bring with them threatens the very fabric of our life and culture.

I'm afraid I sound like a obscurantist but these are some of the thoughts that came to me as I looked at the spectacular laser show in Pragati Maidan. I'm sharing these fears and dreads with you; maybe they will disappear because of this. Or maybe, I'll win a few adherents and together we'll fight these forces. Or maybe, the laser Diwali will vanish like any nightmare with the dawning of the mom.

54

IN QUEST OF SCIENTIFIC ANSWERS TO MIRACLES

There have been two natural (or can one call them super natural?) happenings lately that have eclipsed all others, even the ever-present doing of the politicians: the total solar eclipse and the phenomenon of the idols of Lord Ganesha drinking milk.

There is no apparent connection between the two but for the one given by a DD scientist commentation who waxed eloquent at the sight of the total eclipse. He cried in between bouts of Sanskrit and Bengali as the moon moved in between the sun and the earth to temporarily block out sunlight. And all this coming so soon after the phenomenon of Ganesha drinking milk!' It is difficult to make out what people actually mean when they say something but here the message probably is that while observing the eclipse and carrying out experiments is an indication of our scientific temperament, accepting the fact that an idol made of stone could gulp milk showed us in an irrational mold.

Well, in a way he's right. Our entire study of marble and bronze has shown us that there is no way that an idol made out of these materials could drink milk or any other for that matter. Prima facie, therefore, it does seem ridiculous that on one particular day, a couple of weeks ago, such a phenomenon did take place in Hindu temples all over the world.

Whether stone idols actually took the milk or not could be

a debatable matter but the fact that millions of people all over the world, and not all of them Indians, observed and participated in such a phenomenon and later testified to it is indisputable.

Ill equipped and half baked scientists were quick to cry foul. It's surface tension and mass delusion, they cried.

But in their craze to be classified as modern and, maybe, to catch the next day's headlines, they forgot to apply their minds to two critical questions: why did the phenomenon take place when it did and why was the same thing observed in different places of the globe by completely disparate people?

Seeing is believing and that is the sum and substance of the scientific spirit. If that is so, then is it scientific to ignore the testimony of millions of people on the milk drinking phenomenon?

The scientific explanation of the eclipse came many centuries after man had observed it. At that time if describing it as a warning of the gods was wrong it was equally wrong to deny that such was indeed the case! What I'm saying is that making any statement, of refutation or of acceptance, for a phenomenon without studying it properly is not the scientific way of dealing with it.

Let's take Einstein's theory of gravitation. Before making any remarks for or against it, scientists inquired of ways of proving or disproving it. These methods of course would involve empirical observations which would finally decide the issue this way or that.

It is only when observations had proved Einstein completely right that his theory was given its due place in the scientific lexicon.

Now let's take the observed fact of the idols drinking milk. No doubt it is difficult to understand on the basis of known scientific theories. But facts do not give way to theories but it's the other way around. If a theory cannot explain an observed fact it's the theory that has to go.

The people who raised their voices against the observed fact of the idols drinking milk would do well to ponder over this. Of course, it's possible, that an observed fact would ultimately turn out to be a chimera or a mirage. But we have to prove that and not merely state it.

The eclipse, we now know, is a simply explained natural phenomenon not requiring any supernatural explanations that were once advance to explain it. We know that the earth as a planet of the sun revolves around it and the moon, as a natural satellite of the earth in turn revolves around it. The moon thus has two circular: (lest some scientist takes me on, let me make it clear that I'm using this term not in the mathematical sense motions) one around the earth and the other around the sun.

It is because of these two motions that the lunar and the solar eclipse take place. Lunar eclipse takes place when the earth comes between the moon and the sun, thus preventing sunlight from reaching it.

A solar eclipse takes place when the moon comes between the earth and the sun, thus eclipsing the sun from our view for a short time.

This scientific view of the eclipse not merely explains the phenomenon but also simplifies and demystifies it. Moreover, it can be proved by very simple observations and experiments. Many such phenomenon have been simply explained by scientists, including complicated biological and life generating processes. But many still beg for an explanation.

How about the recently observed fact of a star being older than the universe of which it is part? or of questions like what before the Big Bang? There was a time when hundreds of theories were needed to explain known facts: theories of magnetism, gravitation, motion, genses, structure of the atom, etc. Now most of the known facts can be explained with one single theory. Scientists are now on the search for a unified field theory which will make all other theories in physics redundant and unnecessary.

In due course we may be able to make one theory that would explain phenomenon in other areas as well. May be this theory can explain the milk drinking phenomenon as well. But till that theory comes let us allow a parallel line of knowledge to survive. Kant could bring forward the philosophy of the practical reason to counter some of the deficiencies of the pure reason, why can't we allow the parallel stream, call it religion if you like or anything else, to subsist side by side with science?

In that case the apparent dichotomy of an idol drinking milk while the marble from which it is made refuses to do so will have been resolved.

One is a fact of religion and the other a fact of science. With it will have been eliminated the need for pseudo scientists to make unscientific statements about phenomenon in the other domain.

To the religious his religion and to the scientist his science.

55

THE LARGE EMPTINESS OF SPACE

Would you like to go to space? There are chances that such a possibility may arise in our lifetimes. But before you hop on to a rocket going to space, please pause and try to understand what the hazards are.

Mostly, they result from lack of knowledge and information. I remember how in the early years of air travel, all sorts of ceremonies were performed before a journey. One can hardly imagine a *havan* being performed today before one goes for a ticket by Indian Airlines, unless it is to propitiate the gods to ensure that there is not another strike of the pilots!

With knowledge and experience, most of our fears have gone and that is why we must try to gather knowledge.

About space, most of our information and knowledge is on the basis of speculations. The one most important factor, in space travel is that we are pretty sure that much of it is empty. As we look up at the sky on a clear day and from a deserted and dark spot, we find it crowded with stars and starry objects. But it isn't exactly so.

If the sky above is taken as, say, various peals of onion, all the stars must be distributed on the different peals at various distances, not only from us but also from each other. We know that the universe as such is not static: but that all these star clusters are running away from each other. This implies that once they were very closely clustered around each other; but now they are at increasing distance.

In the 15 billion years that have elapsed since that Big Bang, these distances have become very large indeed. In fact, it is estimated that the closest distance between two such clusters may not be less than many hundred light years, i.e., light will take many hundred years to go from one to the other.

Similar is the position in respect of the stars in these clusters or galaxies. As it is with stars and their planetary configurations. In the Milky Way galaxy, for instance, of which we are a part, there may be many billions of stars and all of them must be many billions of kilometres away from each other. Such is the case with the planetary system too: we must be at least 90 million miles from the sun.

All these features have made the universe so empty that matter may not even occupy one in a billions paces in it. At first, this would appear to make space travel less hazardous and forbidding since there would be less possibilities of accidental collisions.

Wouldn't the roads of Delhi be safer if they were less crowded? So it must surely be with space. But the very factor that makes space attractive for travel also makes for a major hazard. Space is so empty that it is possible for a traveller to go on for billions and billions of years without encountering anything. It's like a train journey in an unending desert.

The biggest hazard of space travel is that we may die before we encounter anything at all. After all, what is a life span of 70-80 years for a journey that may require a billion years to complete!

This large emptiness is a hazard no doubt: but there are ways to encounter it. One obvious way is to increase the speed of travel. Travelling at the speed of most of our rockets today, it is not even possible to reach even the nearest of the stars: at best we can hope to reach some of the planets like Mars or make landings on our Moon. But if we could attain speed close to that of light, many of the stars in the Milky Way galaxy could become accessible to us.

It is quite another matter that such speeds are possible only in the realm of science fiction. But science fiction has a way of coming true. Would then the hazards of space travel go away? Unfortunately no. Because even if space is empty on the large scale, on the small scale it may not be as empty. In addition to the more visible features such as the stars and the planets, which we have seen make out a case for a largely empty space, there may be many more objects that crowd it.

Haven't we all seen shooting stars streaking across the sky and heard of meteorites falling into the ground? We are sure these are not part of the stars and starry clusters that we have been talking of but for sure these are part of the space. No one can deny that these too have to be avoided if safe travel is to be ensured.

But these are too few and too far in between to really constitute a major hazard. But there could be other problems; but one cannot imagine of a single one that man's ingenuity and inventiveness may not be able to overcome.

Unless we are talking of black holes.

There was a time when scientists considered it infra dig to talk of them; and speculations on them were confined to cranks and science fiction writers. But no longer.

It is common scientific knowledge that the heavier a body, the more difficult it is to escape from it. We also know that the higher the velocity of escape from any body, the lesser are the chances of being forced to return.

If we leave the surface of the earth at something more than 7 km/sec speed, we can escape the earth's gravitation for ever. That is, we will not fall back. The escape velocity will be somewhat more for the sun, which is a heavier object than the earth and still more for the other massive and super massive stellar and inter-stellar objects.

Now suppose an object is so massive that its escape velocity is equal to the velocity of light. Such an object would no doubt have to be very massive, but it need not be very large: in fact, it can even be the size of an atom! But in such a case it would have to be very dense indeed.

Now if its escape velocity is more than the velocity of light, it would not be visible since even light could not escape it. But despite its 'blackness', it would still be a massive and very 'attractive' body.

Imagine a space traveller who happened to come near it: poor thing, he would not have any way of knowing about its presence in the area and there is no way he can avoid being sucked into it. To an observer on earth, who is keeping track of the traveller's movements, he will simply vanish: one instant, he was there, the other, not.

Does all this worry you? Let it not. Even if you vanish from the view of the earthlings, there is always a chance of there being a world on the other side of the black hole. And, if there is such a world, time there should be going backward. Think about it. This may not be too bad a prospect for you would have the chance of meeting yourself!

56

BEWARE OF TAMPERING WITH NATURE

Science has placed a tremendous amount of power in our hands; so much, in fact, that we feel we can acquire all of it without any cost. But there is nothing that is a free picnic. Take the case of malaria or the new-found techniques of transplanting animal organs to humans.

In the fight for control over malaria it already seems that mankind no longer has the upper hand.

In the 1950s international health experts thought wonder drugs and insecticides would eliminate malaria completely, just as widespread inoculation programmes have conquered smallpox. For sometime it did seem that such would be the case. In 1947 there were 75 million malaria cases with more than three quarter of a million deaths. By 1965 the cases had come down sharply to less than a lakh with, may be, not more than a couple of hundred deaths. It was natural to assume that soon we would be in control over the most potent of scourges that plagued us over the years.

But it was not to be. Last year the number of infections zoomed to more than 15 millions with many thousand fatalities. And what is most disturbing is the fact that behind this increase is the inexplicable rise in the P falciparum strain which, while it always existed in India, always accounted for a small number of cases. Now it outstrips the more common strains.

Pfalciparum is more difficult to diagnose than the ordinary

strain as it does not alway produce the shivering that is otherwise the hallmark of the disease and may not even show up in the blood test. Most disturbingly, even when it shows the common symptoms, there is a potential trap.

Most people are familiar with malaria and feel that it can be controlled with over-the-table drugs. That kind of self-diagnosis has become dangerous. Pfalciparum has developed resistance to the most widely used anti-malaria drugs, chloroquine and it reproduces with a devastating speed.

People who believe in nature cure and use of herbs and other natural elements for treatment have always been warning against the excessive use of drugs in treatment. But, so remarkable was the impact on disease cure and control, that their warnings were rarely heeded. But now the time has come to give it a second thought.

An area in which science is soon assuming a godly role is in the area of organ transplants. I personally felt the dramatic impact of this new technology when my sister's son received a kidney transplant from his mother to replace both his kidneys that had packed up following a urinary tract problem. The young man, left for dead by one of the leading West Delhi hospitals following this failure, now leads a near normal life.

From kidneys to the heart and then to almost all other organs in the body—that is how the technique has been extended. The only problem, it seemed, was the lack of donors. But now, with the news of animal transplants, this problem too seems to be receding. But the question that arises is: are animal transplants really safe for humans?

Pigs have been used as a source for transplants for items ranging from fatal brain tissue, heart valves and blood vessels to heart, liver and the pancreatic cells that secrete insulin. From baboon's heart, liver, kidneys and even bone marrow have been taken.

While this technology seems revolutionary, there is a small chance that could some day unleash a medical disaster. The danger is that patients could receive a previously unknown microbe along with the transplant. In the past when viruses or bacteria made the jump from animals to humans the results have been chilling. Remember HIV, the virus which causes AIDS?

No one had to worry about such hazards so far because there was no way that such transplants could be made. When even human tissues were not being accepted by the immune system, how could one trick the system to accept a tissue from an entirely different species?

But the advent of genetic engineering threateris to change all this. It is now possible for scientists to alter the genetic make up of animals especially pigs. The organs of such genetically altered animals have successfully been transplant into other animals on an experimental basis and more experiments are on the cards on human subjects as well.

And this is where the danger lies, especially when such techniques become successful. HIV virus somehow crossed the barrier between the baboons and humans; god alone knows how many such virus lie lurking in lower animals. Once these viruses get transferred to a human body and if they are really dangerous, it's conceivable that they could spread to many victims before revealing their deadly nature.

The dangers of trying to tamper with nature have been amply highlighted both in the case of the malaria control programme and the use of animal transplants. Should we, because of this, give up these methods of disease control and let natural processes prevail?

The success of the scientific method in the past has been tremendous, both in terms of the progress made to reduce the tedium and humdrum of life as also to control disease and pestilence. We cannot reverse the flow of time without causing tremendous harm to the cause of development and progress. But at the same time we cannot forget that this development is not without its own problems.

Like the industrial revolution, which gave us untold material, wealth and power but at the cost of the environment, the progress in the medical sciences is also exacting its own price. All this shows that there is a balance in nature and whatever we do disturbs it somehow. In many cases the disturbance may be desirable (as in the case of distribution of wealth) but sometimes the same disturbance may have a price. The pros and cons of disturbing nature's balance need to be carefully weighed.

Ultimately there is no free picnic. What nature gives us in one hand has to be paid for by the other. What one would like to know is whether the price being paid is well worth the benefit.

57

CONSCIENCE IN SCIENCE

It was only the other day as I was reading a science fiction story 'Einstein the Second' written by Laxman Londhe included in the collection of short stories brought out by the National Book Trust? 'It happened tomorrow', that I was reminded of a letter written by Albert Einstein to President Roosevelt about the urgency for the Americans to make the atom bomb. All this forced my attention on the issue of conscience in science.

Einstein, when he was informed of fission being performed in a aboratory by Otto Hahn, a non-Jew German working in Nazi Germany, immediately penned a letter to Roosevelt urging him to start work on the atom bomb before Hitler made one. It is one of history's important footnotes that, when the allies took over Germany, their laborious researchers did not give away any clue about the efforts of the Germans to make the bomb.

It is interesting that but for Otto Hahn's himself telling Einstein about his important research, there was no way for the eminent scientist to know about it. And the reason for giving this information was because of Hahn's implicit faith in the German scientists working in USA of not misutilising this information.

There is no doubt that when Einstein wrote the letter to Roosevelt, he was sure that Hahn would pass on the results of his researches to Hitler which would enable the latter to make the ultimate weapon. On the other hand he felt, that even if the bomb were made by the Western powers, its use would be purely defensive and tampered with conscience.

History tells us an entirely different tale. While Hahn succumbed to the dictates of his conscience and kept the important information to himself, Roosevelt did not do justice to the confidence reposed in him by the US scientific community and not only made the bomb but also used it as a weapon of destruction against the Japanese.

Laxman Londhe puts this true incident to good use in his fictionalised account on 'Einstein the Second'. Here Srinivasan is carrying on research on what even the great Einstein could not finish, i.e., the unified field theory.

In his theory of relativity, Einstein was able to work out the relationship between matter and energy; thus making them interchangeable and interconvertable. What Hahn had discovered in the lab would have been impossible to understand had not Einstein worked out the relationship between matter and energy.

In fact, what Hahn had found was that while breaking up particular atom (fission) there was a certain loss of mass; that is there was a breakdown of the law of conversation of mass. Since Einstein had already given the equation, the famous $e=mc^2$, of conversion of mass to energy, it was easy to understand. This opened ahead of what Einstein had done: Srinivasan is close to achieving a breakthrough in working out the theory which will not only explain the strong forces within the nucleus of the atom but will also explain the weak forces like gravity.

If the theory of relativity gave up power over the atom, Srinivasan's unified theory could give us control over gravity. This would make it possible to travel throughout the universe, and thus be in a position to control it. The problem here is not the conscience of Srinivasan, as was the case with Hahn, but the fact that Srinivasan has cancer and there is no way to make him live long enough for his work to be completed.

The cancer specialist, Chitale is put under tremendous pressure to save him; but there is no way that he can do it. The only way that he can suggest is to let Srinivasan's body die and somehow keep the brain alive.

Srinivasan will not even hear this suggestion: to live as a brain without a body is a possibility that he can't even imagine. He refuses. The dilemma before Chitale now is: should he perform the operation to save the brain without the approval of the subject?

He decides exactly the way the great Einstein had himself decided, wrote that letter to prevent telt. And there was nothing from doing, Srinivasan could do to the all powerful surgeon ring the operation.

So it came about that while Srinivasan's body was allowed to die, his brain was saved and it could carry on the research. It is at this juncture that Srinivasan, albeit in brain form only, started having qualms of conscience.

If a surgeon of the eminence of Chitale could defy the Hippocrates oath and, against Srinivasan's wishes, save his brain, what not could the politicians and bureaucrats do? Einstein's theory only led to spread of evil on this earth; the unified theory could easily lead to the spread of this evil in the whole of the universe!

The story ends very neatly thereafter. On the day fixed for the unified theory to be given by the brain; all the top brass is assembled. And the voice-box, attached to the brain, comes to life. But what emerges is not the theory in any form that could be understood but in the form of a graph that would not be deciphered for the next two centuries.

Srinivasan was lucky: at least his conscience woke up before it was too late. Not all scientists may be equally lucky, as was the case with Einstein, and they may have to suffer the pangs of conscience when it is too late.

It is time for all scientists to get alerted to the fact that science without a conscience is like a time bomb whose controls are in the hands of a soulless monster. Science can no longer be an end in itself; it must satisfy the aspirations of humanity and be in accordance with a universal conscience.

PART 11

OF KHANS AND BOLLYWOOD

58

THE CINEMA CRITIC AS AN ARTIST

Sometimes National Awards for films have a real surprise. For example, when I heard the announcement 'the award for the best film critic has gone to Gautam Kaul'. Really it was a matter of happiness for all the people who are interested in cinema.

Most of the people were interested to know, 'Gautam Kaul, who'?

Gautam Kaul of the Indian Police Service, of course! A writer in uniform!

The announcement clears a long persisting doubt: can a creative mind be put down? If even the debilitating burden of a police uniform could not put down Kaul's creative interests, why should anything else? Or, for that matter, for anybody else.

I knew about Kaul's multifarious interests (including his collection of old records) but had not read any of his comments on films since I was not a subscriber of the papers in which he wrote; so I obtained a copy of his reviews for the last one year. There was a pleasant surprise in store.

These were not reviews at all; it was a treasure house of information and comment on cinema. Where else could one have discovered that the earliest doyens of cinema journalism, people like Babu Rao Patel, V.P. Patel, K.A. Abbas and B.D.Garga in Mumbai and Chidananda Dasgupta in Kalkatta, through their film appreciation, affected the social styles and made people take serious notice of cinema?

I learnt that it was with the release of V. Shantaram's 'Aadmi', with Sahu Modak and Shanta Hublikar in the lead, that the first film centring significantly on a policeman was created. It will surprise present day audiences, used to a very negative portrayal of the police, that Shantaram had created the policeman's character to signify the importance of adherence to one's professional 'Dharma'!

Though more than 400 films have since been made with a role for the policeman, notes Kaul wistfully, their 'total impact has not been appreciable'. But the police woman, on the other hand, has had a more positive portrayal, thanks largely to the high profile Kiran Bedi whose 'professional activities have caught the imagination of Indians'.

If this is so, Mr Kaul, and cinema mirrors reality, as it does in the case of the police woman, then the 'bloody, noisy and brutal' image of Kiran Bedi's male counterpart is also similarly true? One wonders if this critic in uniform would agree that at least it reflects the policeman's image in the eyes of the people, if nothing else!

Gautam Kaul is generally very soft on Indian cinema; but when it comes to a crunch he minces no words. In his piece on 'Why no Oscar for Indian films' he lashes out at the films that are entered for the award. 'Indian films meant for the American market are those which have hi-tech qualities, some polished performance by artists, good camera work and meticulous film editing. Nothing more than that.' He goes on: 'They were not typically Indian, their themes weak...and the films did not have original ideas'. He is talking of films like 'Nayakan', 'Parinda' and 'Anjali', all sacred cows of the art-cum-commercial circuit.

It is also a revelation to learn that out of the six major schools of classical dances, Bharat Natyam, Kathak, Manipuri, Kathakali, Mohini Attam and Odissi, only the first three have been able to make inroads in our films.

Did you know that Sadhana Bose and Sitara Devi were the earliest dancers on the screen? Or that the golden age of classical dances hit Indian films in 1951 with the rise of

Vyjyantimala in 'Bahar'; that she was followed by the Travancore sisters and then by Waheeda Rehman?

The period of classical dances in Hindi movies took a 'bump' with the advent of Helen Ann Robinson, known to generations of movie-goers as simply Helen. Her beauty and the beast cabaret sequence in 'Inteqaam' ranks still amongst her best shows on the screen, imitated, though poorly, by Japanese girls in Tokyo and Hong Kong.

Since then the dance form in films was commercialised and this led to the development of the so-called folk dance cliche, where the story writer provides an interlude for the stars to participate or watch a tribal dance.

Another aspect of film making in India that has drawn scathing criticism from Kaul is the 'tendency to copy'.

'Script writers in Mumbai have never had it so good since this machine called VCR hit the road....Sitting in the cool comfort of one of the many hotels on the Juhu Beach, the venerable scriptwriter is busy "doing research" on the next project for his producer who wants a new subject ready in the next 72 hours.

Kaul lists a long lineage of 'original' copies starting with 'Bhagyawan' which was a frame by frame copy of the Japanese award winning film 'Yukiwarisoo' in 1952. With this the flood gates opened. "Kohraa" (Rebecca), "Do Kaliaan" (The Parent Trap), "Ek Phool Do Kante" (Fanny), "Parichay" (The Sound of Music), "Koshish" (Happiness of Us Alone), "Hum To Tere Ashik", "Raja Jani" and "Man Pasand" (My Fair Lady), "Suhana Safar" (Roman Holiday), "Aitbar" (Dial M For Murder), "Boxer & Rustam" (The Champ), "Qayamat" (Cape Fear), "Armaan" (Casablanca), "Baazi" (Working Tall), "Tumhare Bina" (Kramer vs Kramer), "Love Story" (Friends), "Shaan" (Goldfinger), "Sunayana" (Limelight), "Hamare Tumhare" (Yours, Mine and Ours), "Chanda Aur Bijli" (Oliver Twist), "O Bewafa" (The Other Side of Midnight), "Bereham" (The Night of the Generals), "Masoom" (Man, Woman and Child), "Satte Pe Satta" (Seven Brides For Seven Brothers), "Insaaf Ka Tarazu" (Lipstick), "Zanzeer & Khoon-Khoon" (Dirty Harry), "Dharmatma" (Godfather) and so on.

The list is so long that it should put to shame all but the most shameless; but that must be the case with the so called script writers of Mumbai for the process of copying continues.

Does it reflect a lack of ability on their part or a lack of confidence of producers and directors in their abilities?

In a country where top writers like Bhagavati Charan Verma have written for films and where writers like Sarat Chander and Tagore have formed the inspiration for some of the best films, it is difficult to understand why film makers resort to open plagiarism! Unless they suffer from total bankruptcy.

Cinema as one of the important literary forms should also be created from its roots and should also be rooted in the soil in which it grows. In case our film makers are not willing to behave in a responsible manner, the viewing public must intervene by boycotting such films and ensuring their commercial failure.

It is heartening, though, that while in many ways films may not have lived up to the needs of being an important literary form, film criticism in the hands of Gautam Kaul and his like has come of age and succeeded in creating a literary form and style of its own.

59

OF ACTORS AND ACTING

For his acting in the movie "Khamoshi", veteran actor Nana Patekar has come in for a lot of flak. And the reason is—I have no doubt that Nana is not going to like it one bit—that he took the title of the movie literally and kept his mouth shut. One reads that chairs were broken in certain cinema halls of UP where, it seems, people had gone to hear Nana's commanding voice and not just see his tantrums.

Poor Nana, what else could he have done? After all, the movie wanted him to be dumb and deaf; and if a dumb person could speak, he wouldn't be dumb, would he?

There are even reports that the distributor of the film for Delhi has threatened to demand refund of part of the Rs 1.25 crore that he paid for the territory unless Nana's voice is dubbed into the print!

For a film actor to be told that without his voice he is no good must be distressing, especially if, like Nana, he has first made his mark on the stage. It is on the stage that modulations of the voice play a key role in an actor's performance. Not so in film, which is a medium of close ups and even minor variations in facial expression can be communicated to the viewer.

Film actors take pride in their expressions and many an acting school teaches them to act without dialogues. In fact, Sunil Dutt first made his mark in a movie where not a single dialogue is spoken.

What would be particularly galling to the veteran actor

would be the unflattering comparisons being made with Sanjeev Kumar's acting in the film of the same name; also the fact that the other actors in the film, even the aging sex siren Helen, have won a lot of admiration for their roles.

While Nana was receiving flak, virtual doll, actors like Salman Khan were receiving praise. In fact, it was he who made the last scene where he interprets Nana's gestures in the Church after his daughter's wedding to Salman. But for his voice, this scene too would have left the movie goers in UP breaking their seats in despair!

Salman Khan is good but the real surprise of the movie is Helen. I remember when Helen first appeared on the film firmament; that was the time when Cuckoo held the fort as far as sex sirens were concerned. Please remember that like the almost mandatory dishum dishum, now, a song and dance item from Cuckoo was a must.

Helen swept everything in her conquering march; even Cuckoo could not stop her winning the hearts of the masses. She had what masses love the most: sex appeal. But as to her pretensions for being an actress, the less said the better.

But it must be said for her that unlike Cuckoo, Helen loved to act and played a role in many a film. But she did not make any waves, at least not of the type that she expected. She did get laughs but not for her acting talent but for the very anglicised dialogue delivery.

In Khamoshi, Helen plays a grandmother, a role as far removed from her traditional role of vamp as the stars are from each other. Imagine the plight of the mother of a deaf and dumb child who, far from seeking solace in company, actually shuns it and lives in a shell of his own making. He marries another deaf and dumb person and the two together forge an independent, though rebellious, world.

Helen is a child of the world, loving all its sights and sounds; but is tied by love to the 'silences' that her son has built around himself. She becomes silent herself, resigned to her fate. But then suddenly something happens that changes the world around her: a 'normal' daughter is born to her son, an event which brings great joy and happiness to the deaf and dumb couple.

Now comes the best part of the movie, a period in which the deaf-mute couple celebrates the festival of life through Helen. The colour of the sky, the sounds of the sea and the silences of the heavens suddenly blend together as Helen puts on her dancing shoes and her melodious voice reverberates into the sorrowful and hitherto silent life of her son.

Her joie de vivre is infectious: one wants to start dancing in one's seat. Helen is great; even in her old age, she exudes grace and, yes, let me admit it, sex.

The biggest mistake the director of the movie made was to let her die before the end; with her demise ended the only chance the movie had of becoming a great hit. Which potential it had with the surprisingly good performance of Salman Khan and expectedly brilliant performance of Manisha Koirala, who, now it seems, has finally taken on the mantle of Madhuri Dixit.

Why did Nana fail? This is an issue that is going to keep film writers and film buffs debating for a long time. It can't just be that he was not allowed to use his voice; if voice was that critical a resource for the actor, how would one explain the brilliance of Charlie Chaplin and the other silent stars?

I feel a part of Nana's failure can be laid at the door of the director. Like any other deaf-mute, Nana is too riddled with complexes to behave and act in a rational manner but while he can be *khamosh*, what prevents him from doing *koshish*? I'll commend a visit to a school like the Lady Noyce School for the deaf and dumb in Delhi: what marks out the children here is the *koshish*, element.

A deaf person can't speak not because there's something wrong with his tongue but because he can't hear; since speech has to imitate, not hearing makes him dumb too. But sophisticated equipment can change the scenario somewhat; so there's nothing wrong with a dumb child trying to speak.

It is heart-rending to see a child do that: only squeaks and squalls come out of his throat. But it is elevating all the same, especially when one realises that the only way to communicate is not through speech. Which one of us has not seen a monkey or even a dumb animal communicating?

I only wish Nanal's character had not been made just a negative and angry one; then at least we would have been witness to his desperate strivings to try to communicate. That alone would have added a new dimension to the movie and maybe given a new edge to Nana's acting. Let us hope that the director will take to heart this lesson for his next movie.

In the meantime, I can only sympathise with Delhi-UP territory distributor's desperate attempts to give Nana's voice to the dumb and mute character that he plays.

60

OF BOLLYWOOD AND 'DOCTORED' SCRIPTS

There is an interesting story of one of our own Bollywood film makers who recently returned from the mecca of movie making with the story of how script doctors had vastly improved the chances of the commercial success of Hollywood movies.

Immediately he summoned his army of technicians, hangers on and *chamchas* who, in Bollywood, constitute the creative team and demanded: "I must have the script of my forthcoming film doctored!"

The members of the creative team exchanged anxious glances: Has Sethji lost his head or what, they wondered. How the hell can you doctor a script that has never been written?

Scripts in Bollywood are rarely, if ever, written. In fact producers would consider it a total waste of money were they to be forced to write one.

What would surely warm the cockles, of our desi film makers is the fact that as much as a hundred thousand dollars per week have to be spent to have a script rewritten! I wonder how many of our own producers are willing to pay this much in rupees for the script to be written in the first place?

A number of smash hits have recently been shown in the US, the scripts of which had been 'doctored' by a professional. In fact, so much in the faith that people there seem to have in the ability of these people that even famous and successful directors like Kevin Costner get their scripts doctored.

The idea of engaging a script doctor must be quite foreign to people who consider script writing as an art which some people are endowed with. And, naturally, it is they who have the art anyway. So why waste money and time on engaging a professional when the same money can be spent on choreography or writing lyrics?

It is wrong to think that script and screenplay writing is an art: at least not in the sense that essay writing or poetry is. Or in the sense that writing a novel or a short story is.

It is true that like many other forms of creative work, be it the work of an artisan or that of an engineer, script writing too needs a knack and some innate talent. But like them, it also needs a lot of training and practical experience as well.

It is true in a way that there are distinct features of each one of these literary forms. It is also true that these features can lend themselves to some sort of an analysis and some principles and precepts can be worked out. But all this still doesn't make them into a science in any meaningful way.

For instance, a short story has some distinct features which distinguish it from a novel or an essay. But the mere study of these features cannot make a good story writer. In fact umpteen successful writers have proved that it is not even necessary to have a good knowledge of these features to write a good short story.

But this is not true of a script writer. In many respect the art of script writing is not an art at all: it is a science. And like any other science it has its own set of rules which can be clearly defined and laid down. And though the literature on the subject is not as extent as one would like it to be, it is there and can be had from a good book shop.

At the heart of a good script is the 'dramatic structure', an area which has been written innumerable times by dramatists and even by novelists. No dramatic structure is possible without 'A person with a problem'.

A beautiful girl crossing the road is hardly a subject for a dramatic structure. But when she is noticed by a possible rapist she becomes a 'A person with a problem' and thus a subject for the building up of a dramatic structure.

But the 'person with the problem' alone is not enough. The person should be one who should involve the audience emotionally. If a murderer is running away from the police, he is no doubt a person with a problem, but hardly a person who can involve the audience.

It is not that a person running away from the police can never be a 'hero', take Bhagat Singh as an example. The important thing here is the 'commitment' of the hero or protagonist Bhagat Singh is hero material since his commitment is both strong and with which we can easily identify.

Just like Bhagat Singh is hero material for us General Dyer may be hero material for the British audience. So not only has the script writer not to keep in mind the fact that a needs a committed person with a problem he also has to ensure that both the person and the problem involve the audience for whom the movie is being made.

We have now arrived at three key words in relation to a script: person, problem commitment. But is this enough? No, we have to now devise incidents that involve this person in dramatic situation. And dramatic situations are not merely situations in which the heroine is hanging on a cliff while the hero battles the villains.

The most dramatic situations are the one where the hero confronts himself; that is he is in two minds on which path to take. If he acts in a certain way he ends up in jail; and if he does the other thing his girl friend leaves him. The agony of the hero in such situations will be such that it will involve the entire audience and make them ache along with our hero.

There are many other obstacles to be crossed before the script can be completed; many other rules that tell you about the phasing of the so-called confrontations and how they peak to the final confrontation called the climax, how and what the valleys in between the peaks, called the transitions should contain; there are rules of dialogue writing and composition and many other areas. But remember none of these will work unless you have a person with a strong commitment who has a problem.

The script doctor, I'm sure, does nothing but analyse the script to see that the essential features are there he is a scientist who has no pretensions to be creative. But how useful he is to the ultimate success of film is clear from the box office success of umpteen Hollywood films.

Are you listening Bollywood? Are you now willing to recognise that a script writer is necessary to the making of the movies just as much as the moneyed man and the creative director?

PART 12

THE BIG-SMALL SCREEN

61
BRINGING WORDS TO LIFE

Having made more than 50 stories from world literature for the small screen in last few years, I am still not sure if I can make the 51st. Every time you take a short story it is a challenge; but none was more challenging than the Roald Dahl story 'Lamb to the Slaughter'.

There are always problems when it comes to translating anything to any other media but the most complicated of all is to bring good literature to the small screen.

On the surface the Dahl story is a simple one about a simple woman, already 6 months into her pregnancy. Her sharply focused life seems to have a single objective: to find happiness and joy in the company of her policeman husband.

She has naturally assumed that what is true for her is also true for her husband.

It is, therefore, a great surprise to her when, on return from work one evening, he lets go his apparently long pent up feelings and asks for a divorce.

Dahl, great writer that he is, does not tell what he actually said; all that he writes about is the effect that all this had on her. While writing the screen play I had to know exactly what he must have said: actually this was key to understanding her subsequent actions.

Dahl not only does not write anything about this but does not give any hints also. He is making full use of the media in which he is operating and feels that this may be the best way to give full freedom to the reader's imagination.

This in turn will be conditioned by the background and the environment of the reader.

While writing the screenplay I could not adopt a similar technique; if I had allowed lip movement on the screen without words coming out, this would have an entirely different connotation. On the other hand, if the whole scene were removed, it would be impossible for the viewer to understand her subsequent actions in which she kills him with a violent blow of the frozen leg of a lamb.

This brings to the fore the problems of writing a script for a film or a TV play. The script writer has to now make his imagination run around to pick up the threads that the writer had woven and which he had decided not to share with the reader. While doing this he has to be careful not to jar too much the sensibilities of the viewer and also conform broadly to the intentions of the writer.

This problem creates both an opportunity as well as a challenge. The opportunity comes because he can now create characters who behave and act more in conformity with the expectations of the audience for whom the film is being made. This may often be quite different from the one for whom the story may have been written.

This is especially the case with a story like 'Lamb to the Slaughter'. This story has characters who would normally find no parallel in our country. Superficially speaking, could one imagine of a beat constable in our country who would have roast leg of lamb for dinner?

Since the leg of the lamb is key to the subsequent development of the story, this would prove a fatal flaw to any screenplay.

And this was the major problem that I faced. I knew that this problem had to be resolved before I even thought of picking up the pen. And there were other developments which would have to tie up with whatever solution that I found for this problem.

Ironical that it may seem, it is here that the opportunity came my way. To involve an Indian audience with what was essentially a European situation I had to change the characters and the situation anyway. Once I had done that, I had to find out motives and actions that would suit Indian characters.

Why would an Indian wife murder her husband? That too an husband whom she dearly and fondly loves.

The answer really is obvious once you get down to it; she will do it to save someone she really loves more. It obviously cannot be another man; it must be someone dear to both of them. It is clear that this person must be their child.

Once this decision is taken the rest is easy. If it is child vs father, then the only person who could be endangering the safety of the child must be the father himself. But why should the father do that?

The issue here is not why any father should do that but why our policeman father decides to act against the interest of the child.

These are both interesting thoughts and apart from giving a new interpretation to the original. Dahl story also have the merit of being more intelligible to an Indian audience.

It also gives the script writer an opportunity of delving into the psyche of the police which has lately been the subject matter of much comment.

Many incidents have taken place in the capital recently which have invited comment from many of the leading intelligentsia. This has brought to the fore issues related to the police.

Many years back 'Ardh Satya' discussed some issues relating to police violence and brutality. This film drew the conclusion that while incidents of police brutality come to the fore, the other part of the truth remains hidden beneath the surface.

This made in many respects this film an apologia for the

police and many of their shocking actions. But what this film failed to bring out was the point of view of the victims of police brutality, most of whom are innocent like the wife in Dahl's story.

When atrocities are committed on the innocent how is he to respond? And if he does respond the way that the police officer in 'Ardh Satya' does, what should be the punishment?

The issue raised by Dahi is: is the lamb always to be led to the slaughter or is there a way for it to retaliate as well? It is this issue that has to be dealt with in the film as well.

How well this was done our audiences have had an opportunity to decide since the film version had been shown on our telly already (Jharokha 7.30 p.m. DD Metro, April 21 and 28). But in two parts. But, merit or otherwise, at least it enabled such a key issue to be raised. And that is what good literature and a good film is all about.

62

DD IN SEARCH OF LUCRE

Organisations in India have become money minded and Doordarshan is no exception. It, too, wants to make money, just like any other commercial organisation.

Did I hear right? Did I say like any other commercial organisation! In which case they would have to more than quadruple their income for the premier electronic media is revenue form commercial; and this source too became significant with the advent of the sponsored programmes way back in the early eighties. The first of such programme was the rather famous, even though tame, Hum Log which ran for weeks and weeks and earned millions for the media.

After this there was no stopping doordarshan; their revenues steadily increased till, before the advent of the satellite, it reached the astronomical figure of about Rs. 300 crore. If there was any fear that competition would bring down this figure it was soon dispelled and the figure this year is likely to be of the order of Rs. 400 crore or so.

This seems to be a considerable achievement but remember that the non-plan budget of the organisation (largely used to pay off the establishment costs only) is at least twice that amount! Thus, if Doordarshan were a private organisation it would be losing as much money as it was earning and all this on the current account!

Now let us come to the problem of how to make DD a commercially viable set up. At the very least we will have to earn an extra Rs. 400 crore per annum to meet the current account deficit. This would still leave the problem of paying depreciation on the fixed assets and interest on borrowed capital.

Is it possible for DD to earn an èxtra Rs 400 crore every year? I find a lot of fingers raised. They point out to the money earned recently from the decision taken to auction slots on Chitrahaar and feature films. A feature film can earn as much as a crore of rupees; in this way if we can auction a film everyday, we can easily earn Rs 300 crore in the year. Q.E.D.

Seems simple enough, doesn't it? But is it so? Let us try to view the problem from another angle. Where does the money come from? The total income of DD reflects their income from commercials and this comes from the budgets of one or other of the big companies.

It is estimated that the total money that is budgeted in India every year by the private companies for brand promotion and for promotion of brands is of the order of Rs 1300 crore or so. This money is spent on promotion on various media: the electronic media is only one of the channels for spending the money. The other channels are radio, the print media, hoardings and bill boards and other promotion channels like giving of free samples.

At a very rough guess, 50 per cent of this amount is spent on the electronic media. This high figure is taken because of the higher mileage that this media gives, especially because of the better penetration, higher reach and more impact. Even at this high figure this comes to an amount of Rs 650 crore or so.

It is clear that the maximum that DD can earn is still Rs 150 crore short of the figure that would at least make it meet its current expenditure. And remember that the developmental expenditure of DD is not less than the amount that it spends for its day to day needs.

There is no way that DD can take the entire amount that industry spends for its day to day needs.

There is no way that DD can take the entire amount that industry spends on the electronic media, even if it were the most efficient organisation in the world, which mercifully it is not. With the most efficient management it can best pick up another Rs 100 crore or so over and above the Rs 100 crore or so that it picks up now.

When DD tries new and better methods to increase it revenues, let it remember these limits: there is no way that it can collect more than what these limits allow. What this means is that if DD can collect Rs 300 crore by auctioning feature film slots, Rangoli and Chitrahaar, this cannot be taken as a net ditation to its revenue: this increase will beat the cost of a loss of revenue in some other area. This area is not the Zee channel; nor it is the print media or the giving of free samples: it will have to be some other chunk of DD itself.

If commercials start coming on the film channel; it well mean that much less money available for spots on serials and sports programmes.

Considering that the total cannot go up much, it is idiotic to carry out such cosmetics like auctioning of the film and Rangoli slots. The film may become popular but it will be at the cost of the serial. Let DD realise that by weakening the serial DD is only destroying its own base and independence. The film under no circumstances can be taken as a programme in which DD has played any role whatsoever. On the other hand no serial could have come up without the support and active participation and encouragement of the authorities of DD.

A serial is out and out a DD programme whereas a film is no. Once DD kills the serial it will find itself so much open to blackmail by Bollywood that it may not find itself easy to extricate itself. Let them turn their pages backward; they will find how easy it is for Bollywood to blackmail them.

No, Sir. There is no way that DD can ensure its pre-eminent position by merely trying innovations like auctioning of slots and putting unfair pressure on the makers of serials by insisting on more spots. Let DD not dill the hen that lays the golden egg. Already by auctioning of the feature film it has laid the foundation for the ultimate demise of the Metro channel, so painstakingly built up by the sweat and labour of many like us who spent so much effort and money in the initial period. Wake up DD. Tomorrow may be too late.

63

HOW LONG CAN WE RESIST TEMPTATION?

I can resist everything but temptation. I resisted cable TV for a long time, but then I succumbed. As if it was inevitable, we finally got the cable installed the other day.

It has always been like this with me. I can never stick to my convictions with a strong heart. It had been the same with colour televisions. I had totally barred its entry into my house when it first became popular at the time of the Aslad. But then, peer pressure compelled me to fall in and in both the cited cases, the peers happened to be none other than my own flesh and blood.

And in each of these cases, I realized later, that I was wrong. In the case of the colour television I was opposed to it on national and global considerations. I felt that our poor nation can hardly afford the luxury of colour television when the coverage of even black and white TV as so poor. The priority, instead ought to be on expanding the cheaper black and white television rather than spend money on what would ultimately make TV elitist and class centred.

The fact that about half the television sets in the country are in the four major metros really proves that my fears were right. But I was wrong was in assuming that the country really favoured an egalitarian and classless social structure.

If I had denied my family access to a colour television they really would have been left out of the race and would have become socially ostracized without the country having gained an Iota in the process.

The same would have been the case if I had denied cable connection to my family though I am not sure if they would have been total losers.

My objections to the cable connection were more complicated and weighty than my objections to the colour TV. Having too many channels does not necessarily mean more and better entertainment. In many cases it only means that you do not see any programme in full and spend most of your time merely switching channels.

Moreover, disputes would go up and ultimately result in demands for another. TV, which may be painful for the pockets. I find that though we have had the cable only for a couple of weeks already I can hear demands in this respect.

Now that I have watched cable TV for some time, my earlier view against cable TV in the house has been strengthened, but with a slight variation. Though I do not want cable in my home, I sincerely welcome the introduction of the system. It has undoubtedly introduced an element of competition in the field and that can only have good result in the long run.

Another aspect that one had heard of foreign networks was not really true. At least it doesn't come out of the few channels that I have watched so far. Let us take the much touted BBC news.

All the visuals and the otherwise excellent coverage cannot hide the fact that it is all irrelevant. Whatever they show as news can be called anything but news at least as far as we in this country are concerned. It is true that this may have some curiosity value for us since we come to know things such as this are happening in some part of the world or other. But it is certainly not news.

One must admit though that outside the news segment there is also an occasional documentary or programme that is both informative and interesting. The same is true of other programme on the umpteen number of other channels.

Whatever these channels may lack, one aspect comes out in abundance and that is the technical excellence and professionalism that they have attained. This aspect becomes even more heightened when we watch our own channels, especially the so called national channels.

It's not just the programmes. They may be good or bad depending on the maker and this proportion of good programmes may not be much less than it is on the other channels. But the obvious lack of professionalism comes out most starkly when you hear the in between programme announcements or when one has to watch the clock for long stretches of time or when one is simply floored by looking at the camera black.

Not all DD channels are so bad; the metro channel is a case in mind. One wonders how one set of people can do such a good job and how another set of their colleagues can fail in the same job. One cannot help wondering if factors other than the technical competence of people are at work here.

Another factor that strikes one after watching all these channels is the increasing commercialisation of the media. Almost all good programmes, on whichever channel, are crowded with commercials. And what is remarkable is the fact that most of these commercials are comparable in quality to the best of programmes.

While watching these commercials it does strike how few are the companies that can afford to advertise on TV. I tried to make an inventory and could not count more than a dozen companies who have programmes on air on any day. What one shudders to think is the fate of the media in the hands of so few marketing and media managers of these few companies.

Even under government control, the media, it may be argued, was in the hands of a few dozen bureaucrats; so what if the control has now passed into the hands of a few MBAs and chartered accountants?

No harm, except that the motivations of the two groups are different. While the bureaucrats were supposed to remain within the confines of law and policy laid down by a popularly elected government, media and marketing managers have aims which are much more confined and commercial.

Progress is not a hand malden of logic; nor is it a friend of the past. It has its own inevitability and moving logic. Like it or not, it is there. Either we go with it or allow ourselves to be buried in the graveyard of oblivion.

PART 13

OUR CITY

64

MONUMENTAL DISREGARD

Delhi is a city of monuments: Such as India Gate, the Red Fort, Qutub Minar... and the *Hindustan Times*. Or so a number of hoardings that have suddenly appeared on New Delhi roads would have us believe.

A monument has more than one aspect: But the one that is most glaring is the fact that it is rigid and unchanging, transfixed as it is to an era long gone by. And it is this aspect that struck me as I read the *Hindustan Times* editorial 'Doctor's Collectors' (October 28, 1992).

Apart from being factually incorrect, the editorial displays monumental disregard for the times when, while recognizing that 'the ideology and purpose of administration may have changed in post-independence India, it still insists that there is little provocation for changing its style'!

One would have forgiven the editor for writing for the sake of style had he not gone on from there to give the most damning indictment to date of the much respected Indian scientific and technical community which occupies, at least in numbers, the third position in the world.

'In fact, the experiment of inducting highly qualified technical persons into the administrative services has caused an erosion both in the administrator's paternalistic content and in the individual administrator's value system, resulting in widespread corruption and inefficiency'.

Even knowing that few people read editorials with any amount of seriousness I am still provoked to respond. And that is as much as a sop to my hurt sentiments for the edification of the learned editor, whom I respect.

For one, it is factually incorrect: If there was an experiment to induct experts into administration, it is a secret to me. The fact that a large number of engineers and doctors have managed to get into professional colleges. Unless we remove merit as a criteria for selection, there is no way that we can keep these people out.

For another, I do not agree with people who want more paternalistic content in the administrative system, which is a relic of its Mughal and British past. The memories of the *angrez mai baap* government are too recent to forget. I had taken it for granted that the epoch making events that culminated with the unfurling of the Tricolor at midnight in August, 1947, would destroy the *raison d'etre* of the ancient administrative structure. But it seems that some people insist on clinging to a past that is long dead and gone.

Does a free India deserve no better than an administrative apparatus designed to keep it under colonial servitude?

It may be so that the administrative style that we have inherited has served us well and so should not necessarily need to change, but even so do the new challenges of science and technology not require new responses?

Lord Mountbatten found that the complex apparatus of the Indian secretariat system, based as it was on system of check and counter-checks, was ideally suited to ensure business when nothing was really being done.

Maybe such a system was needed by the British Home Office to ensure its monopoly of power in India. But now?

It is difficult to agree with the argument that changes are not required in the administrative structure, whether it is in its style or substance. There is much that is wrong in our administrative system, but that blame cannot be put on the people with technical qualifications, rather it reflects the failure of the system to utilize the vast reserve of talent and expertise that they have brought into the service.

Instances are aplenty where brilliant engineering graduates are made to rot in home departments of state secretariats when their English and History colleagues are sent to make a mess in state electricity boards and engineering projects!

The role of administration in India has enlarged. Fortunately so has the talent back that is available to it, thanks to the large scale influx of brilliant alumni from the IITs, IIMs and the Medical Colleges. Out of the more than one lakh top grade scientific and technical personnel that come out of our universities, only a few hundred enter the civil services if this is such a loss for the nation, I wonder what the loss is of the failure to utilize the talents and creative energies of the remaining 99,800?

The learned editor can be faulted on the ground of basing his arguments on false and malicious premises, but he can be faulted even more for the simplistic nature of his arguments.

He deals which the biggest problem that Indian administration has ever faced—the problem of widespread corruption—most speciously. His argument is simple: Take the engineer and doctor out of the IAS, thus restoring its 'traditional values' and, hey presto! Corruption will disappear and the quality of administration too will improve significantly!

Corruption is not an issue that can be so simply analysed, nor can its eradication be that simple an affair. But even if it were, to hold the cream of the Indian intelligentsia responsible for it is stretching matters too far.

The professionals are in the IAS because of their merit, to hold them responsible for any ill that the system may be found to have would amount to denigrating meritocracy itself. It is almost a truism to say that it is not the system of merit that the country has chosen to adopt that has led to the ills that beset it but contrarily the lack of it. It is here that Mandal and the like must be taken to task.

Mr Editor, a value system of honesty and integrity is not a monopoly of any class, even those who have imbibed a liberal education, whatever that may mean these days when an IIT graduate does as many as fifty subjects, including Philosophy, History and Psychology, when an average MA is hardly aware of any subject outside the immediate area of his discipline.

Corruption is really a part of the social and political ethos that prevails in the country.

If a doctor becomes a collector, far from being an event to be ridiculed, as your paper has done, it should be an occasion of rejoicing, it is a signal that Indian administration has finally overcome the obstacles of time and has arrived in the modern age. Administration has taken the first important step to coping up with the times.

65

THE FUTURE OF OUR METRO

The rehearsals of the Republic Day parade has upset the entire pattern of traffic in and out of New Delhi and has especially hit those of us who stay close to India Gate. But is this sort of snarling traffic just a problem of the next few days or is it some sort of a premonition for the future? Much as I would like to believe to the contrary, I know that this is just a full dress rehearsal for what the Delhi of the future is going to see on a day to day basis.

Let us compare what the state of affairs in the city is today and what it will be two to two-and-a-half decades later if we do nothing except allowing the present pace of planning and development to continue. A full 50 lakh of us are living in conditions that are little better than slums, with insufficient housing and substandard civic facilities. The people living in subhuman conditions will increase to 2 crore by 2020.

The state of the roads is such that during peak hours, traffic cannot move faster than 10-15 km. per hour with about 30 lakh vehicles, including 8000 Blueline buses, on the road: for the average commuter it means at least two to three hours spent just to get to his place of work and back. By 2020 this speed will be down to 3-5 km. per hour, with more than 80 lakh vehicles, including 30,000 Redline buses, jamming the streets. In such a situation the best part of the working day will be spent on travelling.

There are at present 1.25 lakh industrial units in Delhi which, along with 22 lakh vehicles, discharge 2000 tonnes of toxic and poisonous gases into the air; by 2020 this will go up five times. At the same time, shortages of water and power should go up so alarmingly that we will be lucky to even a couple of hours of water and power supply!

Enough said, let us resolve here and now to do something about it. What do we do?

The key factor that is creating the problem is population. Let us remember that approximately two-thirds of the increase of half-a-million every year is because of immigration; and three-fourths of this is from within a hundred kms of Delhi. It is clear that to contain the population of the city within manageable limits, we have to take concrete steps to halt, if not actually reverse, the inflow.

The NCR Act was passed with exactly such an intention; it shifted the borders of Delhi, though for planning purposes only, from its 1400 odd sq km. to include an area of 30,000 sq km. Now areas such as Daruhera-Bhiwani-Alwar and Bulandshahr-Khurja-Meerut and Sonepat-Panipat are within the NCR. It identified 13 towns in the region for intensive development so that they could become counter magnets for absorbing population which would otherwise come to Delhi.

The main strategy is to develop regional physical and economic infrastructure and establish linkages within the region to attain balanced development of the entire region.

To do this the key area to be tackled are transportation, power, telecommunications and industrial growth. All these require substantial financial and administrative inputs. Let us take power. If we have to make power available in the region at par with Delhi, mere statements will not help. We may have to provide captive power generation in the NCR towns to the extent of at least 50 per cent of their requirements and improving the transmission and distribution. The cost may be of the order of Rs. 300 crore.

In transportation the aim should be to see that the share of buses in commuter movement should be reduced from the present 98 per cent of less than 50 per cent, this has to be done by the development of a fully integrated regional rail transit system. Such a system will also have to integrate the regional towns with the metropolitan rail transport system of the capital, once it comes up. The existing highways coming into Delhi have to be widened and new expressways built for by passable traffic. The cost: Rs. 10,000 crore.

In telecommunications, telephones will have to be available on demand in Delhi and the regional towns; moreover, the entire region will have to be dealt with as a single circle with local call facilities. Cost: Rs 4,550 crore. Most importantly, to facilitate the shifting of economic activities out of Delhi (we cannot keep jobs here and ask people to move out) we have to spend money to improve the living and work environment of the towns in the region.

It was estimated that just to create jobs for five lakh of people and provide housing and other civic facilities for them, we will need to spend over Rs. 60,000 crore in the next 10 years. No doubt of the bulk of the money will come from the private sector—may be a full two-thirds of it—but quite a bit also has to come from government and its agencies. In fact, government investment is a must to catalyse private funding.

The requirements of funds of infrastructure development in the private sector are mainly on account of housing and industry. The public sector requirement of funds are in land acquisition, railway development, and roads.

The total investment of Rs. 38,000 crore in the private and Rs. 21,000 crore in the public sector may seem large; but considering that agricultural land in parts of South Delhi sells for as much as a crore an acre shows that in relative terms the amount is not that prohibitive. The only important point to note is that we have to think of new strategies for mobilization of resources.

One of the key strategies would have to be to use land as a resource. Six acres given to the HUDCO near South Extension have enabled that body to raise Rs. 150 crore; and we have thousands of acres of land waiting to be utilized in the city.

Recently, a 100 acre plot has been earmarked for government housing; why cannot this same plot of land be sold for commercial development and government housing be shifted to Ghaziabad, where land prices are many times lower than in Delhi?

It seems to me that resources may not be a constraint to the development of the NCR; what we do need is to recognize that there is a problem and then to find innovative and bold initiatives to overcome it. If we fail today, we will have no right tomorrow to remark: 'I wish I knew in time!' In fact, then I will be able to say truthfully: 'I told you so!'

66

THE TERRIFYING REALITY OF A MEGACITY

The terrifying fact of life in that in Delhi, that in where we are heading we are surely and not very slowly heading to a megacity status.

Megacities have the uncanny knack of plucking the worst out of the best: from the village, the basti without the surrounding green open fields; from the small town the lack of amenities without the intimacy and social contact that these towns provide; and from the big city the high living costs without the quality of life.

From the village to the town; from the small town to the larger one and thence to the city; all this is a progression spanning several centuries. And much of it is a progression of progress. But much of it is not.

While our villages continue to languish, despite massive community development efforts, in the Moghul period, our cities, at least parts of them that are new, have progressed far out into the twentieth century, with amenities and opportunities for quality of life that are comparable to the best anywhere in the world.

Let us take New Delhi or Mumbai's Nariman Point; or areas in newly growing metropolises like Pune and Bangalore. These parts provide amenities and facilities that are not less than available anywhere else. The general outlook and tenor is comparable to the best in the world. In terms of quality of life, they are centuries ahead of the villages and small towns surrounding them.

While all this is wonderful, this sort of development has another, not totally planned, effect. The well lighted, amenity-filled cities become oasis in an otherwise under served and below standard desert. In fact, they serve as beacon lights for immigration, sort of fibre lamps for invading insects.

These migrating hordes have two clear and hardly disguised effects: they slowly increase the population of the metropolis and at the same time provide it with its own desolate and underserved over crowded areas, or so-called shanty towns.

This effect is as sure as the fact that the previous century has been replaced by a new one. As also the fact that the city will soon grow out of this status by another manifestation of it, which we can call the megacity.

Just as we had a region, with a beautiful city surrounded by a regime of small towns and villages; so we have in the megacity its own structure of towns and villages but with the important difference that they are all within the city.

While it is true that the megacity consists of a number of small but well served and beautiful city-like areas, between which lie a number of these village and small town like areas, it is not as if they can be counted as distinct and independent areas as was the case before the megacity took shape. In fact, all these areas are part of the larger megacity areas, with a symbolic linkage amongst its various parts. It is this relationship that makes the key difference.

Take community relations. Though they vary in all the manifestations above, in the megacity they are not just a sum total of all. It is not that, while the basti there is a relationship of intimacy as in the village and in the small town, it just gets destroyed in the city and the megacity; it actually gets replaced with a new tension and conflict filled relationship, which creates its own social compulsions.

The basti dweller in the village gets an outlet in his green fields and open environment; moreover, his contact with the town and the city is only momentary and periodic, may be confined to a couple of shopping and sightseeing jaunts in the year. But the relationship of the basti dweller in the megacity with his counterpart in the city beyond the road is more intimate and organic; and that is the reason for the hostility and conflict.

If you do not believe me, visit any of the megacities that have come up in the world. Rio de Janiero for instance, which has grown up in the recent past to a city of a population upwards of 4 million. Nowhere else is the community more sharply split as here, with the vast majority living in congested and stinkingly deficient shanties while their more fortunate citymates live in modern and spacious city like areas dotted all over.

Both these are fortresses, with the affluent areas guarded by specially recruited police and the shanties provided their own set of laws and security by the private armies maintained by drug kings and war-lords. These two are constantly at war with each other, with probably no other relationship other than bad blood and acrimony.

All this has inspired Martin ven Crevold to write *Future War*, in which he predicts that most of the wars now will not be fought between two sovereign states or countries, but within the bounds of a country. What it means is that a megacity will consist of nothing but for mutually opposed and constantly warring and hostile factions. The only relationship and link that brings them together will be the fact of the conflict.

What a bleak prospect for a city we have inherited from the likes of Lutyens; a city which while catering to the hopes and aspirations of an entire region can still provide cultural and artistic satisfaction to the vast majority of its inhabitants.

The choice is ours and the time for decision is now. Do we want to be a part of the wars of the future or do we want to enjoy the cultural, artistic and economic freedom that the city provides to us now?

The decision is easy but the path is hard. While we want higher and higher standards of services and amenities, let us remember all of these bright lights serve as a beacon to the immigrants and bring the city a step closer to the holocaust of future war scenario.

But does all this mean that we have no way but to sacrifice our quality of life for the sake of the future generations?

The answer to this question may hinge the happiness and future prosperity of our great capital city. The question is: can we find the answer in time?

67

MAKING DELHI A PLANNED REGION INSTEAD OF A MONSTER CITY

We have seen how megacities have the bad habit of picking the worst features of villages, small towns and big city's. We also saw how Delhi too is headed in that direction. I had promised to give a way out; let me try. Just as the village was the reality of the medieval age and the small town of the era immediately following the industrial revolution, the big city is inevitable in the present age of hi-tech. There is no doubt that Delhi too has to grow, but the main issue is, must it become a megacity?

The time to act is now; a little later may be too late. In the four decades from 1951, Delhi grew from a population of 14.5 lac to 94.21 lac. At the rate at which it is now growing, half a million a year, it should more than double its population every 15 years: at this rate it will attain the population of Rio De Janiero (4 crore) by the year 2020 or 2030. Already the pressure of population is telling. Already we have only 2120 mld water as against our requirement of 2950; and our sewage and waste disposal capacity is not even half of what is required. Our transport needs will be appalling: 16000 buses in 2000 AD against our existing availability of less than 6000.

That we are already on the way to a megacity status will be clear if you knew that the number of squatter settlements have increased to more than three lakhs now; and the ugly fact is that more than 60 per cent of the new population has to reside in slums. A Delhi with a four crore population will have at least three crore people living in squatter settlements and slums! What a terrifying scenario! Need I argue any more about the needs of Delhi?

What we want in Delhi is clear enough: we want to pick up the best of the village, the small town and the city, that's clear enough. But, the issue is, how?

Let us see what makes the village and the small town so attractive. First of all the vast open spaces and the clean and green environment. Then comes the intimacy of contact amongst the various inhabitants; the person to person contact leads to a more humane and personalized social structure that leads not only to less stress but also to better social management. Apart from the congenial social and personal environment, these towns also provide an economical and satisfying life style.

It seems apparent at the outset: a city of the type mentioned above cannot be one big and vast conglomeration; nor can it be a loose confederation of small dispersed townships. An ideal would probably be a central city loosely the Delhi to today, but with less population, symbiotically linked to a number of well designed and populated towns all around, in two concentric arcs.

That is to say that instead of choking the growth of the smaller towns and villages around, let the city fuel it by strengthening its links.

If Delhi can be taken as the inner city, important and growing towns lie in two arcs around it. In the inner grid are towns like Gurgaon, Faridabad, Ghaziabad, Noida and Kundli and in the outer, in an arc about 60 to 100 kms away, are towns like Sonepat, Bahadurgarh, Bulandshahar, Meerut and Hapur. In between are vast open green spaces where there is agricultural activity.

Delhi at present is sucking out the life of these towns; what do we do to make their growth mutually complementary and symbiotic?

Each one of the towns mentioned have their own independent structure and existence with hardly any links either with each other or with Delhi. What to talk of an organic link, they do not even form a loose confederation of sorts. How do we ensure that the organic relationship comes up? There are many steps to be taken.

The first and foremost are the institutional and legal steps. At present these towns form part of three states, with their own power centres, in this case in Lucknow, Chandigarh and Jaipur, and a Union Territory governed directly from Delhi. There must be some sort of political link among them. Ideally, they should be constituted into a state, by detaching them from the states whose parts they are now. This will not only give the necessary impetus to the other steps that are to be taken to establish the organic linkages but also will be a strong psychological blow for the concept. Even if such a step cannot be taken in one blow, the planning unit (NCR Planning Board) now established, should be strengthened administratively by the creation of common banking and developmental structures. Let the Planning Commission make common plan for the region and ensure that enough fiscal resources are available for its implementation.

This alone is not enough. At present the deficiency in services and infrastructure among these towns and Delhi is so stark that this alone operates as a factor for people of these towns to migrate to Delhi. This has to be upgraded by bringing in new resources both in the public and private sectors. There has to be a crash programme for bridging the gap. This may require an investment in these towns of the order of tens of thousands of crores every year for the next 10-15 years.

But even this not enough, in fact, unless we strengthen umblical bonds of these towns with Delhi, i.e., the transport and communication links, there is no way that these towns can attract all this investment. Let these towns be connected with each other and with Delhi with superfast highways and expressways.

The Delhi of the future should not be a crore megacity

with its confrontational and explosive divide between the few post colonies of the haves interspersed with the multitudes crowded in the millions of busties and shanties in between. It should actually be a region with the Delhi that we know enjoying the position of the heart and with its veins and arteries running to the well laid out and planned towns spread out in a radius of 100 kms or so. And in between will be the small and green village 'townships' to serve as its aerial arteries.

In short, let Delhi expand into a four crore population region rather than into a monster megacity of the same population.

68

A HAPHAZARD GROWTH

Planning in India is now five decades old and still nobody could claim that it has made more than a marginal impact on the development process. But there is no doubt that, but for the plans that had been drawn up, the progress would have been more hazardous and desperate than it has actually been.

Nowhere has the planning process failed more as it has, in our burgeoning metropolises. Take Delhi as an example, from the semi urban-semi rural city of *babus* that we inherited from the Raj, we saw it emerge to a centre of commerce and trade in the sixties to the concrete jungle of the seventies and now into a vast ever growing slum with as many as three lakh dry latrines and 900 so-called jhuggie clusters, where more than a fifth of the population lives. Only a few years ago we had drawn up a plan to restrict the population increase in the city so that it would not go beyond a crore and ten lakh but it seems that already we may have exceeded this figure. In the next five years, we will have at least another two million people crowding our already overcrowded slums and so called jhuggie clusters. And so will it be for every subsequent year. If nothing is done, we may be more than two crore Delhities by 2010-2015.

Is there a way of escaping this terrible fate? If past events are any guide, there seems to be hardly any way. Population projections have gone awry in the past; and if anything there are more chances now of things going wrong. There is talk of the metro, of the tram-way; there is talk of creating a corporation for the poor to provide shelter for the homeless in Delhi; and what not. It is interesting that all this talk is for the city of Delhi and is designed to make the city even more attractive for the immigrant by increasing even further the infrastructure gap in his home town and Delhi.

It is clear that every single scheme that the government in Delhi proposed to launch will be counter productive and, far from solving the problems that beset the city, will accentuate them even further. The higher the allocations that we make for Delhi, the higher still will be the amount we will need. And there is no way to reverse this vicious cycle.

No way, did I say? I should have said no easy way, no easy options. At least not till we are willing to change our attitudes, at least change the way that we have been planning so far. We have a separate plan for the railways, there is a plan for surface transport and for roads, there are plans for the states around Delhi and there is a plan for Delhi. Each one of them are considered in isolation and allocations are decided, based on the perceptions and priorities of the powers that are in the concerned departments and minorities.

When the road plan is finalized, priorities are naturally fixed keeping in view the demand and growth projections for the various regions and parts of the country. We have also to keep in view various other facts, especially political factors. The same would be the case when the railways finalize their plan. As for Delhi, their interest would probably be to insure that the freight moving from Punjab should bypass Delhi; why should they bother about ensuring that we have to provide good commuter movement facilities in the region? So their bypass passes by not merely Delhi City but the region as well, thus having a very marginal impact on the development of infrastructure in the region as a whole.

So is with Delhi. And naturally also with other states. Delhi plans it's power transmission and distribution system only with the union territory in view; so it is with the sewage and water supply system, floods, irrigation, housing, land and other aspects.

So it comes about, that for Delhi region we do not have one plan but a subset of many plans, which may be loosely coordinated but are never fully integrated. Is it possible to have a separate plan for the region or are there constitutional and other impediments that stand in the way? Even if the impediments are removed, is there a Delhi region or is it just a figment of the planner's imagination? A mere alignment on some maps!

It is true that Delhi region is not a political and constitutional entity and unless drastic changes are made in the Constitution, cannot be made one also. But at least in one sense the region is a reality that all the legal realities cannot just wish away. Of the two lakh or so immigrants that come to Delhi every year, more than 70 per cent come from the so-called national capital region and only the rest from outside the region, despite all the talk of the Bangladeshis and the like.

The mere fact that Delhi, like it or not, has become a powerful magnet for such a large number of people living in the region shows that Delhi is not just the capital of the country but is also the *de facto* capital of the region. And if this fact is recognized, there is only one planning process possible and that is of planning for the region.

Planning for the region does not mean that now there will be no plan for the NCT of Delhi; or that U.P. or Haryana also will have plans for areas outside the NCR. A five-year plan for the NCR will mean that, while there will be separate plans for each of the states and for Delhi NCT, they will all have sub-components for the region and the sum total of these components will form the NCR plan.

Much more important than the documentation is the very process of approving the plan. There will first be a discussion on the NCR plan with the concerned states, Delhi and the concerned central ministries; only after this has been finalized will there be a discussion on the plan of these various states and ministries.

The advantage here will be that since a consensus will already have been arrived at as far as allocations for the NCR are concerned, these can then be fitted in the priorities of the ministry/state. Thus, state express ways will not be held up due to lack of provisions for land acquisition in the plan of the surface transport ministry; the road grid around Delhi linking up the satellite towns will not be held up due to lack of provisions in the state plans; and so will the rail network be held on due to lack of funds. Desperate situation need desperate solutions. Planning over the heads of the various legal and constitutional authorities may seem desperate; but the situation of Delhi is desperate. Let us act and act fast; time may not be on our side.

PART 14

TROTTING AROUND

69

THE TAJ MAHAL'S CHEMISTRY OF LOVE

It was the third night of the waning moon; the time was about an hour before midnight. The place: just outside the barred gate of the Taj Mahal in the historic city of Agra.

The three quarter disc of the moon was just about visible in the dark sky above; it was clear that soon the darkness of the sky would be dispelled somewhat by the luminous glow of the moon. We strained our eyes to catch a glimpse of the dome of the symbol of eternal love as the first streak of light struck it; but this was all in vain since the large wall made our effort all but ineffectual.

We were not alone in our disappointment. Nearby we saw a middle aged Japanese couple engaged in a similar hopeless pursuit. Both of us knew that this was the only way to see the Taj in moonlight since security measures taken recently decreed that admittance to the monument was restricted only to daylight hours except on full moon nights. And to get a full moon night one would have to wait in Agra for another couple of weeks.

As we turned back in disappointment, we stopped as we heard the call of the Japanese man. Soon he had accosted us and his puzzled glance swung from us to the direction of the Taj. 'I was here three decades back', said he finally in his hesitant English, 'and I had seen the Taj Mahal here; I wonder where it has gone now!'

One didn't know whether to laugh or cry: this Japanese

man had come half a world, with his wife in tow this time, to whisper to her the vows of eternal love on the footsteps of a moonlit Taj; how tragic that he came when terrorism and violence had converted love into a dirty word.

Science it seems has decided to dabble in an area which for long was a preserve of poets and song writers. And instead of the symptoms with which we are familiar—a drifting mooniness in thought and behaviour, the mad conceit of ecstasy and torment—found it was nothing but chemistry and biology.

Scientists tell us that falling in love is a four stage process. The first of these is imprinting in which evolution, genetics, psychological experiences and even smells can trigger romantic reactions. This is followed by attraction, when the brain is charged by phenylethylamine and the neurochemicals dopamine and norepinephrine. These produce feelings of euphoria and elation.

The third stage of attachment comes about when larger amounts of endorphins start to flow into the brain, 'leaving lovers with a sense of security, peace and calm.' The final stage of 'relaxed satisfaction and attachment' come about when the brain's pituitary gland secretes oxytocin, the cuddle chemical.

If love is really so chemical, as the scientists aver, the Japanese couple need not really have come to Agra at all: a trip to their home town's chemistry lab would have sufficed! But try telling that to the Japanese couple. Or to any other. Well, I didn't.

Nor did I rush to the nearest chemistry lab, my faith in science notwithstanding. I took the next best alternative as I'm sure my Japanese friend refused to do: we visited the Taj in broad daylight. And to make up for the loss of the night visit, we visited the Red Fort from where the ailing and aging Shahjehan continued to view the Taj and whisper his eternal love to his beloved Mumtaj.

Taj in daylight is no less fascinating than it is at night; but what one misses at day is the loneliness and the ecstasy and the freedom that it brings. In the day one is only too aware of the world beyond the world of love that Shahjehan had created;

also of the fact that the world beyond is that of congestion and poverty and pollution. And what hurts most of all is the fact of the disappearance of the Yamuna river. Even worse is the fact that not only has the river vanished what has come in its place is nothing better than a 'gunda nalla'.

I spent much of my childhood in Agra and Allahabad; even then the majesty of the river was much to be remembered. What it must have been five centuries back when Shahjehan chose its shore for crafting his dream in marble can only be imagined.

Imagination too is the only option open when one wonders what the city of love, Agra, must have been in those days. Nothing that one sees today can give even a small idea of what the capital of Mughal India must have been in its heyday. Except when one visits the site of the new temple at Dayalbagh.

It's almost unbelievable that such a construction could have been started in our times. And even more surprising that people hope to complete it.

I had seen the start of the work when I was a child, maybe four decades back. At that time when I had seen the plans and the snail's pace at which the work was proceeding I had given up the project as lost. And it was the same now even though in the intervening four decades a lot of work has been done. Will it ever be completed?

This question was uppermost in my mind as I emerged out of its lustily crafted portals. It was then that my eyes fell on the Japanese couple who I had met the earlier night outside the Taj. It was clear that the same question was in their minds too. The Japanese took the hands of his wife in his hand and smiled at me.

In his smile he mirrored my own hopes; really the hopes of our generation. Well, we have failed to protect the legacy of love that was bequeathed to us by our ancestors; is it too much to hope that this new legacy of love that our own generation has started to build would survive the cauldron of hate that was now threatening to boil over?

I wish for the sake of our generation that the Japanese's smile is fulfilled.

70

SIMLA MON AMOUR

Simla has a peculiar fascination for many like me who spent much of their childhood there and still miss not merely the grandeur of the mall and the mystic challenge of the high hills but also the opulence and majesty of this summer capital of Imperial India, replete with its grand hotels and other buildings.

But even more than 24 hours after my return the sense of disappointment has not left me. It isn't just because cars, jeeps and trucks are constantly spoiling the sanctity of the Mall; not even because of the lack of basic civic amenities like drinking water. Both these I had, at least in my subconscious mind, expected, even hoped to find: it was too much to expect Simla to be an oasis of efficiency in the bureaucratic-political desert that the rest of the country has been reduced to.

What was most disconcerting was the sad neglect, sometimes even the spoiling, of most of the wonderful landmarks there. Take the ridge. The beautiful park and the wooden canopy there have been converted into eating places and the other two open spaces now have statues. The only other open spaces, apart from the road, have been converted into a shopping centre (albeit underground) and a parking lot for civil defence vehicles and ambulances.

Most of the old buildings have similarly been left to rot, with not even a single fresh coat of paint being applied. But what was the most difficult to digest was the neglect of the Grand Hotel. It was doubly disturbing since I had chosen to stay there.

The Grand Hotel is really a grand structure, with more than 200 rooms and suites. Its location is ideal too. Just step out and you are in one of the most famous and intriguing of all of Simla's landmarks: Scandal Point.

It is said that it is so named because the late maharaja of Patiala had tried to abduct the daughter of the British viceroy from this point. The angry English government had then banned the former Patiala rulers' entry from the summer capital, a punishment as harsh as any that our erstwhile rulers could think of. Nobody has ever tried to verify if the story is true: who cares? Even if it isn't, one almost wishes it were.

The Grand Hotel was magnificent both in conception as also in its structure. A massive multi-storeyed wooden building, it was modelled on its counterparts in London, Paris and Vienna. Its spacious rooms and suites had all the facilities that one could think of in those days: big fire places, running hot and cold water supply and attached toilets and kitchenettes. And, of course, it was a stone's throw from the Gaiety theatre and the Green room, that still serves as a club for the gentry. And almost on the fashionable Mall.

It was a big disappointment at first to find that the name had been changed: no longer was the Hotel called Grand; it was called the Holiday Home. It was not long that I was put off by the change in nomenclature: after all, a rose is a rose by whatever name it may be called.

By the time I was signing the hotel register, I had not only reconciled myself to the change of name but was actually looking forward to the change in form that it may imply. After all, who would want to stay in a hotel when he has the chance to stay in a Home! And then the chance to have a holiday even when one is on duty is welcome. Holiday Home was now sounding like musical chimes coming in from the distant peaks of the Himalayas.

But just as I stepped into the huge hall, that went by the name of a VIP suite, the stale and moist smell brought back the mood of depression. And it never went away till we were driving over the wide roads of the township of Panchkula on the outskirts of Chandigarh.

The hall led into another one, where a double bed had been laid and then into another one (smaller this time) that went by the name of a bathroom. Spacewise I had stepped into a fair sized flat but in all other respects it was dark and gloomy. !t was fairly late in the night and I thought the best way to dispel the gloom was to get into bed.

The two blankets provided were so thin that your finger could go through them. And, as I discovered, so cold that the cold entered the marrows of my bones. Somehow the dark, dank stink of the night ended with the first rays of the sun and I jumped out of the bed straight into the bathroom for a hot bath. What if the night was cold: I would let it spoil the bright and sunny day!

But I had not reckoned with the management of the holiday home: there was not a drop of water in the taps. I wanted to ring the bell to let out my frustration but there were no bells to be rung; so I rushed to the office to enquire.

The dissipated face of the babu behind the counter took away whatever energy I had and made me mew like a cat. 'You talk of a bucket of hot water? There's not even a cup of hot water for your tea!'

As I staggered out of his room, I could only sympathize with him: after all, what can he do if a major landslip has destroyed one of the main water pipelines into the city? But this one about the cup of tea.... this must surely be his sense of humour. The canteen would provide that cup and maybe, if I'm lucky, I'll get some hot water for the shave too.

The man behind the counter in the dining hall was in one hell of a mood. Not having even water enough for a cup of tea he was blowing hot air all over the place. Escaping from there, I went to the meeting; at least I'd get the tea there.

The meeting went like all meetings go: a lot of hot air and heady talk with neither any light nor any result. But who cared. All I waited for was the inevitable tea break. And it wasn't late in coming.

The VIP speaker looked at his watch, coughed importantly

and then stopped talking. He called his assistant; I waited with bated breath at last the cup of tea. He whispered something into his ear and the assistant whispered back something. The VIP speaker smiled understandingly as he got up.

'I understand many of you want to go for an outing to Kufri; so we have decided to extend the tea break into lunch to enable you to go back to your hotels where you can have your cup of tea and get ready at the same time'.

It was back to the Grand Hotel (sorry Holiday Home) for me to get in shoes. I could only pray that no pipelines had burst in Kufri and the hotels and resorts there had not yet been homes.

71
THE LAST SHANGRI-LA

Have you been to the roof of the world? Well, I have and am no worse for the experience. No worse, of course, unless you consider going without sleep for three nights and having a mild sort of headache for all the 72-odd hours that I was there to be part of the 'no worse' situation!

Leh, the capital of the Ladakh region of the Jammu & Kashmir state, may not be the roof of the world but at 11,500 feet above sea level comes close to it. It is a place of strange contrasts. Much as the mighty Indus flows through much of the valley, it still is afflicted with a dryness which makes it even drier than the deserts of Rajasthan. It is probably the largest region of the country which has lost the largest chunks of land to foreign countries, with about 40,000 sq kms. each in the occupation of China and Pakistan. Large as it is, Ladakh has the smallest density of population in the whole country, less than 2 persons per sq. km.

And so one can go on. The tall, erect and green poplars abound in the midst of the most inhospitable landscape of sandy mountains and the proud happy go lucky Ladakhi people in the mid of the rarefied air that supplies only enough oxygen to carry out the most basic of activities. At least this is so till one gets acclimatized. And getting acclimatized is not a state that one can think of if one is here for a visit of less than a week or so.

Ladakh is often described in travel booklets as the 'Last Shangri-La' and indeed it is so. I have not been to Tibet and, with relations with China being what they are, have no hope of doing so too in my lifetime. Thus I have no way of verifying the correctness of the statement but have no care of doing so too. A full 3 days in Leh, with a couple of visits to the surrounding areas, have given me a glimpse of what I will always believe is Shangri-La.

The first view of the last Shangri-La was when the Indian Airlines airbus was inching its way perilously close to the Himalayan hill ranges, which must have been 20,000 feet or so each. In the valleys in between one did get an occasional glimpse of the small habitats but most of the time it was just barren and forbidding hill slopes and challenging peaks.

I was yet feasting my eyes on these 'Shangrilan' sights when a familiar voice from behind woke me up from my imaginings. 'Nothing but sleep for the first 24 hours and remember no alcohol. Otherwise you will get an ache in your head which will make you shoot a bullet through it!'

This was Gautam Kaul, now heading the Indian Tibetan Border Police Force who occupied a seat in the plane just behind mine. Just one day in Leh and I realize the truthfulness of his statement. The rarefied air there may seem very fresh and pure to start off with but soon takes its toll: even with the 24 hours of no-activity as advised, I still nursed a law but abiding headache which was my constant companion for much of the 3 days that I spent in Leh. For others who were more venturesome and adventurous on the first day, the next 2 days were excruciating and uncomfortable.

I have been so much taken up with the shortage of oxygen that I have not even mentioned of the other aspects of Leh that were in abundance. Especially, the sun. Being on the roof and closer to the gods, one gets sunlight that is richer in ultra violet rays and causes a sun burn even before you can say 'Oh God!' We had left a Delhi where it was raining, literally, 'cats and dogs' and landed in Leh where the 6 inches of rain in the whole year cannot help make it any wetter than it is. In fact, the air there is so dry that the only way of avoiding the skin from getting parched is to keep sipping liquids the whole day!

I have been talking so much about the lack of oxygen, the caky dryness, the stark inhospitability of the terrain that I may be charged with giving an impression that the last Shangri-La of Ladakh is also the 'last to be visited' place. If that is the impression I have given, then let me at the outset admit that it is false and far from my intention. If I have been highlighting only the negatives it is not because there are no positives but because there are so many of them that it is difficult to decide where to start and where not to.

First of all, let's take the people. Colourful yet simple, fierce yet tampered by the love and non-violence of Gautama Buddha, hardy and hardworking yet ones who seem to know how to enjoy their leisure. That's the Ladakhi people for you.

The place. Spectacular and beautiful, it is different from anything that you may have seen. It can best be described in the very philosophical way of 'neti neti'—'not this, not this'. It lacks the vibrancy and colour of Lakshadweep, the starkness of Rajasthan, the green of Kerala, the verdant beauty of the hills of north-east India: in fact, it lacks almost everything that you may have seen in other parts of the country. But still the one single impression of Ladakh both at first sight and later when you come back, is one of a spectacular and stark beauty that is beyond comparison. And in all the 72 hours that I was there I was trying to find out the best way of describing it and I am not sure if I have succeeded.

In one way, 3 days is too short a period for finding out; and in another too long. But whatever it may be I am at a loss for words for describing what I saw in the time when I was in Leh. Generally, what is difficult to describe in words is better stated in verse or in film.

72

PEARL OF THE ORIENT OR GILDED CAGE?

As I stepped out of the Malaysian Airlines Boeing onto the landing bridge towards the magnificent Singapore airport terminal building, the strains of a song from my childhood played onto my lips.

It went something like this: *Dekho ji dekho...sunlo yeh batein... jeewan mein ek baar ana Singapore...*

And here I was, having crossed the prime of my life, now operating on a sliding scale of borrowed time, fulfilling a childhood fantasy. And what a fantasy it turned out to be!

If this was an airport terminal then what the heck is the jungle of Mizoram! Just as one stepped into the terminal, in front there is a cascading waterfall; and all around are orchids, of all colours and descriptions.

This took me back quite a few decades to my first posting in Tripura and my first visit to the Mizo inhabited Jampui and Sakhan hill ranges.

Just as we were about to enter the small hamlets filled village of Laldengabari (this literally means 'house of Chief Denga'), I saw the orchid laden tree: this was perhaps the most exciting moment of my life. I knew that I feasted my eyes on a rare event: orchids. The memory has remained etched in my mind since then especially since orchids are such a rare commodity.

In the Singapore terminal it is unbelievable: not only are there orchids everywhere, they are also of all descriptions and colours imaginable. I had no doubt whatsoever that they were of paper or cloth; of the variety that abound the shops of our own Panchkuin Road. But the illusion was soon shattered as I saw an aged Chinese-looking gentleman carefully plucking the diseased leaves and watering the plants.

He was old but not senile; still I decided to test my hypothesis. On touching one of the leaves, I found that there was no doubt whatsoever; these were real orchids: not one or two or a few dozens but a whole jungle-full of them. The terminal building was choke full of them.

This was only the first of the series of surprises (or was it shocks?) of my Singapore sojourn. Not the least of the surprises was the surprising lack of dust; the road outside the airport was so clean that I almost wished I was not wearing any shoes: they were probably the dirtiest part of the environment.

As one drove through the streets to the hotel, it was difficult to believe that they had become independent only in 1965, significantly a full 18 years after us. But now they were at least a century ahead; considering the progress they had made. It became an interesting mission to explore how all this had been achieved.

It was not difficult; while Nehru, Nasser, Sukarno and Tito were exploring the Middle Path, Buddhist Singapore unabashedly took the capitalist road. We were proudly told that there were at least 160 multinational companies operating there. They had come from all corners of the globe—from Korea and Japan to UK and the USA. There were no restrictions whatsoever; there were no trade barriers, no restrictions on export or import. Anybody could acquire land and set up industries. Big department stores had been set up to exploit the traditional trading character of the city-state.

All that the state did was to facilitate the investments of the multinationals. They had provided the infrastructure, including 90 per cent of the housing and the network of roads and transportation facilities. A large number of government companies are there, Indian style; but they are themselves run on commercial lines. Their task is clearly cut out. As one of the senior officials told us: 'We are aiming at achieving the standard of living of the Swiss'. He was almost wistful as he added: 'We will achieve in 1997 what the Swiss had in 1983'.

My god! How I wish India could have the standard of living of the English of 1900 at the turn of the century! But then that is not our aim: we wish to achieve economic progress commensurate with social justice et al. It is quite another matter that in the process we have probably not been able to achieve either.

It was natural for an Indian to wonder if the 'Singapore model' could be applied to India. If it would enable us to make the same progress, why not?

But one wonders if the success story of this small city state could be duplicated in countries like India and China which are not only bigger but infinitely more complex. For instance, the first issue that would have to be tackled was how to integrate progress in the rural and urban areas. One cannot forget the much touted Mexican and Brazilian models and how the dream there has soured.

Sometime back this factor alone was enough to make us reject the Singapore model; but now with the visible failure of the Soviet system we cannot afford to do so except at our own peril. In fact, this was the reason I was leading this delegation of Delhi factory owners to this pearl of the orient.

Much more impressive than the obvious success of the model to alleviate poverty and visibly raise living standards was the enthusiasm of the officials and others with whom we interacted. We were clearly worried about one aspect of the model: what would be the effect of the unbridled entry of MNCs on the small businesses and industries that had come up in the country?

The development of small businesses has been one of our successes and the main reason for the emergence of a new and resurgent middle class in the country: in Delhi alone there are about 1 lakh small industries employing about a million workers; in addition there would be another half a million small businesses ranging from the roadside *dhaba* to the small tea stall and grocery store. What the impact would be on them on the opening up of the economy to the MNCs is what troubled the members of our delegation.

We asked one of the officials; his reply was reassuring. 'The MNCs are not in competition with the small industry; in fact, they will encourage them to manufacture products which then they can market. Not only will they allow the small units to continue they would positively encourage them.'

The example of Maruti seems to support this contention: this MNC unit supports a large number of small and medium units. But if this is the case, one wonders why we are wasting our time: why not adopt the Singapore model at once and move ahead?

I got the answer a day before I left Singapore. I just chanced to be a member of a group of people on the road discussing something. Suddenly one of the members pointed out that we were more than five people in the group. The local people immediately dispersed, leaving me alone wondering what it was all about. Soon the mystery was cleared.

It seemed that in Singapore more than five people are never allowed to assemble in a public place. A sort of perpetual Section 144.

I suddenly realized what the issue really was: since nothing came for free the decision was clear: how much of our individual freedom and liberty were we willing to sacrifice for the sake of economic progress.

That is the issue we should debate in the days to come.

PART 15
SHORT OF THE GOAL

73

THE OLYMPIAN TRAGEDY

The leap year comes but once in four years; but the Indian Olympian tragedy repeats itself many times in between.

The Olympics will end in a few days but not our misery: before the next Olympics four years from now, there are the Asian Games, the Afro-Asian Games, the SAARC games, and then the cricket series, the hockey World Cup and what not! The cup of our misery will indeed remain full! And much beyond the four-year period!

Olympics, Asiad, World Cup... far from being occasions of joy and celebration, they have become milestones of our national humiliation. Failure in them is not merely a reminder of our weaknesses; it is a cruel destroyer of our dreams and wishful hopes.

We have always believed that India is a sacred land, an ancient land, the chosen abode of the ten *avatars;* how is it then possible for us to fail to achieve anything? Our failure to win a medal is taken not merely as a failure of a few athletes or players but a national calamity which leads to the destruction of our mostly cherished beliefs.

The trauma is similar to the one that the Western world must have felt when Copernicus pointed out that the sun did not revolve around the earth but it was the other way around.

With this statement was shattered the most sacred and sacrosanct of man's beliefs. Earth, which Man the 'crown of creation' chose as his abode was not the centre of the universe;

in fact it was not even the centre of the centre of the solar system! Far from being the 'blessed place' as always believed, it was a dead planet which did not even produce its own light!

So that was it: man was not ... could not be... the crown of creation; he was a minuscule part of the wonder of creation. That was the Copernican revelation.

Losses in international forums whether in sports or in other areas is a similar nerve racking revelation; could we really be the chosen abode if we can't even win in sports?

This upsetting thought bears upon us heavily like some heavy weight and seems to affect our performance day by day.

But how did the West bear the impact of the Copernican revelation?

Well, they refused to wear it like a dead weight around their necks. At least not for a long time. They had soon converted the revelation into a revolution.

The Copernican Revolution soon drove Europe out of the Dark Ages where they had been mired for over a thousand years into the Age of Enlightenment and from there to the Age of Science and Technology.

This new Age in the West is not merely manifested in material attainments, important and obvious that they are: it is apparent in almost all other spheres as well, especially in their thinking and their attitudes.

The fact that we are an ancient country is something that we need not continue to remind ourselves; the fact that we seem to be bogged down in the dead past seems to be staring us in the face. And losses in sports is only one of the pointers in this direction. There are many others.

In this country we believe that success is 99 per cent *sifarish* and only 1 per cent competence. And that may be the reason why we have instant remedies for almost any problem.

Take sports. We were doing badly in almost all spheres, except hockey and sometimes cricket. There was universal agreement that something ought to be done. Bureaucrats of all shades–civil servants, sports administrators, police and army people, and, of course, the politicians—sat around specially designed tables and confabulated. For months and years. And finally evolved the package: at the centre of the package was what bureaucrats like best institutions. And thus came into the being the central and state departments of sports and bodies like the Sports Authority of India.

A massive programme was launched—of course, nobody knew how massive, should be! But the programme was indeed big: sports arenas and stadia, grants and financial assistance, invited coaches, and of course new bodies and institutions! The current plan provision is a full Rs 350 crore.

Where has all this taken us? Ask any sports bureaucrat and he'll give you mile-long statistics of success.

To the credulous, whose information sources are not confined to churned out press notes, who cries 'But the Emperor has nothing on!' sports administrators reply is a big yawn. Bureaucratic bodies care more for prepared statistics than for hard and inconvenient realities. Haven't we heard it said: Lies, damn lies, statistics in that order?

It serves him right; the 'credulous' must really be gullible to pick up the daily paper and throw facts at the bureaucrat; the bureaucrat has enough statistics to drown him for the whole of his waking life!

In any case, Mr. Credulous, how did you expect medals to flow in? Did you not follow the reports on the intrigues and pressures that were exerted by both officials and players to get included into the squad? Shouldn't you have known better what to expect?

Mr. Credulous, how do you expect people who have failed to win any medals at the Asian Games to come out gloriously in the Olympiad! And what about those who did win a medal in the Asiad but have since slided down in their performance?

Performance in sports can be improved somewhat by better selections, better training, better facilities, better incentives to sportspersons. But can that alone be enough to improve the present position (no medals since the Moscow Olympics) so drastically as to put us in the league of CIS, USA, Germany or China?

I don't believe so. So let us leave sports, for the time being, to the time servers and the bureaucrats; let the right thinking people think on other lines and try to draw the right lessons from this failure. Can we not somehow convert this revelation into a revolution?

Can we make our failure to win medals into a Copernican Revolution of sorts? I believe we can.

Yes, we are an ancient land with a golden past and even more glorious traditions. We can be justly proud of all this. We are strongly and deeply rooted in our lofty culture and there is no reason why we should dig ourselves out.

But there is no reason either for us to remain mired in the past; the new revolution in Science and Technology has raised new challenges and presented new opportunities. Let us grab them and give ourselves a push; let the slow and slothful be left behind but let us not allow them to bog us down to their slothful and deceitful ways.

From now onwards let our 99 per cent perspiration make the 1 per cent inspiration that we get from our glorious past more meaningful and effective.

74

THIS COMPETITION IS NOT FAIR

The cricket coverage of the ongoing MCC India series hits. And hits where it hurts the most at the national pride.

For the first time in the history of cricket coverage in India, foreigners are at the cameras, at the editing consoles and giving production cues. And poor Indians at the mike–the likes of Nawab of Pataudi, Bishan Singh Bedi, Abbas Ali Beg, Narottam Puri and Ravi Chaturvedi–have to be content with merely swearing their breaths as they face the humiliation of speaking one thing while the visual shows something quite contrary!

It is not quite infrequent for them to be left stranded in the midst of some cricketing comment as the English controllers take the camera away from cricket to show some village belles carrying water on their heads or on a foray of some Chandigarh street or to show some wisecrack comment on a placard written by some publicity hungry member of the crowd.

The cup of misery of the Indian cricket lovers was full when for a full two days the TV screen refused to show the bowling statistics of the Indian bowlers. (One wonders if this is so because the Indians for a change are doing better than the firangees!) And not once in the ten days of reporting of the two matches played so far have the fall of wickets been shown as a part of the scoreboard!

I heard a pretty one explain the reason for all this in a party in a fashionable south Delhi cocktail party. 'Busji...Doordarshan is 'door' always; at least now we can see the action from close!'

The charge wasn't true; at least for post-Asiad Doordarshan. But what if it was? I wonder how the little fashionable beau would react if her husband failed to perform. Would she rush for replacement to the UK?

When I said as much to the blushing beauty, a smart young man in jeans came to her aid. 'It's competition', he said and smiled as if he had uncovered a major secret for poor ignorant me.

It was unfortunate for the smart young swinger that I wasn't as ignorant as he seemed to imagine. 'Competition between whom?' I asked defiantly. 'Competition is between two equals, not between a merchant and a beggar; or, for that matter, between the citizen of a country just emerging from a colonial economy and that of a citizen of a modern country that is fully imbibed with the spirit of science and technology!' A B.R. Chopra or a Raj Barjatiya cannot compete with a Spielberg not because they are inferior to him as persons or as artists or even as entrepreneurs but because a Spielberg has the backing of superior technology and a stronger, more resilient and sound home economy.

It is the same when it comes to competition of some of our computer whiz kids with a Bill Gates or our Tatas and Birlas with the Donald Trumps and the Henry Fords. Or with their Japanese, English, German or even Korean or Taiwanese counterparts, for that matter!

It wasn't too long ago that traders came across the sea onto our shores ostensibly with the purpose of trading; but stayed back to enslave and rule us. Have we forgotten it or do we really believe that history never repeats itself?

Haven't we heard of competition before in the context of the products of Lancashire mills and the products of our own weavers, be they the weavers of Dacca muslin or the ones who made coarser varieties of cloth? Have we forgotten that our struggle of freedom initially involved nothing but burning of stacks of mill made cloth, which was forced on us in the name of competition in the first place?

Have we already forgotten the lessons of history? Or do

we believe that the only lesson that history teaches is that it has no lesson at all?

No. I believe that a nation ignores the lessons of history only at its peril. Freedom is not a marketable commodity that can be bartered away in the name of competition. Or anything else.

While falling prey to the new fangled concepts we are not only ignoring the lessons of history, we are also forgetting our recent experiences. How can we forget that the recent bank scam, even though its full manifestations are still to come before us, was a direct result of so called marketisation? And what about the fate that is overtaking Doordarshan?

Yes, what about Doordarshan, counters the swinger, with the latest MTV tune still echoing inside him? It is lack of competition that has made it what it is: boring, stale and irrelevant. A spot of competition, even if from foreign satellites, could only do it good.

I must admit the teenager haa a point and I couldn't counter this one so easily. And frankly speaking I didn't try to.

But I've all the time have had a lurking suspicion that the competition that Doordarshan faced was not really fair. It's really difficult to put your finger down to it but it is there–there are clear indications that Doordarshan fights with its hands tied to its back.

It is also difficult to say if the difficulties are of its own making or have been imposed on it. But impediments are there.

I wonder how Zee and all would react if their serial selections were referred to CBI for a probe. Or if their programmer like Saanp Seedi were subjected to parliamentary scrutiny. Or if their programme controllers had to go for funds to the finance ministry, after crossing a dozen or so tables.

If competition has to be between a no-holds-barred private company and hands-tied-behind-back public sector, then let the contest be called off and the former be declared the winner; for there can be no other result possible anyway. Otherwise let the ropes that tie up the latter be loosened, if not altogether removed.

75

IT'S CRICKET NOT WAR

It's India vs Pak again. After 7 years, we are told. And the excitement is such that one hopes that the contest remains confined to the cricket ground alone. And if it does, there is promise of a thrill for every minute that the match is played.

Every contest is interesting, even if it is between imaginary figures on the cinema screen. The interest mounts if the contestants are evenly matched, leaving the final conclusion in some doubt. It reaches a pinnacle when the contest is between two groups, one of which you want desperately to win and the other to lose.

All these conditions are present in an Indo-Pak contest. First the latter. There is no way that any Indian can fail to root for his side; the same is true of the Pakistanis. While wanting our side to win we are equally keen that the other loses. Thus in matches played between Pakistan and some other side we must root for whichever team happens to be opposing Pakistan.

In fact, the feeling is so deep that in a Holland-UAE match, a part of the crowd kept shouting in favour of Pakistan and against India, completely oblivious of the fact that the contest before then made any of the two imagined results completely impossible.

In the Bangalore encounter both these conditions are beautifully fulfilled. If India wins, not only we have the pleasure of seeing 'our' side winning but we also have the double pleasure of seeing the Pakistan being defeated. What a wonderful 'two in one'!

But despite the fulfilment of these conditions, the excitement would have been almost nil if the two sides were unevenly matched. Imagine India playing Pakistan in tennis. There is no way that Pakistan can beat India; so the excitement of such a contest would be almost nil. The same would probably be true of hockey, howsoever popular the game may otherwise be.

Let us take the two sides. There are superstars galore in both. If there is a Sachin here there is a Waqar there; for one Kumble, there are the two Musthaqs on the other side. Azharuddin is more than matched by Salim Malik just as the flamboyance of a Kambli is more than matched by Aamir Suhail.

Even in terms of recent form there is nothing much to choose between the two sides. While Pakistan has faced humiliating home defeats at the hands of the Lankans, we have had no better luck either, having been stretched to the full by teams like Zimbabwe.

While both teams have been humbled recently, they have not lost their reputation of being potential giant beaters. Both the teams have great potentialities; but unfortunately almost the same failings.

So, there you are. You have a readymade script that would have surely have done many an Oscar winning script writer proud. A strong protagonist wanting to win at any cost opposed by an equally strong and determined antagonist. Only one of them can win; this is what thrillers and suspense mysteries are made of.

But this is not the entire story. Unfortunately. There are reports in the press of certain groups making veiled threats of certain people being arrested, and what not. While these no doubt add to the air or mystery and drama, they do somewhat tend to diminish the role of the drama being enacted on the field.

The danger is that such off field drama can take communal overtones, as has been the case for the last 7 years with the Pakistan team refusing to come to India. The first blow to this syndrome was made a couple of weeks back and that too by a fortuitous circumstance.

Australia and West Indies, citing extraneous reasons, refused to go to Sri Lanka to play their matches. To demonstrate to them that things were not as bad as was being made out, a joint Indo-Pak team played a resurgent Sri Lanka side in Colombo.

Suddenly you had Azharuddin leading the likes of Waqar, Mushtaq and Wasim along with players like Sachin, Kumble and Srinath. Though it was a festival match, imagine what the result was: the combined team gave a hiding to Sri Lanka.

But that is not important: the key thing is that two teams that had not played each other for 7 years could still combine as a team and that too a winning team.

I have a feeling that this team could beat any team in the world; maybe it could even take on the combined might of the rest of the world. This fact sets me thinking. What if India had not been partitioned and in place of two mutually hostile countries we were one resurgent and strong country?

For one, instead of our armies facing each other, we would have used our combined strength to face the rest of the world. It is even possible that in such an eventuality we may have not needed these two armies at all and the manpower and resources now deployed in them could have been used for some other useful purpose.

I find a skeptical voice: in that case wouldn't life have been dull since none of us would have an enemy and so no focus for our 'hate attention'!

I'm sorry, I cannot make myself agree with this. Actually since we have focused our 'hate attention' on each other, we have forgotten the other enemies that we have.

Do you want me to list out these enemies? What about communalism for a start? Or casteism? What about poverty, backwardness, illiteracy?

The match played in Colombo was the starting point of a new era; I am not saying that it can turn the clock back by 50 years, but at least let its gains of reversing of the last 7 years of history not be lost in Bangalore.

PART 16
ABRACADABRA

76

WWW. KARGIL.COM

Whenever I think of WWW, it's always Worrel, Weekes, Walcott– the three legendary West Indian cricketers. If I think a little deeper, it could even be Win the War with Walour (sic- sorry for the spelling; it's more important to make a point than to score for your spellings!).

However, the other day when Union Home Minister L.K. Advani mentioned the 3Ws, all these meanings rushed into my mind, no doubt, but still somehow I knew I couldn't be right. Surely Advaniji had some other meaning in mind and sure enough it came out soon enough.

Wimbledon, Washington, War Zone. All these Ws had happened on the same day. Leander Paes' double victory in Wimbledon; the Clinton-Nawaz Sharif joint declaration in Washington; and last but not the least the news from the War in Kargil of the fall of Tiger Hills.

Wimbledon, Washington, War Zone. All these Ws represented a fourth W for Wictory (oops here goes the spelling again!) and a fifth (Wonderful) and a sixth (Wow!) and a seventh ... an eighth and so on and on.

All these wonderful Ws took me on a flight of fancy to the wonderful valley of Kargil, Leh and what have you. Only last year I was there and already it had seemed so distant and far away. But now as Advaniji mentioned it and so the other speakers (Chief Ministers all of them) it seemed so near and invigorating.

My mind rushed back a year. The beauty is spectacular: extremely high hills surrounding green and verdant valleys; mountain peaks so forbidding and rock faces so vertical and sharp; air so thin that one can barely breathe.

It is now that all of this came suddenly to me. How Gautam Kaul had warned me in the plane to avoid all alcohol; take long rests after short mountain climbs; to avoid any sort of exertion in the first couple of days; and so on.

As I thought all this, suddenly it was Kargil all over me; not Kargil alone but a Kargil in which hundreds of young and brave soldiers and officers, just out of their teens not just climbing these forbidding rock faces but carrying 20 kilo back bags and in the fact of intense enemy artillery, mortar and killing machine gun fire.

Col. Singh, the smart officer picked up by the Army Chief to make the presentation to the select and distinguished gathering, carded on in his matter of fact, emotionless tones. "Most expert mountain climbers would be proud to climb just one of these peaks and that too without any weight on their backs. Our jawans have not just climbed these peaks but have done it through sheer and vertical rock faces and in the face of blistering enemy fire.

And after having climbed the cliff and taken the peak they came down again, this time to climb up and conquer the second one."

It takes a while to digest the meaning of all this but when you do your eye lids comic down in salutation as a tear rolls down your cheeks. After a long time I can again hold my head up and say with a matter of fact pride: 'I am an Indian'.

The importance of Kargil for me is not merely the fact that we are fighting a war there with our traditional enemy nor the fact that we are winning it; or even the fact that the whole world, for the first time since we became a free country, is supporting us in this effort. For me Kargil is important because it binds me with the rest of my countrymen. More than any other issue in recent times.

Cricket, no doubt, is a binding factor but then, let us not forget, a vast majority of our country men neither play the game nor even understand it. Secularism, democracy, freedom, socialist pattern of society, planned development, and what have you. All these were at one time in the past great binding ideas but no more. Not only do they mean different things to different people but they themselves have become the foci of disruptive, mutually destructive and hostile forces.

Kargil is not a war between Hindu and Muslim; nor is it a war being fought for the defence of Kashmir. It is certainly not a war for defending an area full of minerals or one which produces a lot of foodgrains or any other valuable commodity. It is also not, unlike the pretty Kashmir valley, an attractive place to spend our holidays. If it is not this, not that, well, for heavens sake, what is it?

Neti. Neti. Not this. Not this. That's Kargil? It is an idea. And an idea that is *Neti Neti.* It is like Kant's Ding An Sich and Krishna's *Nishkama Karma*, with not much of a solid existence but powerful nevertheless. Unlike the deluding Maya of our philosophy, Kargil is existing in our psyche and soul like a mighty volcano, even like an earth-shaking quake.

Even though on the maps it may be shown as a small dot we know it to be a pretty valley surrounded by high and mighty hills of the Himalayas. But if that were all, it would not deserve more than a line or two in my column; certainly not the tons of praise that I seem to reserve for it. Like many ideas that have caught the fancy of our people in the past, even like the concept of 'matrabhoomi' and Mother India, Kargil is going to live on in our mass consciousness for ever.

My emotions were aroused when I read about the eagerness of the young cadets from our Military Academy to rush to Kargil to throw out the intruding hordes. It has been fired by news coming in everyday of how young officers and jawans have taken a hail of machine gun bullets on their chests but carried on nevertheless till they had evicted the well entrenched enemy from their pill boxes and bunkers.

India is a land of peace and *ahimsa* but our non-violence,

as Gandhiji used to say, is not the non-violence of the weak but of the strong. We have not crossed our frontiers; it is the intruders who have and thus have thrown a challenge to our young men and women. Similar crossings took place at the dawn of the millennium; now that the new millennium has begain we are faced with a similar challenge. The response of our youth has clearly shown how well we have digested the lessons of history.

The intruders will soon realize that India is not just 1000 years old today but behind that has a consciousness and a collective psyche that stretches back many more millenniums. And this will be the true message of Kargil for many millenniums to come.

77

THE DIANA SYNDROME

We in this country have been exposed to bizarre happenings, like the mass hysteria generated in the wake of Ganesh idols drinking milk. But life in the West, especially in the stiff upper lip country, UK, is more sedate and settled. It is for this reason that the aftermath of Diana's death is so difficult to understand.

No doubt, Diana's was an exceptional story. An ordinary girl from a moderate though upper class family getting wedded to the heir to the English throne was really a dream come true for anyone. And then to have to come out of the whole thing through a divorce was enough to make her a celebrity of sorts. But none of this can explain the reaction of the masses to her death in a car accident in Paris as she rode with her latest lover, the Muslim son of the owner of the fashionable store, Harrods.

More than a million bouquets were piled outside her Kensington home and elsewhere; more than twice that number of people lined the route that her funeral cortege took and maybe about a 100 times that number witnessed the funeral procession on television. And all this in a country where even VE Day did not witness this sort of mass hysteria!

There is no doubt that for a long time much will be said and even more will be written about all this. It is also possible that 'the whole week of lamentation was an electronically stimulated hysteria, an ersatz binge catered by press and television barons that will be followed soon by a massive letdown and hangover', as one leading paper from the US has reported. But all the same can we get over the fact that something remarkable had happened, something that made the happenings of the week totally unprecedented.

There are a host of opinions emerging about the Diana phenomenon which started off as a sort of 'Cinderella come true story' and ended in the million bouquets and flood of tears. 'Some saw a princess martyred by publicity, hounded unto death by the cameras that loved her so and that then feasted on her funeral...others blamed the family that drew her into its royal orbit, expecting her to glow with the pale fire of reflected glory, and later cast her aside when she blazed forth as a star'

There are other reasons given as well. One of it is the fact that she did not translate her own pain into bitterness and withdrawal but into a genuine desire to comfort the suffering of others—people afflicted with AIDS and leprosy and breast cancer and the mutilated victims of land mines. Another is that while men were swayed by her poise and beauty, for women she was the living embodiment of an atavistic, patriarchal fact of life.

I am not satisfied that any of these arguments fully explain the phenomena, even though they may truly be part of the reason. For really gauging the reason we may have to delve a bit deeper into the human psyche. Let us take our own 'Ganesh drinking milk' phenomenon. Why did it generate the sort of mass hysteria that it did?

Corruption, callousness and criminality is fast sweeping the Indian scene, with not just human institutions falling by the wayside but the godly ones as well. The euphoria of the last 50 years of independence has ended in whiff of smoke of unfilled aspirations and destroyed hopes. Having been deprived of all earthly support systems, our people turned to god (read Kalki) to come as promised and save them. But even this did not seem to be materialising and sense of deep wound and frustration was overcoming the masses.

It is now that rumour about Ganesh drinking milk emerged. People rushed to temples with cans of milk; they did not just want to verify the rumour they actually wanted it to be true. And, lo and behold, they found that indeed it was so. What they wanted to prove, and the milk drinking idols did prove, was that 'god's in his heaven, all's right with the world'.

Is a similar syndrome operating in the Diana phenomenon? I have a lurking suspicion that it is. For meeting the material needs of people, capitalist societies, especially the one in Western Europe and US, are wonderful. They ensure a fairly decent standard of living for every one, except probably the fringe elements who are not interested in such matters at all. I have always wondered what the dreams of such people, who hardly lack any material comforts, are composed of.

Diana is being compared ever so often with Cinderella. The people who do so forget how poor and desperate Cinderella was. Was Diana ever like her? Or is any English woman today like her? Well, certainly not in the absolute sense but relatively speaking maybe.

Capitalist societies may have brought up everybody to at least some sort of a level, they have at the same time allowed some privileged people to travel much faster and much higher. The situation, therefore, is that while 90 per cent of the people will be enjoying a comparable level, the remaining 10 per cent will be even better off than the kings and queens of yore. It is not just the money part that is important; the rich also happen to be the famous.

The Cinderellas in the western society are not poor or lacking in basic material necessities; nor even are they being ill-treated or misused. What they lack is the wealth and fame that the minority of the people have. It therefore, came about that when Diana married Charles, every young woman found her own dreams getting fulfilment in her 'elevation'.

Being a clever and charming woman at the same time, Diana carefully nursed and nurtured these dreams, much in the way that film stars do. And she reaped the same harvest. Like Cinderella, Diana's prince came and made her famous beyond measure, bore two healthy sons and acquired a regal platform to build for herself a lasting image. So clever did she play her cards that soon she had ensured identification with all the young woman and the old, the low and the ordinary.

It was thus that when her prince decided to go his own way, it was not as if only Diana had lost the throne: it was as if all the 90 per cent who had identified with her who were the rejected. The trauma and challenge that such sudden independence that was brought home to Diana was not hers alone; it was shared by all of them who had earlier shared her triumph.

For these people it was Diana alone who died in the car crash; it was as if their own dreams and lives had been shattered. And that is the reason for their grief and tears.

78

THE BIDAII OF MY 'BUNDLE OF JOY'

It is truly said that girls are a bundle of joy; so much so that it is difficult to believe that in many homes the birth of girls is followed by much grieving and sorrow. Whatever it may be, I got my girl after a great deal of waiting, in which period two sons were born. In fact if her birth had been delayed just a few months or if the emergency had been declared earlier, she may have not been born at all. In those troubled days the choice was between a third child and a government house and who does not know what losing a government house means!

Be as it may, Rohini (that's what I called my 'bundle of joy') was born and ever since then has been a source of great pleasure and joy to me and her brothers. In fact, even though with the elapse of time she did grow up and moved up from one class to another, for us she was still the little bonny baby that she was at the time of her birth. Her tiny build, her very quiet, reserved and happy-go-lucky ways only helped to perpetuate this myth. Rohini was a baby and would always remain so, that is the myth that I committed myself to.

What I didn't realise was that behind this myth was the desire to believe that I was and would remain the only man in her life; but like all other myths this one was too destined to be shattered.

Just a few days back my wife, followed by a meek Rohini,

came in and commanded me to shut the TV. 'There's something that Rohini wishes to say!' she commanded. 'And what she wants to say cannot be said with the TV on'.

Till now whatever she had to say could be said with the TV on; what had happened today that this could not be done? I was upset.

Missing the climax of the forgettable Sharukh Khan movie, *Koyla*, that was on the telly at that time, was not something that upset me; this must have been because of the strange expression on Rohini's face. The expression seemed too grown up for my liking.

My wife must have read my expression because she was quick with the retort: "She's not little any longer; in just a few months she will turn 22!'

That's true, I thought. She had just completed her MBA and was now working in a multinational earning almost the same that I was getting after more than 3 decades in the premiere service of the country. That surely couldn't be the work of a baby! Even if she stood behind my wife, like the lamb ready for the slaughter!

She's not a baby and she wants to say something! As I switched the telly off, I feared the worst. I am not so unused to the ways of the world not to realise what happens when daughters grow up and become MBAs. So I was prepared for the worst as I took her little hand in mine and looked at her. 'Go ahead', I said putting up a brave front but all the accumulated fears of the past many years started to surge into my head. Has it happened ? Has the time come?

Her first look at me was convincing enough: She would have to be an actress of the first grade to keep her real inner feelings from filtering down to me. It was clear from her expression that there was a man in her life. If any doubts still remained, her first words removed them. 'Papa, I want you to visit them once', she said in a voice that that was all honey and sugar but full of passion and clear in intent.

Visit the house of the people who are conspiring to rob you of your 'bundle of joy'? Fond hopes. But still I didn't know how to say so. 'What' is the point?' I said. 'If you have made up your mind, then that's it.'

'I still want you to, Papa', was her simple response.

'I will, if there's any choice', I said, looking intently into her eyes trying to figure out if I had any chance whatsoever or if the 'other man' had stolen her away from me forever. For a moment when she was quiet I found my chance and quickly added: 'If there's a choice, then what about that MBA from USA?'

'But I don't know him!' was the effective repartee that shut me up effectively. 'Besides', she added as a sweetener, 'the chap I want you to meet is an engineer as well as being an MBA'.

She had hit the nail on the head: being an engineer-IAS myself, this part was of particular interest to me. And, what is more important is, that she knew it.

It thus happened that the very next day, I and my wife were sitting in the Saluja's drawing room at Gurgaon and peering out at a tall, lanky youngster, with a pleasing look on his face. The first thought that struck me was that indeed Rohini was no baby when it came to choosing a life partner!

Class fellows as they were at the MDI where they did their MBA, they really were 'made for each other'and not just because they were class fellows. Both of them, I found, had the same delicate and dainty look; Harsh, of course, was taller but both had the same slim build and fair complexion.

She had chosen well. As I talked to him, I remembered Rohini's words: 'I can intellectually jibe with him.' I had wondered at that time if she really knew what that meant but now that I talked to him, I know that she had spoken right: I could jibe with him too. This was not the choice of the 'little Rohini' or 'Tukki' as we lovingly call her but that of a very mature person who not only knows her mind but also is an excellent judge.

It is now that I realised how little I knew her; for me for the last two decades she was a mere 'bundle of joy', a plaything, a baby to tell stories to. Though I had seen her grow, I had always refused to believe my eyes. But now my dreams and illusions were all shattered and all because of the 24-year old who sat in front of me.

As I got up and turned towards the door to go to my car, I could already hear the *shenais*; for an instant it seemed that *bidaii* was already underway. I barely kept the tears from gushing out of my eyes as I slipped into the Maruti and pulled the starter; it was as if the parting had already begun.

It is only later that the comforting thought came: I wasn't losing my 'bundle of joy'; maybe I was winning another one in Harsh. I am joining all fathers of little girls to pray that this may really prove to be the case.